Changing Families

A Group Activities Manual for Middle and High School Students from Separated, Divorced, Single-Parent Families or Stepfamilies

Teresa Schmidt, LCSW, BCD

JOHNSON INSTITUTE®

MINNEAPOLIS

CHANGING FAMILIES

A Group Activities Manual for Middle and High School Students from Separated, Divorced, Single-parent Families or Stepfamilies

Johnson Institute
7205 Ohms Lane
Minneapolis, MN 55439-2159
612-831-1630 or 800-231-5165

Library of Congress Cataloging-in-Publication Data

Schmidt, Teresa M.
Changing families: a group activities manual for middle and high school students from separated, divorced, single-parent families or stepfamilies / Teresa M. Schmidt.
p. cm.
Includes bibliographical references.
ISBN 1-56246-087-0

1. Group guidance in education. 2. Group counseling for teenagers. 3. Teenagers — Family relationships. 4. Problem youth — Counseling of. 5. Socially handicapped youth — Counseling of. I. Title.
LB1620.4.S36 1994
373. 14—dc20 93-45455
CIP

Cover and text design: Lindberg Design
Printed in the United States of America
95 96 97 98 99 / 5 4 3 2 1

CONTENTS

Acknowledgments

I would like to thank Thelma Spencer, Ed.D., with whom I collaborated to write *Peter the Puppy Talks About Chemical Dependence in the Family*, one of the books in the *Building Trust, Making Friends* series. This manuscript uses the format that Thelma and I developed in my living room over Christmas vacation in 1988, although the current work is solely my responsibility.

The middle school counselors of York County, Virginia, participated in the field testing of the first draft. Dr. Leslie Kaplan, who was at that time director of guidance of York County Public Schools, made that training possible. The administration, SAP staff, and guidance counselors of Avon High School and Avon Middle School, Avon, Indiana, also graciously provided opportunities for field testing the first draft.

I am grateful for the help and support of my family. My sons, Matthew and Thomas Schmidt, were in the third and fifth grades respectively during the year Thelma Spencer and I developed *Peter the Puppy;* the three of us had just experienced a separation. Living with them as they coped with separation, divorce, remarriage, and a stepfamily spurred my determination to provide materials for school personnel to use with children and teenagers in their position. The boys have always been ready to provide consultation and support, and they managed to reach adolescence at a time when the experience of mothering teenage boys became very useful. They have shown supreme patience over the five years during which I wrote several support group manuals. My husband, Wiltz Wagner, inspired me to maintain high standards for these group manuals, has taken me on motorcycle rides that have kept everything in perspective, and has given much love and affection which have enhanced the current writing.

About the Author

Teresa M. Schmidt, MSW, LCSW, BCD, has been a clinical social worker since 1970. A graduate of the College of William and Mary and the Smith College School for Social Work, Ms. Schmidt has had extensive experience in outpatient settings. Bringing her clinical experience in mental health to Newport News Public Schools, Newport News, Virginia, in 1987, she worked with Dr. Thelma Spencer to develop and implement in a school setting a prevention/intervention group program for children from chemically dependent families. Ms. Schmidt is co-author with Dr. Spencer of the *Building Trust, Making Friends* series: *Peter the Puppy Talks About Chemical Dependence in the Family; Tanya Talks About Chemical Dependence in the Family; Thomas Barker Talks About Divorce and Separation;* and *Della the Dinosaur Talks About Violence and Anger Management.* Ms. Schmidt currently lives in the cornfields of Indiana, where she maintains a private practice, consults with local school systems on leading support groups, and conducts training workshops for mental health and school professionals on the local, state, and national levels.

Introduction

Adolescents live in an important transitional stage. They move from the sheltered home into an arena where peers and outsiders are increasingly more important than their family. They must deal with a number of developmental issues: they need to accept physical changes initiated by puberty, learn how to regulate their emotions, and deal with increasing advances in cognitive ability. Furthermore, they need to confront the growing importance of peer relationships and the reworking of family relationships, and they need to start creating an individual identity.

Imagine a group of adolescents who face these developmental issues in the best of all possible worlds. They have what current theorists call protective factors, factors that help them through these developmental issues. And since they live in the best of all possible worlds, they have these protective factors on four levels. Theorists have described these levels in an ecological-integration framework: the personal, family, social, and societal levels. These students have pluses on the personal level: they are bright, attractive, and able to manage their emotions. They have good interpersonal skills and a sense of their ability to affect positively what happens to them. On the family level, they have parents who are stable role models and good providers. Their parents are able to provide the structure and nurturing that children need, without being either too permissive or too autocratic. They have not had to deal with the stresses of parental divorce, chemical dependence, or family violence. On the social level, these adolescents have good peer relationships, get along well with their grandparents, and are active in school, church, or community organizations. They live in clean, crime-free suburban or rural neighborhoods. Finally, on the societal level, these mythical adolescents live in a world that does not condone violence, either in the family or on the street. This world has solved the issues of racism, sexism, unemployment, and educational and economic inequality. It provides adequate medical and health care for all segments of society and supports families in their parenting responsibilities.

Unfortunately, average adolescents are far from resembling these mythical teens. Typical adolescents are more likely to have encountered risk factors, in addition to protective factors, on all four levels of the ecological framework. On the personal level, adolescents may be victims of parental maltreatment; they may have low IQs and learning disabilities; they may be physically unattractive; they may be aggressive and violent in their interpersonal relationships. On the family level, they may experience parental divorce, chemical dependence, or violence. Their parents may be unemployed and unable to provide adequately for them. On the social level, they may be isolated and uninvolved in any school, church, or community activities; they may have no extended family or social network. Or they may live in a poor urban area near illegal markets like prostitution and drug dealing and look for their sense of community in a gang that thrives on violence. Or they may come from families where men beat their wives and have done so for several generations. And on the societal level, they live in the United States in the 1990s, a time marked by cultural acceptance of family violence, ranging from parents disciplining children by spanking to wife beating; a time when a violent crime is committed every 17 seconds, according to the FBI's crime clock for 1991; a time when violence is seen daily on television and in movies; and a time when many children and families experience social and economic inequalities, poverty, and inadequate health care.

As a helping professional—a guidance counselor, school psychologist, school social worker, Student Assistance Program (SAP) worker, Core team member, school nurse, teacher, or probation officer—you want to increase the protective factors, the positive tools for living that adolescents possess. You'd like to increase the protective buffers that adolescents have in their environment, as they face the developmental issues of their middle school and high school years. You want to help them develop skills to deal with their anger in positive ways, as well as to deal with the stresses of their families. You'd like them to be part of the social support system that you provide for teens. You may also want to help change cultural values so that violence will not be condoned in our society and individual responsibility and interpersonal support will be supported.

*Changing Families: A Group Activities Manual for Middle and High School Students From Separated, Divorced, Single-parent Families or Stepfamilies** has been developed to help caring professionals like you intervene with at-risk adolescents. You will reach them on the social level, within the context of a group. Through the group, you will provide them with a social support system as they learn personal skills to manage their own emotions and to deal with the stresses and possible traumas they may experience in their families.

This group activity manual is targeted for the adolescent who has risk factors on any of the four ecological levels—personal, family, social, and societal. Students who are dealing with a separated, divorced, single-parent family or stepfamily will find membership in a *Changing Families* group helpful in developing coping strategies for dealing with the stresses and issues that they face regularly.

Changing Families uses the same group model as the *Building Trust, Making Friends* series: *Peter the Puppy Talks About Chemical Dependence in the Family; Tanya Talks About Chemical Dependence in the Family; Thomas Barker Talks About Divorce and Separation;* and *Della the Dinosaur Talks About Violence and Anger Management* (Schmidt and Spencer, 1991). That 11-session group model made use of both clinical and educational theory to develop programs for elementary students from chemically dependent, divorced, or violent families, and for middle school students from chemically dependent families.

This complete and easy-to-use manual contains all you need to lead a group of middle or high school students through the program *Changing Families.*

* A companion model called *Anger Management and Violence Prevention: A Group Activities Manual for Middle and High School Students* written by Teresa Schmidt, is also available from Johnson Institute (see page 204). *Anger Management and Violence Prevention* is designed to help students develop coping strategies for dealing with their own and others' anger and learn to clarify their views on violence by looking at the protective and risk factors on each level of the ecological framework.

Part One of this manual contains materials to help you understand the structure of this group model, including group format and progression of session themes. It also provides guidelines and materials to help you initiate and implement the program in your school or agency.

Part Two contains materials to help you understand the most current theories on adolescent development. You will also find information about separation, divorce, and living in a stepfamily and their effects on adolescents, as well as the issues for adolescents living in such families.

Part Three contains the complete group guide for leading a *Changing Families* group. The group guide includes the objectives, necessary preparations, background information and guidelines, all handouts, and detailed step-by-step plans for each of the 11 sessions.

Part Four contains support materials, a list of references and supplementary readings, and a list of important resources. This section will further help group leaders and other staff members make the group process successful and rewarding for everyone involved.

Overall, this manual provides practical and creative ways to help adolescents clarify the stresses they experience from living in a changing family. In theoretically correct and clinically sound ways, it also teaches adolescents concrete problem-solving skills to use in anger situations, and it provides age-appropriate and relevant scenarios in which they can practice using these skills. The manual also helps teens to correct their misconceptions regarding issues about parental divorce and to solve problems that come up in peer and family relationships.

This material was drawn from the following source: Cicchetti, D., and V. Carlson eds. 1989. *Child Maltreatment. Theory and Research on the Causes and Consequences of Child Abuse and Neglect.* New York: Cambridge University Press.

Part One

Establishing A Support-Group Program for At-risk Students

CHAPTER • 1

Dynamics of the Group Model

For a variety of reasons, the most effective and practical setting in which to offer support groups for adolescents may be in the school. First, the families of many at-risk adolescents may be experiencing extreme stress: the stress of family violence, chemical dependence, separation or divorce, or of being a stepfamily, or of chemical dependence. Many families undergoing such stress are in a state of denial and don't seek professional help. Second, even families who aren't in denial often lack the ability or means to make use of professional help. Third, many professional helping facilities, such as treatment centers for chemical dependence or battered women's shelters, aren't equipped to work with children or adolescents. Fourth, the organizational structure of some helping facilities may not allow professionals who do have the skills and training to deal with teens to have access to them. Finally, the adolescents themselves may not be able to put their distress into words, may not know that help is available, or may not want to betray their families by admitting there is a problem and asking for help. Better than any other setting, schools are in a position to offer prevention services—like this program—to the large numbers of at-risk adolescents who would otherwise never receive them.

Schools can offer the group model's services as part of a comprehensive prevention program implemented by pupil services personnel, which include clinical and school social workers, school psychologists, guidance counselors, and chemical dependence counselors. Many Student Assistance Programs (SAPs) and CORE Teams, which are now broadening their focus from chemically dependent students to include students from divorced or separated families, stepfamilies, and violent families, will also find the program's group model ideal to use and easy to implement.

Although the school is a valuable setting for the group model, it may be used elsewhere: mental health centers, private practices, battered women's shelters, chemical dependence treatment centers that provide family services, and agencies that serve troubled teenagers.

This group model, based on the *Building Trust, Making Friends* series, is a dynamic process that helps meet the needs of children and adolescents from at-risk families by providing structure, consistency, predictability, and fun. It incorporates a structured format that remains the same for all group sessions. The group model also presents a specific and definite progression of themes that foster nonjudgmental education about the issues of anger management, violence prevention, separation, divorce, and stepfamilies; corrects misconceptions that students commonly have regarding these issues; and teaches teens effective coping strategies that enable them to let go of futile overresponsibility and begin to take care of themselves.

All this takes place through the media of lectures, discussions, and role plays led by you, the leader. Teens who have trouble managing anger can learn concrete problem-solving skills to help them in anger situations. Other teens will easily identify with the examples the leaders use without feeling disloyal to their own families. The group model enables adolescents who come from families experiencing the severe stress of parental separation and divorce or family violence to recognize that they're not alone, that other teenagers have feelings just like theirs, and that, above all, they *can* learn to manage their feelings and deal with them in healthy ways.

Group Format

The group model follows a structured format for each group session that is both educationally and clinically sound. The three-part format includes the following components.

1. Beginning the Session
   - Review of group rules
   - Centering exercise
   - Feelings check-in
   - Review of basic facts (beginning with Session 2)
   - Review of assignment (beginning with Session 3)
2. Exploring the Material
   - Mini-lecture (the heart of the session)
   - Group discussion
   - Role plays, in a number sessions
   - Homework assignment to practice skills (beginning with Session 2)
3. Wrapping Up
   - Repetition of centering exercise
   - Affirmation
   - Closing activity

Since the format and its components remain virtually constant through all 11 sessions, these components deserve a closer look.

Rules and Rules Contract. Creating an atmosphere in which a group of teenagers (some of whom might not know each other) feel secure and willing to share thoughts and feelings is a major undertaking. Many of the students will not have participated in a group process before, so they'll be unaccustomed to the expectations and the boundaries of a group. Group rules ensure that all group members will be treated with the dignity and respect they deserve. Group rules also establish a standard of behavior for the adolescents and the expectation that students can be responsible for their behavior.

As group leader, you should initially present the rules contract in the screening interview and explain that all members of the group will be asked to sign the contract. In the initial session, you will again go over the rules with the group and explain the consequences of not following the rules. You can decide the consequences, but it often works well to give misbehaving students one warning, and then ask them to leave if they cannot follow the rules a second time. Explain that the student can return the following week and may again receive one warning, but if asked to leave a second time, the student will not be able to attend the rest of the group meetings. The group members are then asked to agree to follow the rules by signing their names to the contract. The rules are then displayed in the group meeting room.

After another review of the rules in Session 2, teens are usually able to follow the rules easily. However, if student behavior deteriorates, you can review the rules at the beginning of the next group session, making sure that the students understand them all. For the sake of group morale, it is important to enforce the consequences if a student cannot follow the rules. As difficult as it is to remove students from the group, allowing them to misbehave amounts to enabling. The consistency of enforcing consequences reminds the adolescents that they're safe in group, that the rules serve to protect them and will be enforced, and that all group members will behave as they have agreed to by signing the contract.

Centering Exercise. This exercise sets the stage for group work. The techniques learned in the centering exercise, which include deep breathing and tensing and relaxing muscles, are not limited to group work only. Once mastered, teens can use them in real-life situations. Repeated toward the end of a group session, the centering exercise not only reinforces learning but also enables the adolescents to calm down—especially if intense feelings arose during the session—and helps them get ready to return to their classroom.

Feelings Check-in. During the feelings check-in, the group members learn to identify, own, and express their feelings in appropriate ways. As group leader, you will validate, accept, and tolerate the students' feelings. For example, responding to a teen who says he wants to kill his father because of a fight his parents had, you might say, "It sounds like you're feeling very angry and upset! Can you tell us what you're so angry about?" After the student responds, you could continue, "Many teens feel angry when that happens in their family. In this group, we're discussing the intense feelings that teens often have when there's a separation or divorce in the family. We want teens to accept their feelings, but to think carefully before they act on them. We'll learn more about how to handle these kinds of problems in later sessions." Again, if a teen is tearful because a relative has committed suicide, you can say, "Many teens feel sad or lonely when a close relative or friend dies, especially if it's by suicide. They might show their sadness by crying or by drawing a picture or writing a poem. After a while, they don't feel as sad. But for a while, they may just need to sit with their feelings. We'll learn more about feelings in Session 5."

By accepting and validating feelings, and by helping the students identify helpful ways to express them, you will consistently teach that feelings aren't bad or dangerous, that they can be felt and expressed, and that they will pass. Thus, the feelings check-in functions both as a corrective and a therapeutic experience for the group members.

Review of Basic Facts. Beginning in Session 2, the basic facts learned in previous sessions are reviewed for understanding. This weekly repetition and clarification is an effective technique to change some deep-seated beliefs that some adolescents have.

Leaders of groups of secondary students can consider this weekly review optional, although for impact the basic facts should probably be reviewed at least every other week. Use your own judgment on the best way to review the basic facts. The session plans suggest asking the students to look at the List of Basic Facts (page 197), which you can staple to the inside of the folder, on the left side for easy accessibility. A second alternative is to write each basic fact on an index card, and to pass the cards out to students. A third alternative is for you (or the students) to make a poster for each basic fact. The posters will then be ready for the presentation of basic facts in session 10. Whether you use the List of Basic Facts, index cards, or posters, have a go-around, in which a group member reads Basic Fact 1, and explains it. If the student has trouble explaining the fact, don't contradict or judge, simply clarify his or her explanation. Repeat the procedure for the next basic fact. Remember that this is a wonderful opportunity to make sure that the students understand and integrate the basic facts that have been taught. It is also easy preparation for the presentation in Session 10 and provides a lead-in for the session material.

Assignment. In each session, beginning with Session 2, you will give the students a homework assignment, which is designed to help the students put into practice what they have learned. Based on cognitive-behavioral theory and the principle of starting behavioral change by observing current behavior, some of the assignments call for group members simply to observe themselves, their friends, and their families to see what thinking they put between feeling and behavior and what problem-solving skills they could use. The assignment is given at the end of each session, and it is reviewed at the beginning of the next session. The review, a go-around where the students report what they have observed, is an important component of this group format. Being expected to put what they see into words will force group members to be more observant, and hearing how other group members are trying to use their new skills provides encouragement and motivation for all. Be nonjudgmental as you conduct the go-around. Remember that behavioral change starts with the smallest concrete steps. Be sure to praise the students' ability to recognize their current style of dealing with family problems, even if you think the style itself is harmful.

Mini-lecture. This component presents basic facts about changing families, the stresses and effects on teens, and how they can cope with the stresses. Combine the lecture material provided with discussion and brainstorming. In some sessions, the students read and discuss scenarios and act out role plays, using materials provided in the manuals. Adolescents enjoy these kinds of activities. Teens who live in families experiencing the strains of family violence, divorce, or separation will be able to identify easily with the material presented without feeling that they are betraying their families.

Discussion. Each session's lecture is followed by questions you may use to initiate group discussion. In the discussion, the students have the opportunity to process the basic facts, and you have the chance to make sure they understand the concepts and issues presented. In some sessions, the discussion questions are interspersed throughout the lecture material.

Activity. The activity reinforces the material presented in the lecture and is designed to engage the students in active understanding of the material. The activities in some sessions enable students in a nonthreatening way to express their perceptions of their situations, but only to the degree they can and want to share them. Role plays and scenarios are provided to facilitate this component of the group session.

Basic Facts. New basic facts are introduced by having the students look at the List of Basic Facts. The basic facts summarize the essential message of the material in a way that is easily understood and remembered.

Affirmation. This gives the students a chance to end the group on a positive note, even if intense feelings have arisen during the session. The affirmation reinforces the content presented in the group session and helps the adolescents learn to choose a positive attitude.

Closing. The closing exercise helps the group develop a sense of bonding, cohesiveness, acceptance, and sharing. It allows for physical touch in a safe, nonthreatening atmosphere, which may be a new experience for many of the adolescents. The same closing exercise concludes each session. Older students who feel uncomfortable holding hands may pass the wish in any appropriate way, such as a touch on the elbow or a pat on the shoulder.

This structured format encourages the students to participate as fully as possible in the group process. Go-arounds, in which everybody gets a chance to describe feelings and experiences, are used extensively to make it easy for students to share in a safe, nonthreatening way. Although the students are never forced to take part and are given the right to "pass," the format allows each group member at least three opportunities per session to speak. The repeated structure in all the group sessions provides a sense of predictability, order, and consistency, which is often absent in the homes of at-risk adolescents.

Progression of Themes

The essence of the group model is the progression of themes.

In the *Changing Families* model, the themes combine to create a program that helps the students become less at risk, while allowing them to save face and never making them feel that they're being disloyal to their families. In fact, the group leader never asks the teens to reveal negative things about their families, nor does the leader ever make negative comments about people who are separated or divorced. The program consistently describes the behavior of people who separate, divorce, or live in stepfamilies objectively and nonjudgmentally. At the same time, the program unfailingly identifies and validates the feelings in adolescents—and in other family members—that such behaviors elicit.

The *Changing Families* group program follows a specific thematic progression:

SESSION 1 : Changing Families and Family Values

SESSION 2 : Why People Get Married and Why People Get Divorced

SESSION 3 : The Effects of Changing Families on Teens and Issues for Teens from Changing Families

SESSION 4 : The Effects of Divorce, Separation, and Other Nontraditional Lifestyles on Families: Family Sculptures

SESSION 5 : Feelings

SESSION 6 : Skills to Problem-solve Anger Situations

SESSION 7 : Anger Management Steps

SESSION 8 : Other Coping Strategies

SESSION 9 : Setting Personal Goals

SESSION 10: Group Presentation—optional

SESSION 11: Developing a Support System

In Session 1, the group manual provides material to help students realize that there are many kinds of families, which may have many kinds of family values.

In Session 2, the students explore why people get married and why they get divorced.

In Session 3, the program, through scenarios, describes the stress or trauma that separation, divorce, or living in a stepfamily can cause families and the effects on teenagers.

Session 4 helps students see the patterns that some families develop in response to separation or divorce. It also helps correct the misconceptions common to teenagers, who discover that although they can't cure the family's problems, they can do some things to help themselves.

Sessions 5 through 7 focus on feelings and emotions. In Session 5, the group participants learn to put thinking between their feelings and their behavior, and to recognize how negative and positive thinking can influence both feelings and behavior. In Sessions 6 and 7, they learn problem-solving skills to use in anger situations, and anger management steps to help them remember to use the skills.

In Session 8, the teens learn coping strategies to deal with problems that come up in their families. They learn to how to maintain a relationship with both parents, how to keep themselves safe in conflictive situations between parents, how to avoid assuming responsibility for someone else's feelings or behavior, and how to do good things for themselves.

Session 9 helps the students learn how to set personal goals. Group members identify ways they can take good care of their bodies, minds, and feelings and can make positive choices.

Session 10 involves an educational presentation by the group members. Audiences can range from a principal or an administrator to a class or an entire grade level. Successfully teaching their peers the basic facts reinforces the students' learning and increases their self-esteem. It helps give the group a sense of cohesiveness and closure. It also raises the education and awareness levels of the audience and provides an opportunity for future referrals.

In Session 11, the students celebrate their learning and growth. They create their own support system that will help them know where to go and to whom they can turn for help should they need it in the future.

Displacement Communication

In its progression of themes, the group model uses a therapeutic technique called *displacement communication* (Kalter, 1990) to help adolescents deal with family stress, while allowing them to save face and remain loyal to their families. Lacking knowledge and perspective, young children often are not verbal or articulate in describing family problems or their reactions to those problems. While adolescents may have greater knowledge and perspective, they still might not want to discuss the problems, both in an effort to avoid or deny their own distress and in an effort to preserve their family's good name. Some adolescents are often unaware of their specific feelings and are unable to name them. They're also unaware of their internal conflicts and end up acting them out by fighting; misbehaving; somatizing, that is, expressing their feelings through physical ailments; overeating; or trying to be perfect.

Recognizing that many adolescents don't communicate directly, the group model combines a direct and an indirect method of communication through lecture material and the scenarios and role plays provided.

The displacement communication model developed by Kalter contains the following six steps:

1. Represent in the displacement figure (an example in a lecture or a character in a scenario; stuffed animals for younger children) the behaviors that signify emotional distress (fighting, crying, chemical use, sexual acting out).
2. Acknowledge how upsetting such behavior is to the displacement figure.
3. Address the displacement figure's underlying conflict or emotional pain.
4. Correct any misconceptions in the displacement.
5. Accept conflicted feelings.
6. Present alternative ways of expressing and coping with conflict.

These steps are incorporated into the group model's sessions.

The sessions' lectures educate the students, in a nonjudgmental way, about the particular issue of divorce or family violence. Family stress and behavior are described. The lectures identify the underlying conflicts and the emotional pain common to adolescents in the family situation. The lectures then correct the students' misconceptions and misperceptions by teaching them the three Cs: children don't **cause** and can't **control** or **change** parental divorce or violence. The sessions teach the students how to identify, accept, and express their feelings in appropriate ways. Finally, the sessions teach alternative coping strategies to enable the students to deal more successfully with their stress.

Adolescents easily identify with the family examples provided in the scenarios. Without having to describe their family situations, the group members can compare their behavior and situations to those described. Due to the material's nonthreatening and nonjudgmental nature, the students are able to use new ideas without feeling pressured. They are able to save face and get help without feeling disloyal to their families.

Benefits of Use

Using this group model for at-risk adolescents can benefit your school on a number of levels, including the logistics level, the individual level, and the system level.

The Logistics Level. Logistically, the model provides structure for new and untrained group leaders. The materials contained in the manual provide everything a leader will need to implement a group, including a Self-referral Group Survey Form for referral development, a Parental Consent Letter, a Screening Interview Outline, and complete guidelines for each session. In addition, considerable background material is provided to explain the theoretical purpose of each session.

The structure of the group format considerably reduces behavior problems during group sessions. Generally, adolescents enjoy participating in these groups and eagerly recommend them to their friends.

The Individual Level. Adolescents who have participated in these support groups have benefited in a variety of ways, including the following: (1) the behavior of group members in school improved, even the behavior of aggressive high school males, who were not seen in the school administrator's office during the course of the group; (2) group members increased their attachment to school, which has proven to be effective drop-out prevention; (3) middle school students were helped to abstain from alcohol, marijuana, and other drugs; and (4) students integrated concepts taught in the group into other situations. The examples that follow illustrate how group members were able to integrate concepts into real situations.

A seventh-grade girl who got into many fights in school began to come to the guidance counselor's office after a fight, to talk about what she should have done differently.

Middle school students in a group based on *Tanya Talks About Chemical Dependence in the Family,* from the *Building Trust, Making Friends* series, recommended a number of their peers for participation in the next group. These friends were drinking and smoking marijuana, and the group members thought they would stop using if they joined a group.

A high school student had parents who divorced at the beginning of her senior year. This girl was attractive, had good grades, and excelled in school activities, but she had difficulty in dealing with parental affairs and the separation. She learned in the *Changing Families* group that she could do nothing to cause, control, or change the divorce and did not have to choose between her parents, but instead could remain friendly with both. She also learned to set limits to avoid being caught in the middle between her divorced parents.

Another high school senior whose parents had just divorced was feeling as though her life had been shattered. Meeting other adolescents, and hearing about their problems and experiences, made her realize her problems were manageable.

A sixth-grade girl whose father murdered her 8-year-old brother taught her mother a relaxing technique learned in group ("Breathing Through Your Feet") to help her get through the trial.

A freshman boy whose father battered his mother, and whose stepfather later murdered her and his stepsister, announced at the beginning of the *Anger Management and Violence Prevention* group that when he got angry, he just liked to hurt somebody, claiming that he had broken someone's arm and had beaten another boy, breaking every bone in his face. This boy was not seen in the principal's office for aggressive behavior at all during the course of the group, and he learned to think rather than to fight when he got angry. During the presentation in Session 10, the boy thanked his former principal for coming, saying, "You usually see me in your office when I've done something bad, and now you can see me doing something good."

Sometimes there is a ripple effect from an adolescent's participation in one of the groups, and family members also benefit. One mother entered therapy because her son smiled when she asked him about his group experience. The child wouldn't discuss the group because of confidentiality, but the mother realized that he liked it and was benefiting from it.

The System Level. The group model recommends in-service programs for administrators and teachers before beginning the groups in the school. Thus, the entire system can benefit from using the group model.

In-services raise the awareness and education levels of teachers and administrators about the issues of chemical dependence, divorce, and family violence that are dealt with in the groups. In-services also help some in the audience to realize for the first time that they are children from such families and to understand some of the problems that they have had or are still having in their own lives. Many who share in the in-service may have friends or relatives who are affected by someone else's chemical dependence, divorce, or violence. Thus, the in-service plants the seeds of recovery for many. Participants may be encouraged to gain further education about these particular issues, to offer informed help to their students who come from chemically dependent, divorced, or violent families, and to seek any professional help they may need themselves.

CHAPTER • 2

Implementing the Group Program

This chapter will help you, the group leader, implement this group program in your school, agency, or other counseling setting. The chapter includes information on acquiring administrative support, recruiting and training staff, developing a referral network, screening candidates, and forming and scheduling groups. You will also find information on informed consent, confidentiality, and self-disclosure on the part of group leaders. Additionally, the chapter will point out effective ways to follow up on the individual, group, and system levels. Finally, it will outline ways you can use the program in guidance counseling and family therapy.

As mentioned, although schools may be able to reach the largest numbers of adolescents, the program may be used in a variety of other settings as well. After deciding where it will best fit in your school's (or agency's) situation, you must undertake the task of getting it started. The first step in doing that is gaining administrative support.

Gaining Administrative Support

If a school is to support a group program, the principal's backing is necessary. If principals establish student support groups as a priority, they will direct teachers to allow students to leave the classroom in order to participate. Likewise, principals will also be prepared to answer questions from hostile, resistant, or concerned parents, although such calls are rare. Principals, however, may feel that they're taking unnecessary risks by supporting groups for at-risk students, especially those from chemically dependent or violent families, and initially may not see any benefits for their school. If you encounter this sort of resistance from principals, discuss with them the program's low-key profile but very real benefits and its long-term results.

Offer an in-service for administrators, teachers, and other staff members to increase their awareness of the needs and characteristics of at-risk adolescents. Describe how offering support groups will benefit the students, their families, the school, and the community. Describe the misconceptions that adolescents from at-risk families often have. Explain how the group will correct students' misconceptions, while allowing them to remain loyal to their families. Recount how young people who learn that they haven't caused, and can't be responsible for fixing, their family's problems will feel better about themselves, will perform better at school, and will be less likely to get into serious trouble either in school or in the community. Explain that learning coping strategies will help adolescents take better care of themselves. Point out that support groups generally help students develop more positive attitudes about themselves and, thus, about learning. School staff members will feel good about referring students to groups that really work. Good groups will give both administrators and classroom teachers more free time to do their jobs.

If you're blessed with wholehearted administrative approval, it's still a good idea to provide in-service sessions for school personnel to acquaint them with the issues for at-risk adolescents. Design a simple presentation describing the purposes of offering a support group program, the role of the group, and the dynamics of the group model, including the group format and progression of themes. The better school staff members understand the purposes of a group program, the better will be their acceptance and support.

Staffing and Training

The authorization to provide prevention and intervention services for at-risk adolescents can come from the superintendent or school board, in the form of drop-out prevention, substance abuse prevention, or violence prevention programs or services for at-risk children. A support group program will be enhanced if implemented by and with trained personnel. Effective staff personnel may include members of Student Assistance Programs and CORE Teams, social workers, psychologists, guidance counselors, chemical dependence counselors, nurses, Drug and Alcohol Resistance Education (DARE) officers, and teachers—all of whom can be trained to lead groups to help at-risk adolescents. Although you'll have to depend on the staffing patterns of your school or agency, keep in mind that the needs of the students will be better met if personnel from various helping professions work together—not engage in territorial battles—to provide services.

The better trained the personnel, the better they'll be able to meet the needs of at-risk adolescents. Training should include the following:

- information about the goals of the group program
- education on specific issues to be dealt with in the groups (chemical dependence, divorce and separation, or family violence)
- instruction on how to lead groups
- ongoing supervision

One training model for leading student support groups might require a three-hour graduate-level course on chemical abuse or family violence, 20 hours of in-service, and 10 hours of supervised experience leading groups. Another model might consist of 15 hours of experiential in-service, during which staff members take turns leading and participating in the entire group program. After this experience, they would be ready to co-lead a group with a certified worker. A third model might have a trainer provide staff development for new group leaders and in-services for school faculty at the beginning of the school year. The trainer assists new group leaders in developing referrals and screening potential group members. The trainer then leads a group, with a new leader observing. When the group is repeated during the second half of the school year, the new leader facilitates the group, with the trainer observing and providing supervision.

A fourth model meets the needs of professionals who are implementing this program by themselves. This model combines the expertise of different professionals as group co-leaders: for example, a teacher can co-lead a group with a chemical dependence counselor. The complementarity of skills, training, and experience will again better serve the needs of adolescents.

Finally, you can also check your local resources for facilities that provide training. These may include chemical dependence treatment facilities, state and local health organizations, colleges and universities, state departments of education, and social welfare agencies. You can also find help by turning to a national organization, such as the Johnson Institute, which specializes in training. (See Resources for Help on page 206.)

Developing Referrals

Once you've gained administrative support and have begun training leaders to lead groups, begin to develop a list of at-risk adolescents who could benefit from being part of a group. You can build this list by looking to a number of referral sources, including the following:

- school counseling/social work case histories
- other school staff
- parents
- students themselves
- the broader community

School Counseling/Social Work Case Histories. Ask school counselors or social workers to recommend potential group members from their caseloads.

Other School Staff. Look for referrals from any and all members of the school staff: administrators, teachers, maintenance personnel, secretaries, DARE officers, CORE Teams, school nurses, or bus drivers. With the help of in-services, all school staff members can learn to identify students who may be at risk. By understanding how the support group program operates and the services it provides, staff members can refer students appropriately.

Parents. Some referrals will come directly from parents who might disclose during an interview or conference their stress over a family difficulty such as divorce, family violence, or chemical dependence. As leaders become more experienced in facilitating these groups, they gain confidence in asking about the presence of these problems in a family conference or history interview. Many parents will welcome the chance to have their children learn skills for healthy living. Introduce the group as an educational and preventive service. To allay parents' fears that the group might be intended to discover pathologies in their families, stress that the group is clearly designed to educate and inform teenagers, to correct their misconceptions, and to teach coping skills. Describe, too, the instructional process, including the use of the lecture material and scenarios. This will help parents recognize that the group experience will be a positive one for their child, not a negative or judgmental one.

Students Themselves. Another referral source is your school's student body. Self-referrals are likely to begin as soon as youngsters become aware that you are offering support groups. Offer classroom presentations on the various groups you plan to offer. Once the students understand what the groups are about, they'll find it easier to self-refer.

Begin your presentation by announcing that you will be offering some groups during the school year, that you want the students to know about. To give the students a taste of what happens in group, lead them in a centering exercise (for example, "Breathing Through Your Feet," page 59, or "The Waterfall," page 155). Then introduce one of the issues, such as divorce. Using a scenario from the *Changing Families* manual, describe some things a typical teenage boy likes to do: sports, dancing, hanging out with friends. Then go on to describe what might happen if his parents are divorced, and his father lives out of state, and doesn't call very often. Ask the students, "What would it feel like if your father didn't try to see you often and didn't pay child support until your mother took him to court?" Then ask "What would you think if your father had remarried, and had young children from a new wife, and he did take care of those children?" Explain that this boy's mother works two jobs, so he has to baby-sit his younger brothers and sisters; consequently, he can't be on the track team, even though he has a lot of talent. Explore with the students what he might feel about himself, about his mother, and about his father. Explain that being in a group would help the teen learn that he didn't cause his parents' separation and can't do anything to change or control it, and that it wasn't his fault that his father was not doing a good job of parenting him. Explain, too, that group leaders can help a student learn how to deal with such feelings in ways that will help the student.

Depending on which groups you'll be offering, repeat the above process by using the scenarios in the manual to introduce an adolescent who is frequently angry or who lives in a violent family, and have the students explore with you what the stresses might be for such a teen. Describe some of the styles of expressing anger, and have two students act out one of the problem-solving skills to use in anger situations. Be assured that adolescents enjoy hearing about how teens might react to various stresses.

After the presentation, distribute copies of the Self-referral Group Survey Form (see page 203), and go through the directions on the form with the students. Ask all the students to put their names on the form, and ask those who are interested in being in a group to mark the appropriate place. If they want to be in more than one group, ask them to number the groups in priority. Then ask all the students to fold the survey form, for the sake of privacy, and hand it in to you. Since the number of self-referrals tends to be high, be sure to tell the students that not everyone may be in a group right away. Assure them, however, that groups will be offered according to time and need.

Broader Community. Sharing information about the support group program with parents, professionals, and other concerned adults at a community forum will lead to referrals from the broader community. For example, once therapists and social workers from treatment centers and mental health agencies know that you are offering groups, they will be able to refer clients to it.

When it comes to referrals, the rule of thumb is "the broader the referral network, the better." The broader the referral network, the better the chance at-risk adolescents will be reached and helped.

Screening Candidates

No matter how students are referred for membership in a group, each candidate should be screened individually before you grant membership. The screening process consists of a brief interview that details demographic factors, the student's adjustment and attitude toward school, and the family or living situation. (See the Screening Interview Outline on page 202.) If the student is self-referred, and if you or other group leaders have no knowledge of the particular family stress, screening will help gather specific information about it.

During the screening interview, make the young person as comfortable as possible, acknowledge loyalty to the family, stress confidentiality, and reassure him or her that such questioning will not take place in front of other group members. Ask respectfully for specific information about the family stress. Listen carefully to the student's reason for self-referral, then use your best judgment about whether or not to include the student in the group.

If you know about the family stress of a particular candidate, and the adolescent is in denial (therefore, generally not self-referred), there's no need to break that denial during the screening interview. Simply help the student see that being part of the group is a way to learn about issues like divorce, chemical dependence, anger management, or violence prevention.

If you feel that the student belongs in a group, discuss the group process, including group format and session topics. Describing the format will prepare the student for what will happen in during the sessions and will reassure him or her about the safety of the group.

Show each prospective group member a copy of the Group Rules Contract (see page 61).

Explain the rules and tell the student that to be in the group, he or she must make a commitment to attend every group session and to keep all the rules. Explain that the rule about making up missed class work is important, so that administrators and teachers will be willing to support a group program in the future. Tell the student that at the first group session, all group members will be asked to sign a copy of the Group Rules Contract. It's important to explain the consequences of not following the rules during the screening interview. Explain that if a student is not following the rules, he or she will be given one warning. If they continue misbehaving, they will be asked to leave the group for that session. The student can return the next week, but if he or she is not able to follow the rules then, the student again will be asked to leave and will not be able to return to the group. Group leaders who are clear about the behavior they expect, and who enforce consequences, help give the group members the structure that adolescents need. This process also sets the stage for good behavior during the group sessions.

At this point in the screening interview, it's important to ask the student if he or she wants to participate in the group and is willing to follow the rules. It is important that the group members have a sense of ownership and investment in the group. Experience has shown that students who are coerced to join a group may remain resistant throughout the sessions.

It's useful to show the adolescent a copy of the Parental Consent Form, and to ask if he or she anticipates any problems. It might be more effective for the leader to call the parent to explain about the group, rather than to send a letter. Adolescents generally have a good sense of an appropriate way to obtain their parents' consent.

The prospect of screening every group candidate individually may seem a bit daunting. But such screening isn't just for your sake; it's also a valuable experience for the student. The screening may also serve as a case-finding procedure, during which cases of alcohol and other drug experimentation or sexual or physical abuse may come to light and can be dealt with properly. Naturally, cases of sexual and physical abuse should be reported immediately to the appropriate authorities. The screening may reveal that the student needs a group experience regarding another family issue. If such is the case, you can make the appropriate referral.

Acquiring Informed Parental Consent

To ensure a group's integrity and success, you need to acquire consent from the parents whose children are candidates for group membership. Procedures for acquiring parental consent must consider the children's needs, the parents' rights to privacy, the school's desire to help its students, and the provisions of the law in order to avoid any legal action being taken against the school.

The simplest way to get informed consent is to have the school mail a letter to the parents of all prospective group members that clearly but simply

- describes the group process
- encourages parents to allow their child to receive the services the group can provide
- informs parents that they must contact the school if they do not want their child to participate (see the Parental Consent Letter on page 198).

If you feel that parents will be resistant, call or visit with them personally to talk about the group. Explain the group format and progression of themes. Emphasize that you're not looking for family pathology or problems, but rather are hoping to correct misconceptions and to teach coping skills. Once the group program is explained well to parents, few are likely to refuse permission for their child to take part.

There will be times when you, another group leader, or a school staff member will identify a particular student who could benefit by participating in a group, but whose parents refuse to allow it. If you've clearly explained the purpose and format of the group to the parents, and they still don't want their child involved, there are two ways you can help the adolescent. First, make sure that the student is present for any in-school presentation about the group, either one you offer as a recruitment tool or one that students themselves might provide (for example, the presentation provided by the optional Session 10). An at-risk adolescent can begin to integrate facts, concepts, and specific skills even when the presentation is brief. Second, you can refer the student to the school counseling services for individual assistance. Some counselors modify these groups to use with students individually. Finally, remember, these groups are not the only help available to at-risk adolescents.

Forming and Scheduling the Groups

You know from your own experience that the best groups—of any kind—are made up of different individuals with varying temperaments and personalities. The same is true for these groups. To the best of your ability, see to it that a group is a mix of adolescents who are outgoing, shy, talkative, quiet, boys, girls, and so on. Because of the wide variation in development among early adolescents, you should not have more than a two-year age spread for middle school students in a group. However, high school groups seem to work even with a four-year spread.

For rich group dynamics and useful interactions, eight seems to be the maximum number of participants for the structured groups of this model. When the group size extends beyond eight, the level of individual attention and sharing diminishes. If you find that more students want to participate, offer more groups as it becomes possible to do so.

The location, size, and atmosphere of a group's meeting room are very important in establishing a safe, welcoming space for students to open up and take risks. Generally, classrooms aren't the most satisfactory places for group meetings; they're almost always too large and filled with too many distractions. Ideally, the meeting room needs to be small, comfortable, and quiet, a place where interruptions and potential distractions are minimal. Privacy is essential so teenagers won't be afraid that others outside the room can see or overhear them. Sitting together at a table will help promote group cohesion and simplify discussion.

Survey your school facility for a good place for group meetings. Obviously, such a space is often at a premium in a school setting, so remember that your most important considerations are privacy, quiet, and regular availability.

Besides matters of space, scheduling must also deal with matters of time. The group sessions are designed to last approximately 45 minutes. Plan to hold them on a weekly basis so that the adolescents have time to integrate the insight and support gained from each session. Weekly sessions are also less likely to interfere with the students' studies and other activities. Although you'll want to make the meeting place and day consistent, you may rotate meeting times so that the students won't miss instruction in the same subject each week. For example, for the first week, schedule the group meeting during the first instructional hour; for the second week, schedule it during the second instructional hour, and so on.

In all matters of scheduling, administrative support is an invaluable aid to help foster teacher cooperation in releasing students from regular classes. Remember, however, that cooperation is a two-way street. Let teachers know that students participate in the group on the condition that they make up all missed work. Likewise, give teachers a schedule of group meetings so that they'll know in advance what class a student will miss, won't plan field trips or tests for those times, and can make arrangements for the student to make up missed schoolwork.

Assuring Group Confidentiality

Confidentiality is the cornerstone of safe and supportive groups. To share problems and deep feelings, group members must know that what they say will be kept in confidence. Experts have pointed out that at-risk children are very reluctant to reveal family problems. For example, there are unspoken rules in many at-risk families: "Don't talk; don't trust; don't feel" (Black, 1981). It's important to realize that the adolescents will not open up if they think that what they share will become common knowledge around school. Group confidentiality, therefore, must be guaranteed.

In setting up a group, therefore, take extra care to assure and protect confidentiality. The students must realize that outside of the group sessions, they may not discuss who else is in their group or what they say. The group members can, however, discuss the facts and information they learn during group. The group leader has responsibilities as well. Except in cases where the law requires such revelation (for example, where a group leader suspects that a child is being physically or sexually abused), it is inappropriate for a group leader to reveal to others anything a student may share. It's a good idea, therefore, to inform the students of this at the very first session.

But what about teachers in the school? Don't they have a right to know when a student will miss class because of his or her participation in a group? Yes, they do. But isn't this a breach of confidentiality? No, not at all. To help maintain confidentiality, you need only inform teachers that the group is part of the school counseling program and that the students in it are going to learn basic facts about alcohol and other drugs, anger management, family violence, or divorce. For even further confidentiality, you might give the group a simple generic name. That way, neither school staff nor anyone else (except specific group members) will know what kind of group a student is in or what the student's specific problem(s) might be. Teachers will only know that one or more of their students are taking part in a group.

In a support group, the students have opportunities to share feelings and to self-disclose as they choose, all the while remaining loyal to their families. Although they have many opportunities to take an active part in every group session, if they choose to pass, they may, and the group leader respects their decision. Meanwhile, through warm acceptance and a nonjudgmental attitude, the leader builds an atmosphere of trust. As the students grow more secure, they feel safe to self-disclose and identify and share feelings, which the group leader helps them express in appropriate ways. Remember, however, that self-disclosure is not the goal of the group. Group members who never say a word in group can still benefit.

Self-disclosure by Leaders

Since the group members aren't required or asked to self-disclose, should group leaders self-disclose? If used correctly, self-disclosure can be a useful group technique with middle and high school students. Even so, leaders should be very cautious and think carefully before self-disclosing. Sharing facts about one's personal life is appropriate only if it's positive role modeling or if it will help illustrate a point effectively. However, leaders should never employ self-disclosure for purposes of eliciting the same from students, nor should they use the group for personal therapy. For example, leaders must not express feelings or share experiences that they haven't adequately resolved or dealt with themselves. If you're ever in doubt whether to self-disclose, a good rule of thumb is to trust your doubt and don't.

Role Modeling by Leaders

Although group leaders should make their own decisions regarding self-disclosure, the group model does ask leaders to share of themselves several times during each group session. Leaders act as role models for important components. Leaders begin the go-arounds for the feelings check-in, the affirmation, and the closing activity of each session. During the feelings check-in, leaders act as role models by sharing appropriate feelings and facts, such as "I'm glad to see you" or "I'm feeling sad because my dog died." During the affirmation, leaders model what it means to take a positive attitude, to choose helpful ways to express anger, and to have a repertoire of coping strategies. Overall, it's important to follow the rule of thumb described earlier. Never share a feeling or issue that has not been dealt with or resolved adequately. Doing so would be poor role modeling.

Following Up Group Participation

Some adolescents who participate in a group will require further services. If, for instance, students have severe behavior problems, it's unlikely that one group experience will enable them to deal much differently or much more effectively with the stress in their lives. Realizing this, be sure to make further help available. That help can come in the form of individual, group, or system follow-up.

Individual Follow-up. A counselor can continue to see students individually. Follow-up counseling sessions can help them learn to integrate the concepts and skills the group presented and to use them in their own lives.

Group Follow-up. For students with serious behavior problems, participating in other group experiences can be very beneficial. For example, students who have been in a support group for children from chemically dependent families, such as the group provided in *Tanya Talks About Chemical Dependence in the Family,* may continue to have difficulty dealing with or expressing their anger in helpful ways. Or the chemical dependence in their families may be accompanied by family violence. Such students could benefit from taking part in the *Anger Management and Violence Prevention* group.

Students are often eager to participate in another group, since they enjoy the familiarity, consistency, and predictability of the group format, as well as the ability to discuss problems openly, in a safe place, with peers that they trust. Students should not, however, participate in more than one group at a time. Instead, encourage them to spread their participation over one or two years.

System Follow-up. Students with particularly intense behavior problems may require the services of a schoolwide helping plan as follow-up to their participation in a group. Such services can include any or all of the following: (1) individual counseling; (2) successive group experiences; (3) a schoolwide plan for anger management (see the Background and Guidelines section for Session 7 on page 138); (4) participation in a peer counseling program; and (5) frequent consultation between counselor and teachers and administrators in charge of discipline, to enable them to help students use their centering exercises, anger management steps, and problem-solving skills in anger situations. Of course, recognize that you may want or need to refer an adolescent or family for outside therapy.

Using the Program in Guidance Counseling

Guidance counselors and other professionals have found the group model's centering exercises, anger management plan, problem-solving skills, and basic facts useful not only when working with adolescents in groups but also when working with them individually. Because the group's concepts, including the basic education about the issues and the correction of typical misconceptions, are clear and easily identifiable, they enhance assessment skills. They also empower counselors to be more effective in individual counseling with students. Instead of just discussing feelings with the students, counselors can impart information and correct misconceptions. Also, the skills presented in the group are effective techniques that adolescents learn, master, and use.

Guidance counselors who have led groups based on this model have been able to teach centering exercises and anger management plans and to use the basic facts and coping strategy scenarios in classroom guidance. They report that students who have participated in these groups are usually actively involved in the classroom discussion, which reveals that adolescents truly do integrate crucial concepts presented by the program (for example, "Divorce is never the child's fault" and "It is never acceptable to use violence to express anger"). Counselors generally report that leading these groups gives them a sense of greater competence, effectiveness, and empowerment.

Using the Group Material in Family Therapy

This group model works well not only in schools, mental health facilities, and treatment centers, but it also works well in family therapy with families experiencing chemical dependence, divorce, and family violence, or with families in which children exhibit aggressive behavior.

By using the group's format and materials, therapists can help family members become aware of and learn the facts about whatever issue has brought them to therapy. The family members can see the impact the issue has made on their family and their feelings about it. The program can help the family learn anger management steps, develop coping strategies, set personal goals, and develop a support system. During family sessions, the helping professional serves as a role model for the parents.

Just as the program corrects misconceptions for children, it also corrects them for parents. For instance, a mother engaged in long-term conflict with an ex-spouse may come to see that it's important for her children to be friendly with both parents, and she will then lessen her part in the conflict. Or a father whose spouse is chemically dependent might come to understand that his wife has a disease, that alcohol or another drug is causing the changes in her behavior, and that her problems aren't his fault or his problems. Likewise, parents who express anger by yelling or who try to control through physical force can learn to use—and benefit from—the program's centering exercises, anger management steps, and problem-solving skills. Finally, all parents can benefit by learning to put thinking between feeling and behavior.

This group model, based on the *Building Trust, Making Friends* program, was developed for caring professionals like you who are concerned about at-risk adolescents. It will help you enhance the emotional growth, safety, and self-esteem of these young people. It will also give at-risk students the chance to obtain the skills they need to maintain their physical and emotional health and to correct any misconceptions they may have developed. Living healthfully and well is a risky business. All children, especially at-risk children, deserve the chance to take that risk.

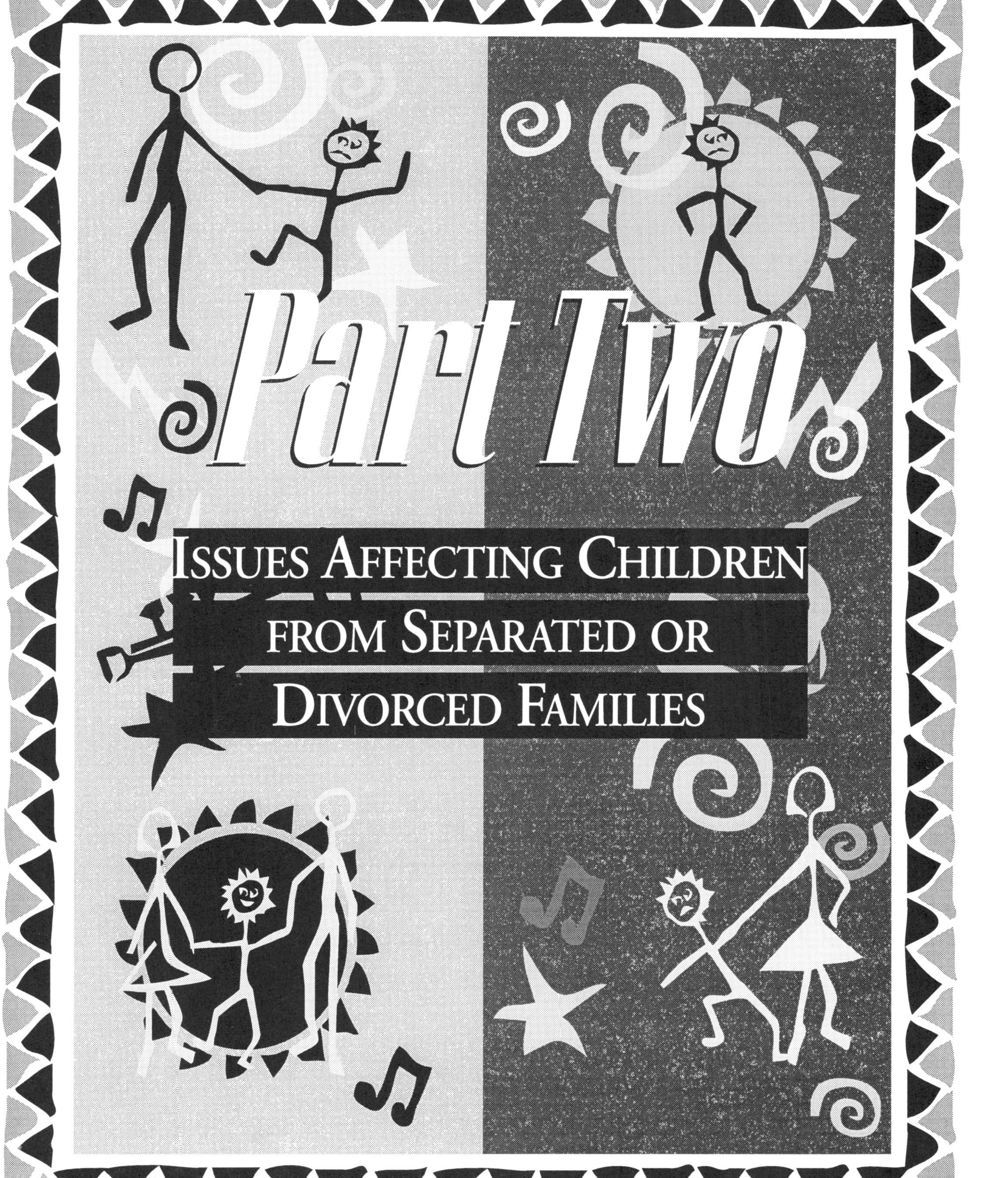

Part Two

Issues Affecting Children from Separated or Divorced Families

CHAPTER • 1

The Influence of Divorce and Separation

Among the many stresses facing at-risk children today, separation and divorce seem to be the most prevalent. As the divorce rate reaches 50 percent, it has been estimated that 40 percent of all children will experience a parental divorce (Kalter, 1990).

The effects of divorce on children have been well documented. On the scale of childhood traumas, divorce is considered second only to the death of a parent. The reactions of children of divorcing parents have been compared to the stages of grief (shock, denial and repression, anger, depression, and acceptance). Experts have discovered that children may also experience shame, low self-esteem, a feeling that they are responsible for the divorce, and an obsessive desire to reunite their parents (Francke, 1983).

Children from divorced or separated families are at risk for developing the following problems: angry and aggressive behavior, sadness, depression, impaired academic performance, and difficulties with intimate relationships in adolescence and adulthood (Hetherington, Stanley-Hagan, and Anderson 1989). Studies of the long-term effects of divorce on children reveal that as many as 30 to 50 percent may have long-lasting difficulties in cognitive, emotional, social, and/or behavioral development.

Stages of Divorce—Effects on Children

Research (Kalter, 1990) has shown that divorce is a process that may be divided into three stages:

1. The immediate crisis stage
2. The short-term aftermath stage
3. The long-range stage

As Kalter describes, the effects of divorce on children differ depending on the stage of the divorce process.

The Immediate Crisis Stage. During this first stage, children are often subject to intense parental conflict, anger, and hurt. Parents may feel guilty, remorseful, unlovable, and depressed.

Frequently, there is financial distress. Many parents have diminished parenting capacities (at least temporarily) and are often less attentive to their children, less patient, and more irritable. During this stage, children experience two major losses: (1) the loss of the belief that their parents will never get divorced, and (2) the partial or complete loss of their relationship with the noncustodial parent.

The Short-term Aftermath Stage. This stage can last for as long as two years after the immediate crisis has passed. During this stage, children experience stress due to continued hostility between parents, parental neediness, the loss of relationship with the noncustodial parent, decreased attention from the custodial parent (who may be working or attending school), and parental dating, which may evoke sexual conflicts, as well as result in decreased parental attention.

The Long-range Stage. Continued parental hostility remains a major source of stress for children in this stage. Such ongoing conflict puts children at significant risk for developing emotional and behavioral disorders. A parent's remarriage is also a cause for significant stress during this stage. A new stepparent can create conflict in children regarding loyalty to their own parent of the same sex, jealousy due to the remarried parent's diminished attention, anger over the loss of hope for the parents' reunion, and resentment over the stepparent's attempts to discipline them.

Effects of Divorce on Children at Different Stages of Development

Just as the effects of divorce on children vary according to the different stages of the divorce process, so do they vary according to children's different stages of development. Children's developmental stages can be classified in many different ways. Three stages relate to the goals of this program:

1. The early elementary stage
2. The later elementary stage
3. The adolescent stage

Kalter again describes how separation and divorce affect children at all three stages.

The Early Elementary Stage. Early elementary children (ages 6 to 8) have enough cognitive and abstract-thinking ability to have fantasies regarding abandonment by the noncustodial parent. These children are still egocentric and tend to blame themselves for the divorce. Although they enjoy sufficient emotional independence to attend school, they still need a stable home base. Early elementary children have a powerful attachment to both parents and a strong sense of family; they feel divorce as a significant loss.

In the *immediate crisis stage of divorce,* early elementary children may act very sad. In spite of their defenses of denial and anger, these children may cry, have difficulty concentrating in school, and withdraw from their peers. During the *short-term aftermath stage,* their denial generally breaks down. The major stressors of parental warfare, depression, or diminished attention from a busy custodial parent, can cause these children to display anger, to assume head-of-household chores, or to feel abandoned. In the *long-range stage,* early elementary children may become fearful or angry with peers (especially if parental warfare persists), or they may suffer a disruption of a close relationship with a parent who remarries.

Distress in early elementary children can appear as sadness, depression (sad thoughts, withdrawal, lowered self-esteem), anger, and general anxiety that reveals itself in nervous habits, fear, and a loss or failure to achieve developmentally, such as, for example, a return to bed-wetting.

The Later Elementary Stage. Children in the later elementary stage of development (ages 9 to 12) are gaining psychological maturity. Unlike early elementary children, they can develop internal conflicts regarding a divorce. Instead of simply having frightening fantasies or self-blaming beliefs, these children have conflicted loyalties and a more elaborate system of psychological defenses.

During the *immediate crisis stage of divorce,* later elementary children can act as if they are emotionally detached. They may give no explicit signs that the separation or divorce bothers them. However, their behavior demonstrates that they are, in fact, experiencing distress. Boys may act aggressively at school or at home with siblings. Girls may employ a defense called "reaction formation"; namely, they convert a feeling into its opposite. For example, instead of expressing their anger through aggression, girls might become overly solicitous and helpful. The internal conflict for later elementary children (boys and girls alike) at this stage is anger at parents versus love of parents. This ambivalence can be very threatening and confusing to children.

During the *short-term aftermath stage of divorce,* parents may tend to rely more on later elementary children to help around the house, especially if the parents are suffering from depression. Children then experience the internal conflict of wishing to help the distressed parent and wishing to be involved with their peers. If parents have continued discord, children often feel guilt and shame over disloyalty. They also struggle with the internal conflict of trying to remain loyal to both parents while feeling driven to take sides in the parental conflict. Both of these cause stress in children and can interfere with their development. For example, children may feel so responsible for parental conflict that they fail to achieve the normal developmental task of acquiring independence from the family and the ability to form relationships with peers and others outside the family.

During the *long-range stage of divorce,* later elementary children may experience a number of stresses connected to parental dating: less attention from the parent; having to confront the parent's sexuality—that is, realize that the parent is a sexual person with sexual desires and needs, not just "Mom" or "Dad"; and struggling with loyalty conflicts, namely, being torn between affection for one parent's new partner and loyalty to the other parent.

Signs of distress in later elementary children may appear in behavior and feelings that seem unrelated to the divorce: anger with peers; verbal aggressiveness and noncompliance with parents; somatic complaints, which protect the children against their anger and their longing for an inattentive parent; and social withdrawal. Defenses for later elementary children include intellectualizing, denial, displacement, somatizing, converting one feeling to another, and identifying with an absent parent.

Intellectualizing means that a child focuses on the thinking regarding a trauma or stress, but doesn't experience the accompanying feeling. Denial is pretending that a feeling or an event is not happening. An example of displacement is the behavior of children who express their anger at their parents by fighting with siblings or peers. Children who experience many physical complaints, such as stomach aches and headaches, may be somatizing. Children who are very angry at an absent parent may convert that feeling to another one and profess feelings of love, concern, and forgiveness instead. Children who identify with an absent parent might carry that identification so far as to adopt the parent's mannerisms instead of longing for the parent.

All of these defenses are self-protective and unconscious. They should not be confronted directly. Instead, Kalter recommends using displacement communication techniques to help children identify their stresses and feelings and change their behavior, while enabling them to save face and preserve family loyalty.

The Adolescent Stage. Because adolescents are already experiencing tremendous changes in their physical, mental, and emotional lives, the divorce stakes are higher for them. Adolescents' reactive behaviors can include chemical abuse, sexual acting out, and running away.

Adolescents respond to the *immediate crisis stage of divorce* with shock, anger, dismay, and sadness. They lose the familial structure that is so necessary for their development. They experience a much more rapid shift in their perceptions of their parents than children from intact families—for example, they react very judgmentally if a parent has had an extramarital affair. And, they often revert to the egocentric thinking that they are to blame for the divorce.

During the *short-term aftermath stage of divorce,* adolescents generally accept its finality. Still, they may vehemently protest the symbols of the divorce, such as selling the family home. In the *long-range stage,* adolescents experience the cumulative effects of continued parental warfare and the absence of the noncustodial parent. With a parent's remarriage, adolescents often find themselves in conflict over their affection for the parent's new partner versus their anxiety over their own sexuality.

Adolescent boys who live with single mothers and who have little father contact may be prone to hypermasculine behaviors and conflicts with their mothers in order to prove their masculinity. In such cases, a mother needs to strive for reasonable compromise in order to acknowledge and respect her son's sense of emotional independence from her. In fact, reasonable compromise is helpful with almost all adolescents, male or female.

Teenagers show distress through anger, depression, and somatic complaints. Their defenses are internalizing (intellectualizing, denial, displacement, somatizing) and externalizing (fighting, vandalism, stealing, chemical abuse, and sexual acting out). Parents can help adolescents cope with the effects and stresses of divorce by reducing environmental stresses such as parental warfare and by using displacement communication and reasonable compromise.

Helping Children Cope with Divorce

Although 30 to 50 percent of children from divorced families have long-term difficulties in cognitive, behavioral, social, or emotional development, 50 to 70 percent of these children suffer no long-term pathological effects and adjust well once the initial crisis has passed.

Much research has been done to help children minimize and cope with the stresses of divorce. Overall, experts emphasize three things to help children manage the divorce process:

1. Children need to maintain regular, consistent, and predictable contact with both parents.

2. Children need a conflict-free zone in which they are shielded from parental conflict, including put-downs, arguments, threats, and tension.

3. Parents need to improve their parenting skills through practicing good listening habits, paying attention to their children's feelings, setting reasonable rules and limits, and spending time with their children.

No matter what their age, children from divorced families need to understand that they don't cause, can't control, and can't change the family's problem (the divorce). By being consistent, predictable, and nonjudgmental, the group process of *Changing Families* empowers children who live in divorced families to make positive changes in their own lives.

This material was drawn from the following sources:

Despert, L. 1953. *Children of Divorce.* New York: Doubleday.

Diamond, S. 1985. *Helping Children of Divorce: A Handbook for Parents and Teachers.* New York: Schocken Books.

Dolmetsch, P., and A. Shih. 1985. *The Kids' Book About Single-parent Families.* Garden City, NY: Dolphin.

Francke, L. 1981. *Growing Up Divorced.* New York: Linden Press/Simon and Schuster.

Gardner, R. 1981. *The Boys and Girls Book About Divorce.* New York: Bantam Books.

_______. 1981. *The Parents Book About Divorce.* New York: Bantam Books.

Hetherington, E. M., M. Stanley-Hagan, and E. Anderson. 1989. "Marital Transitions: A Child's Perspective." *American Psychologist* 44, 2: 302-12.

Jewett, C. 1982. *Helping Children Cope with Separation and Loss.* Harvard, Mass.: The Harvard Common Press.

Kalter, N. 1990. *Growing Up with Divorce.* New York: The Free Press.

Kubler-Ross, E. 1969. *On Death and Dying.* New York: Macmillan.

Lansky, V. 1989. *Divorce Book for Parents.* New York: New American Library.

Wallerstein, J., and S. Blakeslee. 1989. *Second Chances: Men and Women and Children a Decade After Divorce.* New York: Ticknor and Fields.

Wallerstein, J., and J. Kelly. 1980. *Surviving the Breakup: How Children and Parents Cope with Divorce.* New York: Basic Books

CHAPTER • 2

Adolescent Development and Intervention Models

Chapter 1 explored the stages of divorce and the effects on children at different developmental levels. Chapter 2 will review issues in adolescent development, will look at the effects of maltreatment on the developmental tasks of childhood and adolescence, and will describe the theoretical bases for the concepts, methods, and techniques in this manual.

Adolescent Development

The theory of lifespan developmental psychology looks at child and adolescent development in a comprehensive way (Coleman and Hendry, 1990). While psychoanalytic theory examines adolescent development as a time of turmoil in the individual, and sociological theory looks at roles and role changes, the lifespan approach posits that there is a human ecology: individuals live in families, and both individuals and families develop in the context of their geographical, historical, social, and political settings. Both individuals and families grow and develop and change, and they reciprocally influence each other as they do so. Theorists are increasingly looking at individuals as producers of their own development, active agents in shaping or determining their lives.

The ecological framework used by many researchers consists of four levels: the personal (ontogenetic) level, the family (microsystem) level, the social (exosystem) level, and the societal (macrosystem) level. Adolescence is a time of enormous change in at least three of the four levels of this framework; the changes on the personal level will be reviewed here.

On the Personal Level: Adolescent Changes

Physical Development

Early adolescence is marked by impressive physical changes, beginning at puberty. The word *puberty* comes from Latin and means the age of manhood. During the growth spurt, height and weight increase; the weight of the heart nearly doubles; there is accelerated growth of the lungs; and physical strength and endurance show a marked increase, especially in boys. There is extreme variation in this growth spurt, as it starts at different ages for males and females. In girls, the growth spurt can begin at 7 or 8, or not start until 12, 13, or 14. The average age of rapid growth for girls starts at 11 and peaks at 12. For boys, the average age of rapid growth starts at 13 and peaks at 14. Sexual maturation also differs from boys to girls. For boys, the first sign of the approach of puberty is an increase in the rate of growth of the genitals, followed by the appearance of pubic hair; the appearance of facial hair accompanies the beginning of the growth spurt. In girls, the menarche, or first menstrual cycle, usually occurs after the peak velocity of the growth spurt.

The enormous growth and the body changes affect the identity and self-concept of the early adolescent. The variations of growth can have an impact on these teens. For boys, early maturation has social advantages. Early maturing boys have been found to be more relaxed, more popular, less dependent, and more attractive to both adults and peers. The situation is less clear-cut for early maturing girls. Some studies have shown that they are less popular and more likely to show signs of inner turmoil; others report enhanced self-confidence and social prestige. In addition to the social significance of their growth, children in puberty must also adjust to the physical effects of their growth. Early adolescents are frequently clumsy as their coordination tries to catch up to their changing bodies. Their focus on their bodies is indicated by studies that show they describe themselves in terms of physical characteristics, whereas older adolescents describe themselves by their intellectual or social aspects.

Thinking and Reasoning: Formal Operational Thinking

The development of thinking and reasoning in adolescents moves them from thinking like children—in concrete ways—to thinking like adults—in abstract ways. Coleman and Hendry describe Jean Piaget's stage of *concrete operations,* ages 7 through 11, when children's thought is relational. Children begin to master notions of classes, relations, and quantities. Conservation and seriation is possible, enabling children to formulate hypotheses and explanations about concrete events. Children formulate a hypothesis originating from the concrete data, rather than from internal resources. And, once the hypothesis is formulated, children in the concrete operations stage are reluctant to change the hypothesis, tending instead to alter the data.

As adolescents move into the stage of *formal operations,* they are able to utilize a number of important capabilities: one of these is the "contrary to fact" proposition, described as a shift in thinking from the real to the possible, which facilitates a hypothetico-deductive approach to problem solving and to the understanding of propositional logic. Adolescents develop the ability to think about mental constructs as objects that can be manipulated and they can master concepts, such as probability and belief.

Coleman and Hendry (1990) describe a study of concept-formation where children of 8 to 9 years and adolescents between 13 and 14 were shown pictures of wheeled and nonwheeled tools and vehicles. Shown a wheeled and a nonwheeled object, the child was asked to choose one item, and a light went on when the wheeled object was chosen. Only half of the younger children came to the conclusion that choosing a wheeled object made the light go on, and it took them nearly all of the 72 trials. By comparison, all the adolescents solved the problem, and many did so in as few as 10 trials. The adolescents thought of hypotheses, tested them, and discarded them if they did not work. The younger children came to a hypothesis based on the data (tool versus nontool or vehicle versus nonvehicle) and were unable to give up the hypothesis even though they failed on most trials. These children were unable to differentiate the hypothesis from reality.

Coleman and Hendry point out that the change from concrete to formal operations occurs slowly in adolescents, and there may be shifting back and forth. Some adolescents may develop formal modes of thinking in one area, such as a verbal area, and later in other areas, such as mathematic and scientific areas.

Social Cognition

Social cognition theorists look at the child's concrete thinking and egocentrism and compare them to the adolescent's formal operational thinking, which allows the adolescent to think about the thought of other people. Coleman and Hendry describe Robert Selman's stage theory of social cognition, which involves role taking, perspective taking, empathy, moral reasoning, interpersonal problem solving, and self-knowledge. Selman's stages describe early adolescence (ages 10-15) as a time when the teen has the capacity for a more complex type of social cognition. The teen moves beyond simply taking the other person's perspective (in a back-and-forth manner) and is able to see all parties from a more generalized third-person perspective. By age 15, the adolescent may move to a still higher and more abstract level of interpersonal perspective taking that involves coordinating the perspectives of society with those of the individual and the group.

Self-concept Development

Adolescents experience great change in self-concept as a result of (1) the major physical changes of puberty, which affect body image; (2) the intellectual growth, which allows for a more complex and sophisticated self-concept; (3) the increasing emotional independence from parents and the need to make important choices about values, friendships, sexual behavior, alcohol and drug use, and occupation. Adolescent self-concept involves issues about *gender identification* and *sex roles.* Studies show children generally have distinct ideas about these issues; there is much more ambiguity in early adolescents; and older adolescents, approaching adulthood, again have a stronger perceived gender identity.

Researchers have looked at ***self-esteem,*** an aspect of self-concept, as rising from

1. *competence* or success in meeting achievement demands
2. *social acceptance,* or attention, worthiness, and positive reinforcement received from significant others
3. *control,* or feelings of internal responsibility for outcomes
4. *virtue,* or adherence to moral and ethical standards

Some adolescents will value competence in sports, while others will value popularity. Studies show that early adolescents have the most difficulty with self-esteem, with girls worrying more about body image and same-sex popularity. There seems to be a general rise in self-esteem during adolescence.

Self-concept literature also discusses the concepts of *locus of control* and *self-agency.* These concepts portray individuals as having the capacity to engage in purposive, goal-oriented, if rule-bound, action, rather than as passive products of socialization. People who have an external locus of control have a passive world view, regarding important events as being essentially independent of their actions. They tend to have outer self-esteem, based on the perceived opinion of others derived from the occupation of a particular position in the social structure. In contrast, people who have a sense of self-agency, an internal locus of control, believe that they have some control over their lives and that their fates are in their own hands. They tend to have inner self-esteem, deriving directly from the experience of themselves as agents who can make things happen in the world and attain their goals, regardless of obstacles.

Erikson's (1968) description of forming an idea of identity as a major task of adolescence is another aspect of self-concept, pertaining especially to older adolescents. Erikson describes four states of identity. Adolescents in the state of *identity diffusion* have no commitment to a vocation or set of beliefs and are not actively trying to make a commitment. Teens who have not experienced their own identity crisis and are committed in goals and beliefs, but largely as a result of choices made by others, are in the state of *identity foreclosure.* Young people in a state of crisis, who are actively searching among alternatives in an attempt to arrive at the choice of identity, are in the state of *moratorium.* Finally, teens who have had a crisis, who have resolved it on their own terms, and who have a firm commitment to an occupation, an ideology, and social roles, are in the state of *identity achievement.*

On the Family Level: the Effects of Maltreatment on Developmental Tasks

Teens and their families must cope with two major developmental tasks during the adolescent years. First, the family must adjust to the adolescent's physical and cognitive growth, and second, the family must prepare the adolescent to leave the home and enter the adult world of work and love.

Cicchetti and Howes (1991) provide a framework for looking at how families can help adolescents master their developmental tasks. They see development as a series of tasks that are age- and stage-appropriate, but which remain critical to the child's continual adaptation. For instance, attachment, the major task of infancy, continues to be relevant as children reach the tasks of later years, such as emotional regulation, autonomy, peer relations, and school adjustment. Cicchetti and Howes believe that some families provide *potentiating,* or *risk, factors* increasing the likelihood of the child developing incompetence at these tasks, while some families provide *compensatory,* or *protective, factors,* which increase the probability of competence in the child's developmental tasks. Cicchetti and Howes describe the effects of maltreating parents on the developmental achievements of young children in five areas: attachment, emotion regulation, autonomous self, peer relations, and school adjustment. The adolescent's behavior and adjustment will be affected by how competently he or she mastered these early developmental tasks.

Task 1: Attachment

The task of infancy—to form secure attachment relationships with the primary caregiver—is especially affected by the characteristics of the caregiver. An adequate caregiver will be sensitive and responsive to the infant's needs. Mothers who are inconsistent in their accessibility and responsiveness to their infants tend to have babies who are both anxious and angry. Mothers who tend to withhold close bodily contact, especially at times of high infant intensity, have babies who are anxious and avoidant of their mothers. Children who have insecurity and fear in these initial relationships may expect maltreatment in later relationships and may continue to express their own anger or avoidant behavior in later childhood and adult relationships (Crittenden and Ainsworth, in Cicchetti and Carlson, 1989).

Task 2: Emotion Regulation

Emotional self-regulation—the ability to modulate and initiate both positive and negative affect (or feelings)—is another early childhood task that continues to be important throughout the rest of the lifespan. Cicchetti and Howes believe that "the use of emotional language helps one control nonverbal emotional expressions, which in turn enhances regulation of the emotions themselves" (Cicchetti and Howes, 1991). Parents who use emotional language by putting feelings into words help their children learn to organize and control their emotional expressions. Maltreated children are overly aware of aggressive stimuli, an adaptive coping mechanism to alert them to signs of immediate danger. However, such awareness of aggressive stimuli is not adaptive when children are in nonthreatening situations.

Task 3: Autonomous Self

The toddler develops a sense of being a separate individual with personal thoughts, feelings and behaviors, a foreshadowing of the adolescent move to independence. Maltreated toddlers show evidence of low self-esteem, not smiling when they see themselves in the mirror and talking less about themselves. In a tool use/problem-solving situation, maltreated 2-year-olds show increased anger, frustration with their mothers, and noncompliance, revealing a difficulty in making a smooth transition to autonomy. Maltreated children in grades 1-3 see themselves as more competent and accepted than other children, and more competent than their teachers perceive them to be. Such inflated self-perception may reflect unrealistic coping strategies that help them gain a sense of personal competence and control in chaotic home settings, but may eventually cause them to feel like failures. By grades 4-6, maltreated children view themselves as less competent and accepted, and more in accordance with teacher ratings, showing a lower self-worth.

Task 4: Peer Relationships

Positive peer relationships can be buffering factors in the lives of maltreated children. However, maltreated children tend to display more disturbed patterns of interaction with peers, showing higher levels of physical and verbal aggression and a higher degree of withdrawal from interaction. Both patterns lead to increasing isolation and peer rejection.

Task 5: Adaptation to School

This final childhood task involves integration into the peer group, acceptable performance in the classroom, and appropriate motivational orientations for achievement. Maltreated children may have unmet physical needs and concerns over safety and may tend to search for acceptance. They may show dependence on teachers, score low on tests of cognitive maturity, and show less readiness to learn in school. In contrast, the optimum state for the child is a secure readiness to learn: a dynamic balance between establishing secure relationships with adults and feeling free to explore the environment in ways that will promote cognitive competence.

Obviously, an ambivalent attachment relationship, an inability to regulate emotion, a failure to develop a sense of autonomous self, poor peer relationships, and poor adaptation to school in early childhood will make chances for a successful, competent, or even adequate adjustment in adolescence more difficult. Adolescents who had problems in the earlier developmental tasks may have problems negotiating the pubertal changes and the movement to independence. The next section addresses the impact of families on the achievement of adolescent developmental tasks.

Task 6: Adjustment to Physical, Social, and Cognitive Changes

Gabarino (in Cicchetti and Carlson, 1989) describes how the family structure can affect the way families deal with adolescent changes. *Authoritarian families* are paternalistic and harsh and use rigid and domineering childrearing styles. Parents tend to avoid feelings and use high levels of force. Authoritarian parents tend to allow their adolescent little freedom, and there is increased conflict over spending money, friends, social life, and activities outside the home. If the parental discipline has been severe, without much love and affection, teens may become overtly aggressive and may seek peer acceptance through membership in a delinquent gang.

Permissive families tend to be overindulgent, making few demands upon children, setting few limits, and demanding a high level of emotional gratification from them. Some permissive parents tend to be too protective and overinvolved, hampering the child's drive for emotional independence.

In contrast, *authoritative families* (which are different from authoritarian families) grant just enough autonomy so that the adolescent can develop a sense of self-governship and control; they also provide enough structure so that the teen is not overwhelmed by responsibility or lost with no direction. Authoritative parents use negotiating techniques, are flexible, and are able to adapt general principles and techniques (setting rules, offering encouragement) to their particular adolescents.

Taking into account that development is an interactive process between children and families, Gabarino points out that it is more difficult to parent teenagers than to parent younger children. Many adolescents have attained adult size, and some are larger and stronger than their parents; this presents a problem for parents who have used physical force to control their children. Adolescents are also more likely to be able to reason like adults and are less willing to accept parental decisions without questioning them. Both size and reasoning ability can be problematic for authoritarian families. Teens are more likely to have significant relationships outside the family, with teachers, coaches, and peers. These outside influences, especially the development of a love interest, can be very threatening to some parents, particularly overcontrolling parents who have tried to control by intrusion. Finally, Gabarino reports that it is far more expensive to raise teenagers than to raise children, causing stress for families with a marginal economic status or for permissive families who have tried to control through indulgence.

In comparing maltreatment in children and adolescents, Gabarino reports that adolescent maltreatment equals or exceeds the incidence of child maltreatment; it includes all forms of abuse and neglect, but psychological and sexual abuse are prevalent. Females are more likely to be abused in adolescence than in childhood, whereas the risk for males peaks early and generally declines through adolescence. Adolescents at high risk for maltreatment are less socially competent and exhibit more developmental problems than peers. On the family level, some adolescent maltreatment is a continuation of child abuse but some is a deterioration of unwise childrearing patterns or the inability of the family to deal with new challenges in adolescence. Families at high risk for adolescent maltreatment are more likely to contain stepparents, but there are fewer socioeconomic class differences than for child maltreatment.

Finally, Gabarino cites studies showing that families at high risk for adolescent maltreatment tend to be multiproblem families, with high rates of divorce and separation, financial stresses, and family conflict. They are authoritarian families with paternalistic, harsh, rigid, domineering styles of childrearing. The parents deny their feelings to each other or to the children. They use high levels of force. Overindulgent families are also at high risk for adolescent maltreatment. As mentioned, these families place few demands upon children, set few limits, and demand a high level of emotional gratification from the children. When teens seek to form primary attachments outside the home and to act impulsively, overindulgent parents react with excessive force. Maltreated adolescents describe their parents as being more punishing. Abusive families are chaotic and enmeshed, whereas nonabusive families are flexible and connected.

Task 7: Independence

In addition to the family task of adjusting to the physical, emotional, social, and mental changes of adolescence, the second task of adolescence is to prepare the adolescents to leave the home and enter the adult world of work and love. Wallerstein and Blakeslee (1989) addressed this issue in their long-term study of families after divorce. They found that the move to independence is gradual for adolescents in intact families, as the adolescent's "primary emotional investment fluctuates from home to school, from friends to parents, from past to future. With time he establishes an independent stance, a more detached relationship with parents" (page 83). Adolescent boys who lived with their mothers tended to have complex relationships with them, wanting love and closeness, but fearing becoming too close. For them, the move to independence is hampered by the absence of a male figure, such as a father or stepfather, who could give them help and support to make the break. Adolescent girls living with their divorced mothers also had more difficult moves to independence. Often, girls become overly responsible, taking on adult household responsibilities, becoming their mothers' confidantes and therapists, and ignoring their own adolescent needs for establishing peer relationships and emotional independence outside of the family. They also are impaired in their move to leave home. Wallerstein and Blakeslee stress the enormous amount of support that adolescents need to leave home with proper preparation, without staying longer than they should to help.

The Role of the Group in Helping Adolescents Adjust to Separation, Divorce, and Stepfamilies

This material is presented in a group model for a number of reasons:

1. Group experiences reduce the adolescent's isolating belief that he or she is the only one whose family has been separated, been divorced, or become a stepfamily.

2. Group experiences help adolescents learn to identify, validate, tolerate, and express their feelings appropriately.

3. Group experiences help adolescents become aware of their self-talk and help them learn what other adolescents are thinking.

4. Group experiences help adolescents become aware of their patterns in relationships and in dealing with their families' problems.

5. Group experiences help adolescents learn and practice changing their behavior in relationships and in expressing anger.

6. Group experiences help adolescents correct their common misconceptions, such as that they may have caused the family divorce, or that they are bad if they get angry with their parents.

7. Group experiences help adolescents develop empathy by learning that others have problems too.

8. Group experiences help adolescents learn and practice coping strategies for getting along with peers and family members.

9. Group experiences help adolescents learn that they can ask for help and can take care of themselves.

The curriculum in this manual is geared to the adolescent who lives in a family that is separated, divorced, a stepfamily, or another nontraditional family. The students learn that

- They are not to blame for the divorce.
- They can't reunite their parents.
- They don't have to take sides in a divorce, even if the parents continue their conflict.
- They aren't to blame if their parents are absent or inattentive.
- They don't have to choose between parent and stepparent.

The curriculum also encourages the adolescent to develop his or her own protective factors, coping strategies, and resiliencies to cope with the family stress in a healthy way.

As students learn to deal effectively with their issues, and learn how to deal appropriately with the stresses of family separation or divorce, their sense of competence and control should increase, as well as a more powerful sense of an internal locus of control, a sense that they can have an impact over what happens in their lives.

This material was drawn from the following sources:

Cicchetti, D., and V. Carlson, eds. 1989. *Child Maltreatment: Theory and Research on the Causes and Consequences of Child Abuse and Neglect.* New York: Cambridge University Press.

Cicchetti, D., and P. W. Howes. 1991. "Developmental Psychopathology in the Context of the Family: Illustrations from the Study of Child Maltreatment." *Canadian Journal of Behavioral Science,* 23 (3) (July 1991): 257-81.

Coleman, J. C. and L. Hendry. 1990. *The Nature of Adolescence.* New York: Routledge.

Crittenden, P. M., and M. D. S. Ainsworth. 1989. "Child Maltreatment and Attachment Theory." *In Child Maltreatment: Theory and Research on the Causes and Consequences of Child Abuse and Neglect,* ed. D. Cicchetti and V. Carlson, 432-63. New York: Cambridge University Press.

Gabarino, J. 1989. "Troubled Youth, Troubled Families: The Dynamics of Adolescent Maltreatment." *Child Maltreatment: Theory and Research on the Causes and Consequences of Child Abuse and Neglect,* ed. D. Cicchetti and V. Carlson, 685-706. New York: Cambridge University Press.

Wallerstein, J., and S. Blakeslee. 1989. *Second Chances: Men and Women and Children a Decade After Divorce.* New York: Ticknor and Fields.

Part Three

Group Guide for Changing Families

Session Plans

Changing Families: A Group Manual for Middle and High School Students from Separated, Divorced, Single-parent Families or Stepfamilies is designed for children in grades 6-12. It is intended to help children from separated, divorced, single-parent, stepfamily, or other nontraditional families to identify the issues and stresses found in these families and to learn the coping skills they need to survive and remain healthy.

This guide contains 11 group session plans for facilitating a support group for middle and high school students:

SESSION 1 : Changing Families and Family Values

SESSION 2 : Why People Get Married and Why People get Divorced

SESSION 3 : The Effects of Changing Families on Teens and Issues for Teens from Changing Families

SESSION 4 : The Effects of Divorce, Separation, and Other Nontraditional Lifestyles on Families: Family Sculptures

SESSION 5 : Feelings

SESSION 6 : Skills to Problem-solve Anger Situations

SESSION 7 : Anger Management Steps

SESSION 8 : Other Coping Strategies

SESSION 9 : Setting Personal Goals

~~SESSION 10: Group Presentation—optional~~

SESSION 11: Developing a Support System

Each plan begins with an **Objectives** section, which sets a clear direction for the group session.

The next section, **Session at a Glance,** outlines the session and suggests the amount of time to be spent on each of the plan's components. If you go over the plan carefully in advance, this section can serve as a quick reference as you move through the session.

The **Preparation** section lists materials needed and gives directions for getting ready for the session. (Note: when directions in this section call for copies of various materials, most may be found in blackline master form at the end of each session. Other support materials, such as the Screening Interview Outline and the Parental Consent Form, are found in Part Four of this manual, "Support Materials," pages 193-206.)

The **Background and Guidelines** section will enrich your understanding of the session's focus and key concepts, as well as guide you through the plan itself.

For the most part, the plan's structure follows the same format for each session and unfolds in three stages. **Beginning the Session** is the first stage and includes a review of group rules, a centering exercise, a feelings check-in (Session 1 substitutes an ice-breaker), a review of basic facts (starting with Session 2), and a review of the homework assignment (starting with Session 3). The second stage, **Exploring the Material,** includes the lecture, discussion, activity, new basic facts, and homework assignment. **Wrapping Up** is the third stage and includes a repetition of the centering exercise, an affirmation, and a closing activity.

This format provides the students with a total experience that is structured as well as welcoming and accepting, instructional as well as creative and enjoyable, challenging as well as affirming and fun. Since the format remains the same for each session, it meets the needs at-risk students have for structure, consistency, predictability, and fun. Each group session is designed to take approximately 45 minutes, but can be shortened or extended to meet local circumstances.

If you are a new group leader, you should follow up each session by filling out a copy of the

Process and Progress Form (see page 199). This form lets you evaluate the session's effectiveness and track the students' progress. It also serves as a useful tool when training new group leaders. If you are an experienced leader, you may follow up each session by filling out the Progress Notes (see page 200). No matter what your experience is, it is a good idea to keep some form of notes on each session.

You may feel that some sessions in this curriculum contain enough information to be scheduled over two meeting times. You may find this especially true for sessions 3, 4, and 8. If you have the time, simply follow the session plan as given but only present half of the plan during one session time. Also, some sessions may offer an alternative suggestion to the given activity. This allows you more choice and flexibility in leading your group. It also can help you tailor the sessions to the particular needs and idiosyncrasies of the group members.

Session 10 is an optional session. Its structure varies from the other sessions, in that group members will present facts they've learned about changing families to an invited audience. You may or may not choose to involve the students in this session. For this session to be successful, you should schedule two meeting times to present it. Use the first time period as a practice session to help the group members decide on the type and content of the presentation, to make all necessary preparations, and to practice their presentation. Use the second time period to conduct the actual session. Again, to guarantee success, plan ahead for Session 10. Read the Background and Guidelines material for Session 10 now to help you decide if you want your group to develop a unique project.

These session plans have been carefully crafted and tested. Use them carefully, creatively, and confidently. Everything you need is here.

SESSION • 1

Changing Families and Family Values

Objectives

To help the students:

- recognize that there are several kinds of families
- understand that all families have values

Session at a Glance

1. Welcome and Group Rules (Group Rules Contract)—4 minutes
2. Centering Exercise: "White Water Rafting"—3 minutes
3. Ice-breaker—5 minutes
4. Mini-lecture—6 minutes
5. Discussion: discuss scenarios—10 minutes
6. Activity: write definition of family and list family values—7 minutes
7. Basic Facts: read Basic Facts 1 and 2; discuss—2 minutes
8. Centering Exercise: "Breathing Through Your Feet"—3 minutes
9. Affirmation: share something you liked about the group—3 minutes
10. Closing: pass a silent wish—2 minutes

Preparation

- Make a copy of the Group Rules Contract (see page 61) for each student. To save time at the copy machine, also make copies of The Feeling Wheel (page 72), the handouts for each session, and the List of Basic Facts (page 197).
- Copy the group rules onto a large sheet of posterboard that you can display in the group meeting space during this and future sessions.

- Have a large manila folder for each student; print the student's name on the folder.
- Include in each student's folder:

  —a 3" x 5", lined index card

  —the Group Rules Contract

  —Handout 1A ("Scenarios")

  —Handout 1B ("Family Values")

  —the List of Basic Facts stapled to the inside of the folder, on the left side, for easy reference
- Place the folder, a pencil, and crayons or markers at each student's place.
- Make a poster to use during the session's ice-breaker. On newsprint, list the following questions:

  —What is your name?

  —Your age?

  —Your year in school?

  —Who lives in your house?

  —If you could be anywhere, where would you like to be?

  —What do you want to do after high school?

  —What are three words that end in "-ing" that describe you?
- Read through the session plan before meeting.

Background and Guidelines

As you present the session, make sure that you give a nonjudgmental explanation of separation and divorce, single-parent families, stepfamilies, or other nontraditional families. Nothing is more detrimental to adolescents from nontraditional families than to hear a group leader say, "It's wrong for parents to separate or divorce." Statements like this demonstrate that a leader hasn't emotionally accepted the reality of today's world, one in which 50 percent of all marriages end in divorce and in which many children live in nontraditional families.

There are many different types of families in today's world, including traditional families, separated or divorced families, single-parent families, and stepfamilies and blended families. And within these different family structures, there are numerous arrangements regarding the custody and visitation of children. You need to recognize this in order to accept whatever situation the students may live in and to help them accept their situation as one that may be common, unusual, or unique. Never label any situation as "wrong," "bad," or "abnormal," even if you personally hold strong beliefs against that lifestyle. If you are aware of the particular living situations of the students in your group, you can create family scenarios similar to those situations in order to give the students a basis for reacting.

The lecture and activity in Session 1 are designed to help the students become aware of their beliefs about what makes a family, and to help them identify the values that families hold. This session begins to help them realize that all families have stresses.

Overall, your task is to empower the students by helping them learn about the changing families of the 1990s; by helping them realize that nontraditional families can have strong family values and can provide children with excellent parenting; by helping them recognize and deal with the effects of divorce and separation on their own families and themselves; by helping them choose helpful ways to express their feelings; and by helping them learn and practice coping strategies that will enable them to take good care of themselves. The structure and format of this session and those that follow are designed to help you do this. It's left to you to add the important human touch that makes for trust, comfort, understanding, cohesiveness, and fun.

Beginning the Session

Welcome the students and have them sit at a table. Explain that this is the group about changing families. Everyone in the group will have a chance to discuss the changing families of the 1990s as well as the issues that adolescents who live in separated, divorced, or single-parent families or in stepfamilies must deal with. They will learn coping strategies to deal with the stresses of their families and new ways to feel better and to take care of themselves. Stress that this is not a class and there will be no grades. You expect everyone in the group to have fun as they learn how to cope with the stresses of changing families.

Group Rules

Ask the students to look at the folders in front of them. Explain that they will use their folders every time they meet and that everything they need will be in these folders. Ask the group members to take their copy of the Group Rules Contract out of their folders. Meanwhile, display the poster you made listing the group rules. Tell the students that just like every group, their group has rules—use examples of groups like band, sports teams, yearbook staff. For the group to work well, everyone needs to follow the rules. Even though the students will have encountered these rules in their screening interview, take a moment to go through them now to check for understanding:

1. I will keep what we talk about private. We call this confidentiality.
2. I will stay in my seat.
3. I will keep my hands to myself.
4. I will wait for my turn to talk and listen carefully when other people talk.
5. I won't tease or put other people down.
6. I can pass during go-arounds if I want.
7. I will come to every session.
8. I will make up the class work I miss.

Explain that some of these rules may seem childish and that you really don't expect them to have trouble staying in their seats or keeping their hands to themselves.

Emphasize the importance of coming to every session and coming on time; also stress how important it is that they keep up in their class work, since you will need the teachers' cooperation to allow you to have groups in the future.

Draw attention to the first rule regarding confidentiality. Remind the students that no one will know what they share in group, with some important exceptions. If they share in group information about suicide, homicide, child abuse, or sexual abuse, you are required by law to report that information to ensure their safety. Once the students understand this and other rules, ask them to sign and date their Group Rules Contracts.

Ask the students to place their contracts in their folders. Explain that they will be using the folders to hold all their group work, that new materials will be added to the folders each session, and that you will keep the folders until the end of the group sessions, when the students can take them home. Tell the students that they can draw on their folders while waiting for the sessions to begin. (High school students often draw and color the names of their boyfriends and girlfriends!)

Keep the group rules poster and display it every time the group meets.

Centering Exercise

Since most of the students will be unfamiliar with a centering exercise, give them—and yourself—time to get into it. Explain that each group session will begin with a centering exercise, a way to relax and let go of the stresses and frustrations they may have encountered during the day. Point out that some of the centering exercises will help reinforce what they learn about feelings and anger management. Also point out that the centering exercises are techniques that the students can use on their own to manage stress and anxiety. Mention that some students create their own centering exercises, and that two students in Virginia developed the one called "The Rainbow" (see page 185).

Begin by inviting the students to relax and telling them that the name of this exercise is "White Water Rafting."

WHITE-WATER RAFTING

Okay, close your eyes. Imagine that you're floating down a river in a one-person boat, an inflatable kayak called a duck. You've been placed on the river by a guide, who has told you that this is a safe stretch of water. He's given you the equipment you need—a paddle, a helmet, and a life jacket—and has shown you how to use them. The guide has told you that he will meet you a few miles down the river and to enjoy yourself. When you first start paddling, you go around in circles, but soon you can make the kayak go in the right direction.

Right now, you're floating along in a long, calm pool of the river. No one else is around. The sky above is very clear and bright blue. The surrounding mountains are steep and green. It's a beautiful wilderness area. You feel very safe in the calm pool, so safe that you take off your life jacket and helmet. You lie back in the kayak and put your feet up, soaking in the sunshine and listening to the quietness. You feel very relaxed.

As you float along, you hear a noise. The sound is coming from around a bend in the river. You can't see what's making the noise. As you drift closer, the sound grows louder. It's the sound of rushing water. You begin to worry. You wonder if your guide placed you in the wrong part of the river. As the sound gets even louder, you worry more, wondering if it's a waterfall. You feel your heart beating faster and faster.

You sit up at attention. You fasten your life jacket and buckle your helmet. You grab your paddle, and get yourself ready for whatever lies ahead. As the noise becomes even louder, you slip around the bend in the river. It's white water, all right!

The kayak leaps into the white water, giving you a great ride around the rocks and through the rushing water. Waves break over the top of the kayak, but they don't stop you. You're feeling strong and excited. In a moment, you've passed through the rapids and

Exercise continued.

you're floating gently in another of the river's calm pools.

You feel excited, confident, satisfied, and proud of yourself. You were able to get through something that was frightening because it was unknown. Using the tools you'd been given and the skills you developed, you got through successfully. You feel so good that you are sitting on top of the world! So let that excitement, pride, confidence, and satisfaction wash all over you right now.

Mention that students who participate in groups sometimes feel scared at the beginning because they don't know what group will be like. Say that you expect them to have feelings of pride, confidence, and satisfaction by the time the group is over.

ICE-BREAKER

Involve the students in an ice-breaker. Have them pull their index cards from their folders. Ask the group members to write their name (what they want to be called), age, and grade in the center of the card. In the upper right-hand corner, have them write who lives with them in their home. In the lower right-hand corner, ask the students to write where they would be if they could be anywhere they wanted to be. In the lower left-hand corner, have them write what they would like to be or do when they finish school. In the upper left-hand corner, have them list three "-ing" words that describe themselves (for example, laughing, smiling, listening, talking, playing the piano, and so on).

When the students finish writing, have them form pairs—if a student is left out, pair yourself with that student. Explain that they are to interview each other. They will then go around and introduce their partners to the group, telling the group their partners' names and the other things they learned about them. To role-model for the students, begin by sharing the information about your partner.

This safe and nonthreatening activity helps the students feel comfortable about sharing information and introduces them to the go-around technique, which will be used throughout the program.

Exploring the Lecture

MINI-LECTURE

Changing Families and Family Values

Present this material in lecture form suitable for your audience.

There has been lots of discussion about what it means to be a family in the United States in the 1990s.

Some people think that a family consists of a mother and a father and 2.2 perfect children.

Other people think that a family can consist of a single mother and her children, or a single father and his children. Some families are stepfamilies. Some teens live in two or more families—living with a mother and stepfather at times and with a father and a stepmother at times. Sometimes teens live in a blended family—with children from two or more previous marriages.

Some teenagers live with relatives, like grandparents or an aunt or uncle. Their parents may have had some problems that made them unable to care for their children.

In a typical classroom or school, it is no longer true that most students live in a traditional family with a mom and dad who have never been divorced.

What is a family? People usually think a family consists of people who have a blood relationship, like children or brothers or sisters, or a legal relationship, like people who marry and stepbrothers or stepsisters. People usually think that blood and legal relationships imply some responsibility, like the parents caring for the children. People also think of families as having an emotional component—the people love each other and care for each other.

What are family values? There has also been a lot of discussion lately about *family values.* Most people use words like *commitment, caring, sharing, responsibility, churchgoing,* and *work ethic* when they discuss family values.

Allow discussion here, using the following questions to help the teens focus their ideas and participate.

- What is a family?
- What should go into the definition of family?
- Does a family consist of people living together?
- If so, are people who are roommates, who never do anything with each other, a family?
- How many people does it take to have a family?
- Does a family have to include a mom and a dad and children?
- Would you say that teenagers who live in single-parent families or stepfamilies are living in families?
- Do you think stepfamilies or separated, divorced, or single-parent families are abnormal, defective, or worse families than traditional families?
- If a married couple does not have children, are they a family?
- What are *family values*?
- Are family values the same for everyone?
- Can it be that only a traditional family can have family values?
- What about other values, such as mutual respect, politeness and decency, tolerance, acceptance of differences, open-mindedness?

Are these values that stepfamilies or separated, divorced, or single-parent families might have?

- Has "the family" deteriorated in recent years, or do we just believe the myth that families used to be better?
- Do all families experience stress, or does stress only occur in nontraditional families?
- What are some stresses that might exist in traditional families today?
- What are some stresses that might exist in nontraditional families today?

In the discussion, be accepting of whatever opinions and beliefs the students have. Some students may have very strong religious beliefs and believe that separation or divorce are wrong.

If the above questions don't generate sufficient student discussion, use the scenarios in Handout 1A to help the students focus their thoughts. It is often easier for teens to clarify their beliefs if they have a situation to react to.

The scenarios show that different families have different stresses and that both traditional and nontraditional families have stresses.

The scenarios also illustrate that different families have different values. Handout 1B, to be given out after the scenarios have been discussed, calls for the students to work up a definition of family for themselves and to list the values that they would want their ideal family to have. They should be able to do this easily after identifying the values described in the scenarios.

If you choose to use the scenarios, tell the students that you will ask one of them to read a short description of one of the many kinds of families that exist now, and that you will then discuss whether this is a family and why or why not, what the values are, and what the stresses are in the family. Tell them that after discussing the scenarios, they will then write their definition of family and will make a list of the values they would want their ideal family to have.

Ask the students to take Handout 1A out of their folders. Ask a student to read Scenario 1.

Scenario 1

JT is a 16-year-old junior at Cornfield High School. His father is an engineer, and his mother is a nurse at a downtown hospital. He has a sister in college and a brother in middle school. JT plays in the marching band and is on the reserve soccer team. JT's father drinks a lot and is always on his case: he complains that JT doesn't do his chores well enough; he doesn't like JT's friends; and he thinks that JT should get better grades. JT's parents fight a lot about his dad's drinking. Sometimes JT wishes he was away at college too.

Use the following questions to encourage discussion:

Is this a family?

Why or why not?

What are the values in this family?

What are the stresses in this family?

Ask a student to read Scenario 2.

Scenario 2

Tammy is a 15-year-old sophomore at City High School. She has a 9-year-old sister who is a fourth grader. The girls' parents are divorced, and they live with their mother. They see their father, who lives in another state, every couple of months. Their mother is very strict and insists that the girls do their homework right after school. They also have to help with the chores every day. Tammy's mother is a lawyer who works late frequently. When she has to go away on business trips, she gets a college student to stay with the girls. The girls love to go shopping with their mother. They like to cook dinner with her and enjoy trying new recipes. They also like to go on trips with their mom; their favorite was the time they went white water rafting in West Virginia.

Use the following questions to encourage discussion:

Is this a family?

Why or why not?

What are the values in this family?

What are the stresses in this family?

Ask another student to read Scenario 3.

Scenario 3

Adam and Allison are a freshman and sophomore in high school. Their parents are divorced. They used to live in another state, and they spent equal time with their mother and father. Then their mother married a man who lives here, and she moved to join him. Now Adam and Allison live with their mother, stepfather, an older stepsister, and two stepbrothers who are in elementary school. (They are also real pests.) Their mother and stepfather are just getting used to living with each other. Their mom is having a hard time finding a job and is irritable. They don't think their stepfather likes them. There are a lot of quarrels among the children in this family.

Use the following questions to encourage discussion:

Is this a family?

Why or why not?

What are the values in this family?

What are the stresses in this family?

Ask another student to read Scenario 4.

Scenario 4

James is a junior in a suburban high school. He gets good grades, is a jock, and has a lot of friends. His parents are very religious and very conservative. His father is a plant foreman, and his mother is a housewife who does a lot of church work. James's older brother, Simon, who is in college, has just announced to the family that he is gay. His parents think that homosexuality is immoral and even evil. They have told Simon that they won't consider him to be their son until he stops being gay.

Use the following questions to encourage discussion:

Is this a family?

Why or why not?

What are the values in this family?

What are the stresses in this family?

Ask another student to read Scenario 5.

Scenario 5

Kimberly is a 16-year-old junior in a city high school. Her parents are very liberal and don't believe in a lot of rules. Kim can stay out as late as she wants, and her parents let her have beer parties. Her friends love to come over because her parents are so cool. They're so cool that they smoke marijuana every night, so they don't cook dinner very frequently. Kim loves to listen to music a lot, but sometimes she wishes her parents would let her listen to it by herself. Sometimes she wishes her parents would do more than lie around the house—like, you know, clean it. The smell in the bathroom is getting pretty bad, and the chicken salad in the fridge is turning green.

Use the following questions to encourage discussion:

Is this a family?

Why or why not?

What are the values in this family?

What are the stresses in this family?

Ask another student to read Scenario 6.

Scenario 6

Marcie is a 17-year-old senior who lives with her grandparents. Her father is in jail, and her mother moved to Australia. Marcie's grandparents won't let her do anything. She can't stay after school to be in any activities because she has to come home and help her grandmother clean. They don't want her to date because they're afraid she'll turn out like her mother, who was 16 when she got pregnant. They even get upset if she talks on the phone with friends. Her grandparents don't want her to mention either her father or her mother.

Use the following questions to encourage discussion:

Is this a family?

Why or why not?

What are the values in this family?

What are the stresses in this family?

Ask another student to read Scenario 7.

Scenario 7

Anna is a 17-year-old senior who lives with very traditional parents. Anna, who is white, went to the Model UN and met a handsome young man named Lamar, who is African American. When Lamar came over to pick Anna up, her parents almost had a stroke. The next day, they told her she would be grounded until she stopped seeing Lamar.

Use the following questions to encourage discussion:

Is this a family?

Why or why not?

What are the values in this family?

What are the stresses in this family?

Ask another student to read Scenario 8.

Scenario 8

Larry is a 16-year-old who lives with an aunt and uncle. His father is in the army and spends time with Larry whenever he's on leave. His mother lives in another state and makes no effort to contact Larry. Larry's father loves motorcycles and is teaching Larry how to ride. They like to go to the drag strip together, and Larry got to compete in the High School Elimination series. He could go nearly 85 miles an hour on his dad's little 250 Ninja. Larry's father also got him a .22 rifle. He takes him to the shooting range and Larry is trying to improve his target shooting. Larry really misses his father when he has to go back overseas.

Use the following questions to encourage discussion:

Is this a family?

Why or why not?

What are the values in this family?

What are the stresses in this family?

Ask another student to read Scenario 9.

Scenario 9

Richard is a 16-year-old junior whose parents are very wealthy. His parents send him to the best schools and the best camp, and they give him music lessons and tennis lessons. He always has to have the latest shoes and the newest CDs. He went skiing in Colorado over Winter break and plans to go to Cancun for his senior trip. Richard doesn't spend much time with his parents because his father is always working. His mother always nags him to do his homework. She wants him to go to Harvard, where her father and his father went. When he got low scores on the PSATs, his mother signed him up for a test-taking course. Richard refused to go.

Use the following questions to encourage discussion:

Is this a family?

Why or why not?

What are the values in this family?

What are the stresses in this family?

Close the discussion by telling the students that there are no right or wrong answers to these questions. You want them to begin to think about the many types of families today. Even families that may be considered "normal" or traditional may experience a lot of stress. Families that may be considered "abnormal" (single-parent or nontraditional) may have very strong family values and do a very good job of raising children.

ACTIVITY

Have the students pull out Handout 1B ("Family Values.") Ask them to think about their definition of family and write it down. Then they should list the values they think an ideal family should have. Then go around the group and ask each student to share his or her definition of family and list of ideal family values.

As the group discusses, you can use the go-around technique: go around the group, making sure that each student has an opportunity to add to the discussion. Encourage participation, but don't force it. Remember the sixth group rule, which allows a student to pass. Accept all ideas and answers, explaining or clarifying information where necessary to reinforce learning. Afterward, be sure to thank the students for their participation.

BASIC FACTS

Ask the students to look at the List of Basic Facts. Tell the group members that each week they will learn new basic facts that carry the message of the session in easily remembered sentences. Explain that you will review the basic facts learned so far at the beginning of each session, and that you will ask them to explain what each means. Have students read the first two basic facts:

1. There are many different kinds of families, and each kind is special.

2. There are traditional families, separated or divorced families, single-parent families, stepfamilies, and blended families.

Briefly discuss each fact, checking for understanding. Correct any misconceptions.

Wrapping Up

CENTERING EXERCISE

Settle the students and introduce them to a new centering exercise, "Breathing Through Your Feet." Tell the students that they can use this centering exercise anywhere, and that no one will know that they are using it. It's an effective one to use if they're angry and want to calm down. It's also helpful to use when they experience some anxiety, for instance if they feel nervous about giving a report in front of the class.

BREATHING THROUGH YOUR FEET

Imagine that you have tiny holes all over the bottom of your feet. Your shoes are dotted with tiny holes, too. Now, breathe air up through those holes—all the way up to your ankles, through your knees, past your waist, right into your stomach. Hold that air in your stomach. Feel how refreshing it is. Now push the air all the way back down your body--down through your legs, past your knees and ankles, all the way down and out through your feet.

Lead the students through this process five times, for a total of five deep breaths; give directions softly; make sure that the students inhale and exhale evenly and slowly. If students have been angry, you can have them breathe in calm, peaceful, relaxed air, and breathe out anger, frustration, worry, or anxiety, and again breathe in calm, peaceful, secure air. Finally, conclude the exercise by saying:

You've learned the technique of breathing through your feet. This technique can give you power. Whenever you feel angry, or scared, or anxious, you can use breathing through your feet to help you calm down and relax.

(Adapted from *The Stress-Proof Child,* by Saunders and Remsberg, 1984.)

AFFIRMATION

Involve the group in an affirmation. Stand and join in a circle with the students, holding hands. Go around and have each student share something he or she liked about the group. Start the affirmation yourself: "One thing I liked about the group today was . . ."

CLOSING

Remain standing in a circle with the students, holding hands, and lead the group in the closing activity. You'll use this same activity to end all group sessions.

Tell the students that you're going to make a silent wish for the student on your right. Then when you've made the wish, gently squeeze that student's hand. The student makes a silent wish for the person on his or her right, then gently squeezes the student's hand, and so on. Continue around the circle until a wish and squeeze come back to you. Usually, students follow the lead of group leaders who expect them to perform this activity. However, if the adolescents in your group don't want to hold hands, allow them to stand next to each other in a circle, and to pass the wish by a pat on the shoulder or the elbow, or in any appropriate way they choose.

Collect the folders. Explain to the group that you will keep the folders until the next group session.

Fill out a copy of the Process and Progress Form (see page 199), or if you are an experienced leader, the Progress Notes (see page 200), as soon as you can after leading the session.

Group Rules Contract

1. I will keep what we talk about private. We call this confidentiality.
2. I will stay in my seat.
3. I will keep my hands to myself.
4. I will wait for my turn to talk and listen carefully when other people talk.
5. I won't tease or put other people down.
6. I can pass during go-arounds if I want.
7. I will come to every session.
8. I will make up the class work I miss.

____

Name

____

Date

Scenarios

For each of the following Scenarios, 1 – 9, address these questions in a discussion.

1. **Is this a family?**
2. **Why or why not?**
3. **What are the values in this family?**
4. **What are the stresses in this family?**

Scenario 1

JT is a 16-year-old junior at Cornfield High School. His father is an engineer, and his mother is a nurse at a downtown hospital. He has a sister in college and a brother in middle school. JT plays in the marching band and is on the reserve soccer team. JT's father drinks a lot and is always on his case: he complains that JT doesn't do his chores well enough; he doesn't like JT's friends; and he thinks that JT should get better grades. JT's parents fight a lot about his dad's drinking. Sometimes JT wishes he was away at college too.

Scenario 2

Tammy is a 15-year-old sophomore at City High School. She has a 9-year-old sister who is a fourth grader. The girls' parents are divorced, and they live with their mother. They see their father, who lives in another state, every couple of months. Their mother is very strict and insists that the girls do their homework right after school. They also have to help with the chores every day. Tammy's mother is a lawyer who works late frequently. When she has to go away on business trips, she gets a college student to stay with the girls. The girls love to go shopping with their mother. They like to cook dinner with her and enjoy trying new recipes. They also like to go on trips with their mom; their favorite was the time they went white water rafting in West Virginia.

Scenario 3

Adam and Allison are a freshman and sophomore in high school. Their parents are divorced. They used to live in another state, and they spent equal time with their mother and father. Then their mother married a man who lives here, and she moved to join him. Now Adam and Allison live with their mother, stepfather, an older stepsister, and two stepbrothers who are in elementary school. (They are also real pests.) Their mother and stepfather are just getting used to living with each other. Their mom is having a hard time finding a job and is irritable. They don't think their stepfather likes them. There are a lot of quarrels among the children in this family.

Scenario 4

James is a junior in a suburban high school. He gets good grades, is a jock, and has a lot of friends. His parents are very religious and very conservative. His father is a plant foreman, and his mother is a housewife who does a lot of church work. James's older brother, Simon, who is in college, has just announced to the family that he is gay. His parents think that homosexuality is immoral and even evil. They have told Simon that they won't consider him to be their son until he stops being gay.

Scenario 5

Kimberly is a 16-year-old junior in a city high school. Her parents are very liberal and don't believe in a lot of rules. Kim can stay out as late as she wants, and her parents let her have beer parties. Her friends love to come over because her parents are so cool. They're so cool that they smoke marijuana every night, so they don't cook dinner very frequently. Kim loves to listen to music a lot, but sometimes she wishes her parents would let her listen to it by herself. Sometimes she wishes her parents would do more than lie around the house—like, you know, clean it. The smell in the bathroom is getting pretty bad, and the chicken salad in the fridge is turning green.

Scenario 6

Marcie is a 17-year-old senior who lives with her grandparents. Her father is in jail, and her mother moved to Australia. Marcie's grandparents won't let her do anything. She can't stay after school to be in any activities because she has to come home and help her grandmother clean. They don't want her to date because they're afraid she'll turn out like her mother, who was 16 when she got pregnant. They even get upset if she talks on the phone with friends. Her grandparents don't want her to mention either her father or her mother.

Scenario 7

Anna is a 17-year-old senior who lives with very traditional parents. Anna, who is white, went to the Model UN and met a handsome young man named Lamar, who is African American. When Lamar came over to pick Anna up, her parents almost had a stroke. The next day, they told her she would be grounded until she stopped seeing Lamar.

Scenario 8

Larry is a 16-year-old who lives with an aunt and uncle. His father is in the army and spends time with Larry whenever he's on leave. His mother lives in another state and makes no effort to contact Larry. Larry's father loves motorcycles and is teaching Larry how to ride. They like to go to the drag strip together, and Larry got to compete in the High School Elimination series. He could go nearly 85 miles an hour on his dad's little 250 Ninja. Larry's father also got him a .22 rifle. He takes him to the shooting range and Larry is trying to improve his target shooting. Larry really misses his father when he has to go back overseas.

Scenario 9

Richard is a 16-year-old junior whose parents are very wealthy. His parents send him to the best schools and the best camp, and they give him music lessons and tennis lessons. He always has to have the latest shoes and the newest CDs. He went skiing in Colorado over Winter break and plans to go to Cancun for his senior trip. Richard doesn't spend much time with his parents because his father is always working. His mother always nags him to do his homework. She wants him to go to Harvard, where her father and his father went. When he got low scores on the PSATs, his mother signed him up for a test-taking course. Richard refused to go.

Family Values

Write your definition of family.

List the values that you think an ideal family should have.

SESSION • 2

Why People Get Married and Why People Get Divorced

Objectives

To help the students:

- learn one reason why people marry and one reason why people divorce
- describe something they can do with each parent that makes them feel happy

Session at a Glance

1. Group Rules: review if necessary—2 minutes
2. Centering Exercise: "The Icicle"—3 minutes
3. Feelings Check-in: look at Feeling Wheel—5 minutes
4. Basic Facts Review—2 minutes
5. Mini-lecture—7 minutes
6. Discussion—10 minutes
7. Activity: draw or write one thing you do with your mom and one thing you do with your dad that you enjoy; discuss drawings—5 minutes.
8. Basic Facts: read Basic Facts 3 and 4; discuss—2 minutes
9. Give Assignment—3 minutes
10. Centering Exercise: repeat "The Icicle"—3 minutes
11. Affirmation: share something that you do with a family member that you enjoy—2 minutes
12. Closing: pass a silent wish—1 minute

Preparation

- Display the posterboard copy of the group rules.

- Have posters with Basic Facts 1-2 available, or the List of Basic Facts, already in the folders, or index cards with a basic fact on each one.
- Arrange to have chalkboard and chalk, or newsprint and a marker, available.
- Staple the student's Group Rules Contract to the inside back cover of their folders.
- Include in each student's folder:
  —the Feeling Wheel
  —Handout 2A ("Scenarios for Session 2")
  —Handout 2B ("Things I Can Do with My Parents That I Enjoy")
  —Assignment 2
- Place each student's folder, a pencil, and crayons or markers at his or her place.
- Read through the session plan before meeting.

Background and Guidelines

As a group leader, it's important for you to recognize that teens have different perspectives on the breakup of a marriage. If a marriage was filled with violence or abusive confrontations, teens may be relieved at the separation, seeing it not as the end of a relationship, but as the cessation of hostilities. If a marriage in which parents have had a distant and withdrawn relationship breaks up, however, teens may be stunned. Adolescents who have been unaware of any conflicts between the parents may have a very difficult time accepting the separation. Also be aware that adolescents may have more knowledge of parental affairs than younger children do. They may be making judgments about their parents and dealing with the internal conflict of loving them but not approving of their behavior.

Never assign blame for the dissolution of a marriage. When it comes to separation and divorce, the only assumption you can make is that only the separating couple can fully understand the reasons for the breakup. Other people affected by the separation, including the children, may just have to accept what they can't change. No matter whether parents and children attempt to assign blame for a separation, *you* must accept—both intellectually and emotionally—that a decision to separate is a complex one. You will do a great service for the students in your group if you role-model that blaming is not helpful. While teens may be very judgmental toward their parents, it is important for counselors to accept their feelings and judgments, but to maintain a greater perspective: that you do not know the whole story or why parents do what they do. The rule of thumb is to be accepting of how difficult the breakup and not knowing the reasons for the breakup might be for the teens involved.

In this session, the group members begin to realize that they are responsible for their feelings, their thinking, and their actions. Adolescents (and adults) can't control the kinds of feelings they get, but they can look at their thinking (their "self-talk") and, if it is negative, change it to positive. They also can choose to do something to make themselves feel better.

If you understand that you, too, are responsible for doing what you need to do in order to feel better, and if you have an extensive repertoire of behaviors for helping you feel better (exercising, listening to music, talking with friends, playing sports, taking a bubble bath, and so on), you'll be more effective as a group leader. So be ready to share with the students the variety of behaviors and activities you use to feel better.

In the discussion, emphasize the concept that teenagers can do good things for themselves—both on their own and with a variety of others—even if they live in a nontraditional family. Be sure to reinforce this concept (saying, for example, "If you feel sad or angry, you can do something that will make you feel better"). Understanding this concept is crucial for building a foundation for the coping strategies that will be described in later sessions.

Be aware that adolescents who live in nontraditional families may need to be very flexible. For instance, teens whose fathers or mothers are absent or inattentive may have a difficult time at father-son dinners, mother-daughter luncheons, and so on. Encourage these adolescents to accept their feelings of loss and anger, and then encourage them to problem solve: can they, for example, ask a relative or neighbor to take them to the dinner or luncheon? This session's art or writing activity ("Things I Can Do with My Parents That I Enjoy") demonstrates this. If you wish, you can tailor the activity to better fit the group members' particular situations. For example, students who have no contact with one parent (either mother or father) can select another person to use for that part of the activity.

Beginning the Session

GROUP RULES

Have the folders at the appropriate places. Welcome the students and begin with a quick review of the group's purpose and rules. Remind the students that they are meeting to discuss the changing family styles of today's world, the stresses these styles create for teens, and how to better cope with those stresses. Draw attention to the poster listing the group rules. If you feel that it is necessary, call on different students to read them one at a time.

Check for understanding before moving on.

CENTERING EXERCISE

Make certain that the students are comfortable and quiet. Ask if anyone used the exercise "Breathing Through Your Feet" in the past week. Then lead them in the following centering exercise called "The Icicle." Tell the group members that this is another centering exercise that will help them to calm down, relax, and be able to think if they get angry or upset. They can use this exercise without anyone else knowing.

THE ICICLE

Close your eyes. Tighten the muscles in your feet and legs really tight; make your feet and legs as stiff as an icicle. *(Pause.)* Now let that cold and stiff icicle melt. Let it melt, drip by drip, into a calm, peaceful puddle. Let your legs get loose and very relaxed, and imagine what they would feel like as part of a puddle. *(Pause.)* Now tighten your chest, stomach, and trunk area; make it as stiff as an icicle. *(Pause.)* Now let that icicle melt, slowly, drip by drip, into a puddle. *(Pause.)* Put your arms straight out in front of you, make fists, and pretend that your arms are icicles. *(Pause.)* Now let those icicles melt; let them drip into a puddle, and imagine what they feel like as they drip into a calm, peaceful puddle. *(Pause.)* Tighten the muscles in your shoulders, neck, and head; tighten them into a stiff, cold icicle. Make them very stiff and tight. *(Pause.)* Now let them relax and melt, slowly, very slowly, into a puddle. *(Pause.)*

Now make all the muscles in your whole body just as stiff and tight as you can. Make your whole body into an icicle. *(Pause.)* Now let yourself melt, from the tip of your toes to the top of your head. Let yourself melt, drip by drip, into a puddle. Let yourself get very loose and relaxed, like smooth water in a puddle. Imagine that your whole body is a calm, quiet, peaceful puddle. *(Pause.)*

Remind the students that they can use this technique in class and at home, to help them put thinking between their feelings and their behavior.

FEELINGS CHECK-IN

Do a feelings check-in with the students. Have the students take out their Feeling Wheels. Tell them that every week, they will look at the wheel and decide how they are feeling that day. Then everybody will give a brief description of how he or she is doing. Tell the students that if they want, they can color in the section on the Feeling Wheel that describes how they're feeling today. Remind the teens that they might have more than one feeling, since it's possible to have more than one feeling at a time. If they're having a feeling that isn't named on the wheel, they can add a bubble to the outside of the wheel and name the feeling there.

When the students finish, have a go-around. Begin by sharing your own feelings. Then invite each student to share his or her feelings. Teenagers often list many feelings. In the interest of time, ask them to name the feelings they have, but then pick only two to discuss. Be sure to accept each student's feeling(s) and to affirm each student. Explain that they will be using this same copy of the Feeling Wheel every time they meet. Ask the students to return the wheels to their folders.

BASIC FACTS REVIEW

To help the students review their last session and the basic facts learned so far, show them Basic Facts Posters 1 and 2; or ask them to look at the List of Basic Facts and review the first two; or use index cards, on which you have written basic facts, one to a card.

In a go-around, ask a student to read Basic Fact 1 aloud and explain what it means. If the student has trouble explaining the fact, don't contradict or judge, simply clarify his or her explanation. Repeat the procedure for the next basic fact. This review ensures that the students understand and integrate the basic facts that have been taught. It is also easy preparation for the presentation, and provides a lead-in for the session material.

Exploring the Material

MINI-LECTURE

Why People Get Married and Why People Get Divorced

Last week we talked about the many different family styles in the 1990s and what the values are in some families. We discussed some of the stresses for teens who live in these changing families.

Today, we're going to spend some time talking about why people get married, why they get divorced, and how you think family values relate to separation and divorce. We're also going to discuss how teens are responsible for handling their own feelings, some ways teens can do that, and some ways they can maintain positive relationships with their parents.

Why People get Married

Ask the students to brainstorm some of the reasons people get married. Write the reasons on a chalkboard or on newsprint. These are some typical responses:

- they're in love
- they like to be with the other person and do things to please them
- they want to leave their parents' home and they can't support themselves
- they're afraid to be alone
- they expect somebody else to make them happy
- they got pregnant

Ask the students which of these reasons they think are negative. Which are positive?

Why People get Divorced

Ask the students if they think married people stay the same throughout a marriage.

(No, people usually grow and change during the course of a marriage. Sometimes people change. They are no longer "in love", and they don't like to be with each other as much. They may stop trying to please the other person.)

Ask the students to brainstorm why people get separated or divorced. Write these reasons on a chalkboard or on newsprint. Some common responses:

- they don't love each other anymore
- they love someone else
- one spouse may behave in a way that makes the other feel hurt or angry. A spouse may be alcoholic or verbally or physically abusive.

Which of these reasons are positive? Which are negative?

Ask the students how they think people might act if their marriage is not a happy one. Typical responses:

- they may feel very hurt
- they may stop talking to each other
- they may yell and fight a lot
- they may even try to physically hurt each other

How do the students weigh staying in an abusive marriage with a desire for personal happiness or safety? Use the following scenarios to focus discussion. Ask the students to pull Handout 2A ("Scenarios for Session 2") from their folders. Call for a volunteer to read Scenario 1.

Scenario 1

Cynthia is a 30-year-old woman with two children, Heather, 13, and Bill, 10. Her husband, Fred, works in an automobile factory and is active in the union. Fred drinks heavily, sometimes six to eight beers a night. He has been drinking heavily for at least 10 years, but he doesn't think he has a drinking problem. He yells at Cynthia a lot. When he gets angry, he sometimes throws furniture around. Fred and Cynthia have had several separations over the last five years. Since Cynthia's parents divorced when she was nine, she didn't want to put her children through a divorce. The last separation occurred six months ago, when Fred beat her up and she asked him to move out. Three months ago, Heather and Bill told Cynthia that their dad had moved in with another woman; before he moved out, Fred would call the other woman whenever Cynthia was gone.

Should Cynthia get a divorce?

Why or why not?

Scenario 2

Jeff is a construction worker who loves his job. His wife, Estelle, is a stay-at-home mom who volunteers at school and is a Girl Scout leader. She loves to decorate the house for Halloween and Christmas. Jeff's brother told him that he had an affair with Estelle. Jeff was furious and confronted Estelle, who denied that she had ever had an affair. Jeff believed his brother and moved out of the home. He asked Estelle for a divorce.

Should Jeff get a divorce?

Why or why not?

Scenario 3

Jane, a teacher, is married to Frank, a computer programmer. Frank is very secretive, comes home late, and doesn't like to do things with the family. Jane finds out that Frank has stolen thousands of dollars from his company and that he has done a lot of things without telling her. He admits he took the money, but he doesn't think that it's a big deal. Frank gets a second job in order to pay the money back. Jane sees him even less than usual.

Should Jane get a divorce?

Why or why not?

Scenario 4

Norma is married to Robert, a very quiet man who likes to read. He isn't very friendly and would rather be by himself than with other people. Robert has two sons, and he likes to play sports with them. Norma spends a lot of time at work because she likes her job. She grows very close to Sam, a man she works with. Sam is friendly and outgoing, and they laugh a lot when they work. Norma feels like she is falling in love with Sam. Sam tells Norma about his problems with his wife, Susan, and that he doesn't love her anymore. He admits that he really loves Norma. Robert gets mad that Norma works so much. He wants her to be at home, but he still doesn't talk to her much when she is at home. Norma gets very depressed and feels trapped.

Should Norma get a divorce?

Why or why not?

Scenario 5

John is a successful businessman who is married to Mary, a secretary. They have two daughters. John travels on business a lot. Mary sometimes finds credit card bills for jewelry that he never gave her and bills for flowers that were not sent to her. Once, John told Mary that he had a venereal disease—he got it from a woman he was having an affair with—so that Mary could go to the doctor to see if she was infected. Mary gets angry because John is gone so much and because he doesn't help much with the house or the kids. She is hurt that he doesn't spend much time with her, either.

Should Mary get a divorce?

Why or why not?

Scenario 6

Jacob, a successful doctor, is reaching his mid-40s. His wife has spent her life taking care of their three children and being a "doctor's wife," active in charities and women's clubs. Jacob falls in love with a young nurse at the hospital. She is beautiful, thin, physically fit, active, and athletic. She is fun to be with, and he feels 20 years younger when he is with her. He sees his wife as old, overweight, complaining, uninteresting, and deadly boring. Jacob feels that he has a chance to start his life over, if only he could leave his wife.

Should Jacob get a divorce?

Why or why not?

Remind the students that there are no right or wrong answers to these questions. You just want them to understand that a decision to separate or divorce is usually a complex one and that there are no easy answers.

People can choose to handle their feelings positively.

Remind the students that they have some choices about how they handle their feelings, even if they live in one of these changing families. They can't control which feelings they get, but they can control their behavior, and they can change their thinking from negative to positive. In a changing family, they can choose many family members to do things with that will make them feel happy.

List some things teens can do to feel better if they wake up in a cranky or down mood:

- ask their dad to play football
- ask their mom to go for a walk
- call their grandfather and tell him a joke
- call their best friend
- put on their favorite music and dance
- go motorcycle riding with their stepfather
- shoot baskets with their uncle or friends

It's important for teens to begin taking some responsibility for how they handle their feelings. They are also old enough to begin taking some responsibility for their relationships with their parents, or at least for their part in those relationships. While adolescence is a time that teens increase their interest in activities with their peers, they generally maintain a need for the support of their parents. It's important for teens, if possible, to do their part to maintain good relations with their parents. We will talk more about these issues in Sessions 3 and 4.

Tell the students that for their activity today, they will draw a picture or write a paragraph about one thing they like to do with their mom and one thing they like to do with their dad.

ACTIVITY

Have the students retrieve their copies of Handout 2B. Read aloud the title at the top of the sheet: "Things I Can Do with My Parents That I Enjoy." Ask them to draw a picture or write a list of at least one thing they do with their mom and one thing they do with their dad that they enjoy. If a teen has no contact with a particular parent, invite the teen to choose someone else. Remind the students that you are not looking for artistic talent; instead, you are interested in their ideas.

When the students finish, have another go-around. Invite each student to explain his or her drawing or read his or her paragraph to the group. Afterward, have the students put their crayons and drawings or paragraphs in their folders.

BASIC FACTS

Tell the students to look at the List of Basic Facts. Ask a group member to read facts 3 and 4.

3. People usually get married because they love each other and want to be together.
4. People usually get separated or divorced because they no longer want to share their lives.

Briefly discuss each fact, checking for understanding. Correct any misconceptions.

ASSIGNMENT

Explain to the students that they will have a homework assignment after the rest of the sessions. These assignments are intended to help them put what they learn in each session into practice. They won't get graded for the homework, but they will get more out of the group if they do the assignments. The assignments are designed to take only a minute or two each day. Tell the group members that each week you will ask them what they learned by doing the assignment.

Have the group members take Assignment 2 out of the folders. Read the directions: "Each day, write down several different things that you can do to feel better if you wake up in a down mood." Explain again that you don't want the students to spend too much time on this, but you do want them to observe their ability to choose to do things that they enjoy.

Wrapping Up

CENTERING EXERCISE

Settle the students and then repeat "The Icicle."

AFFIRMATION

Involve the group in an affirmation. Stand and join in a circle with the students, holding hands. Go around and invite each group member to share something that he or she can do with someone in their family, something that makes them feel happy. Start the affirmation yourself: "One thing I can do with someone in my family to enjoy myself is. . . ."

CLOSING

Remain standing in a circle with the students, holding hands, and lead the group in the closing activity. Tell the students that you're going to make a silent wish for the student on your right. Then, when you've made the wish, gently squeeze the student's hand. The student makes a silent wish for the person on his or her right, then gently squeezes the student's hand, and so on. Continue around the circle until a wish and squeeze come back to you. If necessary, the students can pass the wish in any appropriate way they choose.

Collect the folders. Fill out a copy of the Process and Progress Form (p. 199) or, if you are an experienced leader, the Progress Notes (p. 200) as soon as you can after leading the session.

Feeling Wheel

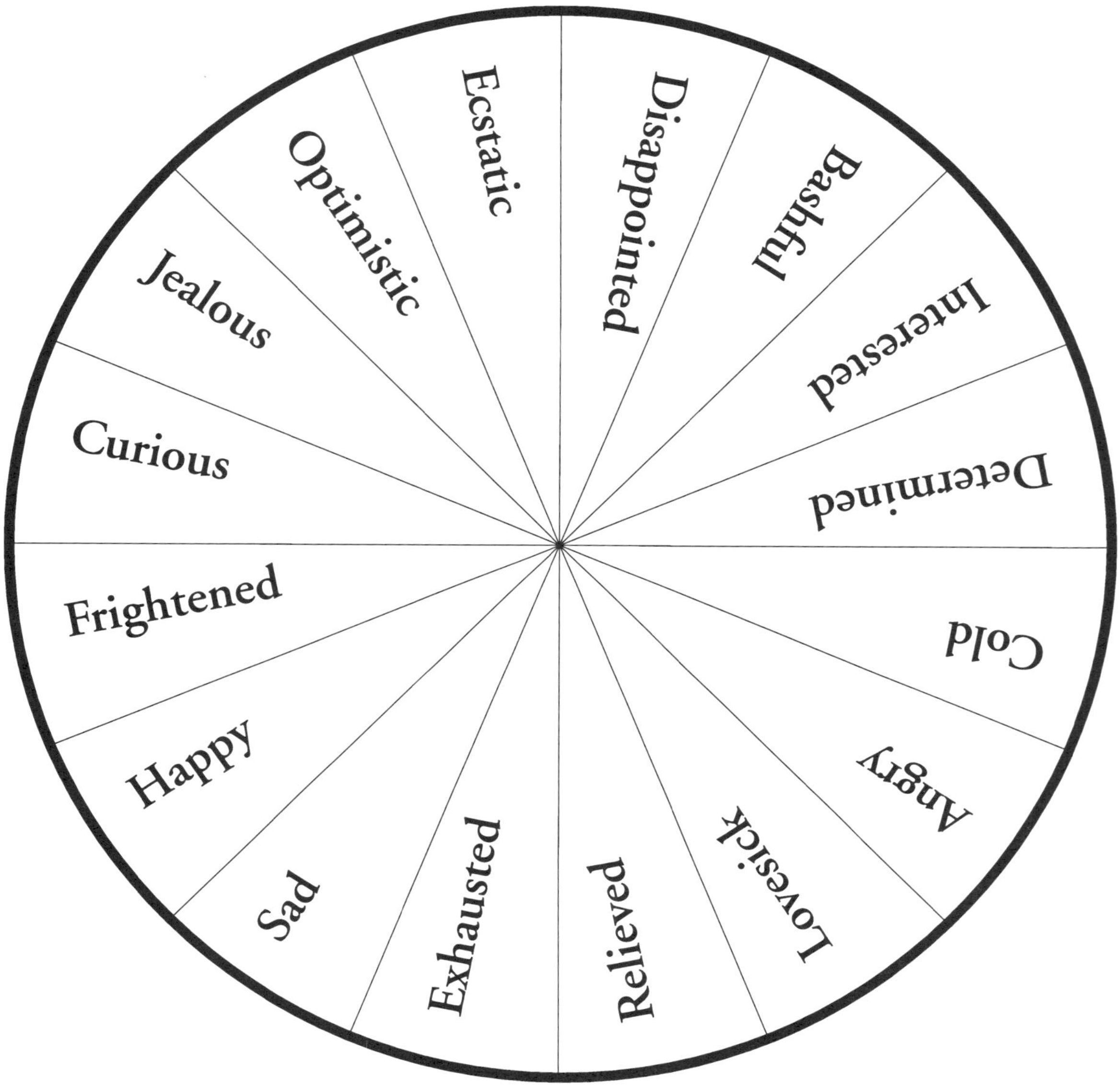

Scenarios for Session 2

Scenario 1

Cynthia is a 30-year-old woman with two children, Heather, 13, and Bill, 10. Her husband, Fred, works in an automobile factory and is active in the union. Fred drinks heavily, sometimes six to eight beers a night. He has been drinking heavily for at least 10 years, but he doesn't think he has a drinking problem. He yells at Cynthia a lot. When he gets angry, he sometimes throws furniture around. Fred and Cynthia have had several separations over the last five years. Since Cynthia's parents divorced when she was nine, she didn't want to put her children through a divorce. The last separation occurred six months ago, when Fred beat her up and she asked him to move out. Three months ago, Heather and Bill told Cynthia that their dad had moved in with another woman; before he moved out, Fred would call the other woman whenever Cynthia was gone.

1. Should Cynthia get a divorce?

2. Why or why not?

Scenario 2

Jeff is a construction worker who loves his job. His wife, Estelle, is a stay-at-home mom who volunteers at school and is a Girl Scout leader. She loves to decorate the house for Halloween and Christmas. Jeff's brother told him that he had an affair with Estelle. Jeff was furious and confronted Estelle, who denied that she had ever had an affair. Jeff believed his brother and moved out of the home. He asked Estelle for a divorce.

1. Should Jeff get a divorce?

2. Why or why not?

Scenario 3

Jane, a teacher, is married to Frank, a computer programmer. Frank is very secretive, comes home late, and doesn't like to do things with the family. Jane finds out that Frank has stolen thousands of dollars from his company and that he has done a lot of things without telling her. He admits he took the money, but he doesn't think that it's a big deal. Frank gets a second job in order to pay the money back. Jane sees him even less than usual.

1. Should Jane get a divorce?

2. Why or why not?

Scenario 4

Norma is married to Robert, a very quiet man who likes to read. He isn't very friendly and would rather be by himself than with other people. Robert has two sons, and he likes to play sports with them. Norma spends a lot of time at work because she likes her job. She grows very close to Sam, a man she works with. Sam is friendly and outgoing, and they laugh a lot when they work. Norma feels like she is falling in love with Sam. Sam tells Norma about his problems with his wife, Susan, and that he doesn't love her anymore. He admits that he really loves Norma. Robert gets mad that Norma works so much. He wants her to be at home, but he still doesn't talk to her much when she is at home. Norma gets very depressed and feels trapped.

1. Should Norma get a divorce?

2. Why or why not?

Scenario 5

John is a successful businessman who is married to Mary, a secretary. They have two daughters. John travels on business a lot. Mary sometimes finds credit card bills for jewelry that he never gave her and bills for flowers that were not sent to her. Once, John told Mary that he had a venereal disease—he got it from a woman he was having an affair with—so that Mary could go to the doctor to see if she was infected. Mary gets angry because John is gone so much and because he doesn't help much with the house or the kids. She is hurt that he doesn't spend much time with her, either.

1. Should Mary get a divorce?

2. Why or why not?

Scenario 6

Jacob, a successful doctor, is reaching his mid-40s. His wife has spent her life taking care of their three children and being a "doctor's wife," active in charities and women's clubs. Jacob falls in love with a young nurse at the hospital. She is beautiful, thin, physically fit, active, and athletic. She is fun to be with, and he feels 20 years younger when he is with her. He sees his wife as old, overweight, complaining, uninteresting, and deadly boring. Jacob feels that he has a chance to start his life over, if only he could leave his wife.

1. Should Jacob get a divorce?

2. Why or why not?

Things I Can Do with My Parents That I Enjoy

Draw or write one thing you do with your mom that you enjoy.

Draw or write one thing you do with your dad that you enjoy.

Each day, write down several different things that you can do to feel better if you wake up in a down mood.

THINGS I CAN DO TO FEEL BETTER

Day one

Day two

Day three

Day four

Day five

Day six

Day seven

Other feelings or comments

SESSION • 3

The Effects of Changing Families on Teens and Issues For Teens From Changing Families

Objectives

To help the students:

- identify ways teens might behave if their parents separate or divorce, or if they live in a non-traditional family
- understand that divorce is never the children's fault
- realize that children usually love both parents, even if the parents no longer live together

Session at a Glance

1. Group Rules: review if necessary—1 minute
2. Centering Exercise: "The Pyramid"—3 minutes
3. Feelings Check-in: look at Feeling Wheel—5 minutes
4. Basic Facts Review—4 minutes
5. Assignment Review—3 minutes
6. Mini-lecture and Discussion of Scenarios for Session 3—20 minutes
7. Basic Facts: read Basic Facts 5 and 6; discuss—2 minutes
8. Assignment—1 minute
9. Centering exercise: Repeat "The Pyramid"—3 minutes
10. Affirmation: share an issue described today that you have experienced—2 minutes
11. Closing: pass a silent wish—1 minute

Preparation

- Display the posterboard copy of the group rules.
- Have posters with Basic Facts 1-4 available, or the List of Basic Facts already in the folders, or index cards with a basic fact on each one.

- Add the following material to each folder:

  —Handout 3 ("Scenarios for Session 3")

  —Assignment 3

- Place each student's folder, a pencil, and crayons or markers at his or her place.
- Read through the session plan before meeting.

Background and Guidelines

This session focuses on the effects on adolescents of living in a changing family. The scenarios describe: 1) a family in the immediate crisis stage of separation; 2) a family in the long-term aftermath of divorce, where the children live in a single-parent family, with no contact with the other parent; 3) a family where there is ongoing parental conflict; and 4) a stepfamily.

Since the students in your group are likely to be living in a variety of changing families, it's a good idea for you to review the material in Part Two, Chapter 1, which describes the three different stages of divorce and the major issues for adolescents at each stage (see pages 33-36).

The scenarios will allow the students to compare and contrast their own experiences, although they may do this without disclosing it to the group. It's important for you to be aware of an overall perspective.

IMMEDIATE CRISIS STAGE

The scenario in which Martha learns of her parents' plans to divorce describes the immediate crisis stage of divorce. For some adolescents, this is a major crisis and a major loss. They react to it as they would to a death, often with shock and denial. However, it's probably best not to expect teens to experience the usual feelings associated with the divorce process (anger, depression, acceptance) in a precise order. In other words, adolescents will probably experience intense sadness, anger, loneliness, guilt, hurt, and so on, at many different times in the divorce process. The intensity of their feelings will alternately increase and decrease.

Therefore, during the discussion, it's a good idea to point out that feelings are transitory and differ in intensity. (See the centering exercise, "The Clouds," in Session 5, page 112, for a useful metaphor.) Like clouds in the sky, feelings—happy or sad—come and go and may come back. Adolescents, and some adults, sometimes try to hold on to happy feelings, or they expect to feel happy all the time. It might be helpful to set up the expectation that feelings concerning separation and divorce will be strong at times but will eventually clear up. This foreshadows what the students will learn about feelings later on in Session 5 and helps them recognize that they can learn to handle the intense feelings that accompany living in a family that's going through the process of divorce.

Martha's parents are calm and nonblaming as they announce their separation. They reassure Martha that the separation is not her fault and reaffirm that they will both continue to be her parents and to love her. They set up custody so that Martha will see both parents on a weekly, in-depth basis. Martha's parents make it relatively easy for her to maintain a loving relationship with each of them. Such is not the case with all divorces and custody arrangements.

Be aware that some adolescents have separation experiences that differ significantly from Martha's. Some marriages end with a great deal of overt conflict; some end with internal hurt. Thus, some parents are relieved to be out of an unhappy or abusive marriage; some are very angry at their partners. In the same way, some adolescents are relieved; some are astonished; some are heartbroken.

Even when told that they're not at fault for causing a divorce, some adolescents don't believe it. They blame themselves for their parents' problems. This is especially true if the parental conflict wasn't overt. In trying to make sense out of the absence of external conflict, some adolescents tend to blame themselves. Therefore, it's important that you help the students understand that a separation or divorce is not their fault. The first basic fact of this session teaches this, but your nonblaming, nonjudgmental, and accepting attitude will teach it even better. The students need your help to recognize that the major loss they've suffered is due to an adult decision, not to anything they have or haven't done. The decision to separate is usually painful and difficult, and parents generally give it a lot of thought: teenagers, however, may be quite unaware of this process. That is why the students need help accepting their parents' decisions and learning how to deal with the many feelings and stresses that accompany a separation.

SINGLE-PARENT FAMILIES OR ABANDONMENT BY NONCUSTODIAL PARENT

Teenagers living in a single-parent family and dealing with parental inattention or abandonment by the other parent have their own set of feelings and issues. Adolescents living in single-parent families may have more responsibility to help around the house and care for other children. They may enjoy some of their new status and responsibility and like helping their parent, but they may feel internal conflict because they have less time to spend with their peers and less time to enjoy normal adolescent activities. These teens may have fewer resources (both materially and financially) due to abandonment by one parent. Their custodial parent feels more responsibility and stress and may have less to offer teenage children in terms of emotional support and day-to-day living support (providing clean soccer uniforms and chauffeuring to band and sports events, etc.). Teens may blame themselves for their noncustodial parent's abandonment, or they may not understand why that parent can move on to a new family and take care of other children. Finally, teens may idealize the absent parent and try to identify with him or her by adopting their characteristics; they might hold out the reunion fantasy, which may inhibit their ability to form a relationship with a surrogate parent, such as a stepparent. Sons of single mothers, especially if they have little contact with their father, may adopt hypermasculine behavior and cause conflicts with their mothers in order to prove their masculinity.

ONGOING PARENTAL CONFLICT

Adolescents who are dealing with ongoing parental conflict may be caught in the middle and feel that they have to divide their loyalties and choose between parents. Sadly, divorce can bring out a lot of anger in parents. Sometimes, angry parents want their children to be as angry as they are. They may even want their children to cut off their relationship with the other parent. By recognizing this pressure on the group members, you can help them see that although parents are responsible for the parent-parent relationship—a relationship that children shouldn't interfere in—adolescents have their own relationship with each parent, and neither parent should interfere with the teen's relationship with the other parent. Give the students permission to keep their relationship with each parent separate from the parents' relationship with each other.

Other teens believe that they can do something to make their parents stop fighting. Some teenagers increase their acting-out behavior in order to divert the parents' conflict. Others may try to be peacemakers or therapists for their parents. Such efforts may be self-destructive for teens, and are most likely to be doomed to failure. So, also let the group members know that they do not have the responsibility—or ability—to help the parents improve their relationship. We will touch on this more in Sessions 4 and 8.

STEPFAMILIES

The issues for adolescents living in stepfamilies arise during the long-range stage of divorce. A major issue for teens is loyalty. They may believe that developing affection for a stepparent would mean that they are being disloyal to the natural parent. Remarriage sometimes results in a relocation, which means less time with the noncustodial parent, which can create feelings of loss or anger. Another common issue is jealousy of the closeness between the remarried parent and the new spouse, since it usually means diminished attention from that parent. Resentment bordering on rage is common when the stepparent tries to take on a disciplinary role. Finally, rivalry and jealousy often occur in blended families, where both parents have children.

Today's session describes some of the problems and issues teens might face in these different divorce situations and clarifies some of the feelings teens might experience. The next session will help correct misconceptions that are common for adolescents living in changing families.

Beginning the Session

Group Rules

Have the folders at the appropriate places. Welcome the students and, if necessary, begin with a quick review of the group's rules. Remind the students that they are meeting to discuss the changing family styles of today's world, the stresses these styles create for teens, and how to better cope with those stresses. Draw attention to the poster listing the group rules. If you feel it is necessary, call on different students to read them one at a time.

Check for understanding before moving on.

Centering Exercise

Lead the group in the following centering exercise called "The Pyramid."

THE PYRAMID

Today's centering exercise will help you learn how to get through periods of very intense feelings, such as panic. Imagine that you are in Mexico, exploring some ancient Mayan ruins. It is amazing to see what those primitive people could build in the jungle in the 700s. One of the massive structures they built was a pyramid, about 500 feet tall, with a steep stone staircase on each of the four sides, and a temple on its flat top. You decide to climb the pyramid so you can get a better view of the other ruins and of the surrounding jungle. You start climbing up, and you move up the stairs very quickly. But, about halfway up, you are suddenly struck with a sense of panic, or terror. It's as if you're suddenly overcome with a fear of heights. You are sure that if you try to go down, you will fall off the pyramid and die; if you move up, you will fall off and die. You are paralyzed. The only thing worse than moving is staying where you are. There is nothing to hold onto except for the steep stone steps, so you bend down and slowly move up the steps one at a time, holding on to the next step as you go.

You finally make it to the top of the pyramid. You remain bent down and, touching the floor with your hand, you make it over to the temple, which you hold onto. You go around to the third side of the pyramid, where there is a very thick wire cable that begins at the temple and goes down the surface of the stairs. You realize that if you don't go down, you will have to stay on top of the pyramid forever. You sit down on your behind, and you hold onto the cable, and slowly inch out to the staircase. You go down the stairs one at a time, holding on desperately to the cable. Other people are coming up the pyramid, and some of them have stopped as if they are paralyzed. Others are coming up holding onto the cable. As you go down the pyramid, you breathe easier and easier. You know you are safe as long as you can hold onto the cable.

Finally, you get to about 12 steps up from the bottom. You feel safe at this point, and you can let go of the cable. You stand up and walk erect down the rest of the steps. You feel relief, because you didn't fall off and die. But you also feel proud, because you got through a period of panic by grounding yourself, by finding something to hold onto. You feel safe and secure now. You decide that if you are ever in a situation where you feel panic, you will just imagine that you are holding onto that cable on the pyramid's staircase, and you will remember the sense of being grounded, which helped you feel safe and secure, even during the period of panic.

FEELINGS CHECK-IN

Do a feelingss check-in with the students. Have them take out their Feeling Wheels. Ask the group members to decide how they're feeling today. Remind the students that if they want, they can color in the section on the feeling wheel that describes how they're feeling. Also remind the teens that they might have more than one feeling, since it's possible to have more than one feeling at a time. Tell them that if they're having a feeling that isn't named on the wheel, they can add a bubble to the outside of the wheel and name the feeling there.

When the students finish, start a go-around. Begin by sharing your own feelings. Then invite each student to share his or her feelings. Teenagers often list many feelings. In the interest of time, ask them to name the feelings they have but to pick only two to discuss. Be sure to accept each student's feeling(s) and to affirm each student. Ask them to return the wheels to their folders.

BASIC FACTS REVIEW

Review Basic Facts 1-4. Use posters, the List of Basic Facts, or index cards.

In a go-around, ask a student to read Basic Fact 1 aloud and explain what it means. If the student has trouble explaining what the fact means, don't contradict or judge, simply clarify his or her explanation. Repeat the procedure for the next basic fact. This review ensures that the students understand and integrate the basic facts that have been taught. It is also easy preparation for the presentation and provides a lead-in for the session material.

ASSIGNMENT REVIEW

Ask the students if they brought their assignments from last week. Remind them that they were to write down several different things that they can do to feel better if they wake up in a down mood. In a go-around, ask each student to share what he or she does to feel better. If the students have forgotten to do the assignment, ask them to think of things they can do to feel better if they wake up in a down mood. Mention that the purpose of the group is to help them cope with issues they confront in daily life. Remind them that they will have a simple assignment each week that will help them choose better ways to cope with stress.

Exploring the Material

MINI-LECTURE

The Effects of the Changing Families of the 1990s on Middle and High School Students

So far we have discussed the changing families of the 1990s, the values in different kinds of families, the stresses in these families, the reasons why people get married and why they get divorced, and how teens can be responsible for their feelings.

Today we are going to talk about four different kinds of families and the effects on teens who live in these families. We're going to look at the issues for these teens, how the teens feel, what they may think or believe about themselves and their families, and the ways they might behave. The scenarios we'll discuss include 1) a girl whose parents announce they are separating, 2) a boy who lives with his mother and siblings and never sees his father, 3) two teens whose parents separated years ago but are still fighting, and 4) two high school students who live in a stepfamily.

Ask the students to retrieve Handout 3, and ask one of the students to read Scenario 1.

Scenario 1

Martha is a high school sophomore who lives with her parents and younger brother. She's on the school volleyball team, gets pretty good grades, fights with her brother, and has a best friend, Sharon. Her mother is an office manager for a group of doctors, and her father is an insurance salesman. Martha likes to sew with her mother, and she loves it when her father comes to her volleyball games. One morning before school, Martha's parents tell her and her younger brother, Thomas, that they are going to get a divorce. They say they don't want to be married any more, for adult reasons, but that they will always be parents to Martha and Thomas and will take good care of them. The kids will spend part of each week with their father, who will move to another house in a nearby neighborhood, and part of the week with their mother. Martha couldn't believe what her parents were telling her. It was true that her mother never seemed very happy and that her father didn't talk much; but her parents never fought like some of her friends' parents. She just couldn't believe it.

Initiate discussion of this scenario by asking the following questions:

What are some *feelings* that Martha might have had that day? (Expect answers like shock, confusion, loneliness, anger, guilty, blame, hurt, sadness. Accept all feelings that the students might suggest.)

What might Martha have *thought?* (She might have thought that this was a dream, that it was her fault, that her world was ending. She might have wondered who would drive her places, whether she could still go to college, if she would ever see her father again.)

How might Martha have *behaved* at school that day? (She might not have been able to concentrate, she might not have felt like eating her lunch, she might have withdrawn from her friends, she might not have felt like going to volleyball practice, etc.)

There are several issues for teenagers like Martha, whose parents announce that they are going to separate.

LOSS. What kinds of losses do teenagers experience when their parents separate?

(Teens lose their family, their security, their sense of history and of a future, of oneness.)

How do you think teens deal with the issue of loss?

CHANGE. What are some of the things that change when parents separate?

(Many things change: one parent usually moves out, so the teens see that parent less. The other parent is often worried, sad, angry, or busier, so the children may not get as much attention from that parent. Both parents may be very angry and more irritable with the children.)

How do you think teens deal with the issue of change?

THE REASON FOR THE SEPARATION. Teenagers often want to know the reason for a separation. Sometimes teenagers are aware of a parent having an affair or having a drinking problem. Sometimes teens are aware of physical or verbal abuse. If teens aren't aware of any underlying reason, they often want to know why in order to make sense of this tragedy. Sometimes teenagers blame themselves: they may think the parents split up because of the teens' poor grades or their fighting with sisters or brothers or getting into trouble in school.

How common do you think it is for teens to want to know the reason for a separation?

INTENSE FEELINGS. Another major issue, for some teens, is that their feelings seem overwhelming: the shock, the disbelief, the sadness, the anger, the panic. They might not know how to deal with the intensity of these feelings. We'll be discussing feelings in Sessions 5, 6, and 7.

Accept whatever ideas your group members come up with on these topics. Some students may want to share their experience of parental separation. If so, draw out their feelings and how they handled them at the time. Remember that such sharing in group is extremely beneficial for the other group members.

Now, move on and ask a student to read Scenario 2.

Scenario 2

Jack is a 14-year-old freshman in high school who lives with his mother and three younger brothers and sister. Jack's mother is a nurse's aide who works in a hospital. In order to make ends meet, she has a second job in a nursing home. Because his mother is working so much, Jack has to spend a lot of time taking care of his brothers and sister. He has to make sure they're up in the morning and ready to get on the bus, has to make lunches, and has to fix them something to eat for dinner. When they fight, he tries to get them to stop. Jack's father left his family several years ago and moved to New York. He married another woman, and they have two small children. Jack's father calls Jack and his brothers and sister about once a year. He comes to visit about once every other year. He only started sending child support after his mother went to court. Jack's grades are usually Cs and Ds. He's starting to hang around with the guys who are always getting into trouble at school. He's been sent to the office twice himself for talking back to a teacher. *(But Mr. Smith is so stupid!)* Last week, he was caught shoplifting. Whenever his mother tries to talk to him, he just yells at her. *(He's not going to let her tell him what to do!)*

Initiate discussion of this scenario by asking the following questions.

What kinds of *feelings* might Jack have? (He might feel hurt, angry, lonely, lost, deprived, depressed, or guilty.)

Do you think Jack is aware of his feelings? Why or why not? (Accept all answers.)

Teens in Jack's situation often have many *thoughts or beliefs*. Which of these do you think are true, or correct, thoughts or beliefs?

1. He might think his father doesn't love him any more since he has other kids.
2. He might think there is something he did to make his dad mad.
3. He might blame his mother for driving his father away.
4. He might think that if he moved to his dad's everything would be better.
5. He might think it's his responsibility to help his mom, since his dad left and he's the oldest.
6. He might think it's not fair that he has to help out at home so much, when his friends don't have to help at all.
7. He might think that he'll be a wimp if he is too nice to his mom.

Point out that we don't know what really happened in Jack's family; you just want their opinions about which of these beliefs are correct.

What kinds of *behaviors* is Jack having? (His grades are not very good. He helps at home, but he's starting to talk back to his teachers and to his mom. He's getting sent to the office and is shoplifting. He's hanging around with kids who get into trouble a lot.)

Why do you think that Jack is getting into so much trouble? (Accept all answers, but try to make the connection that he might be hurt and angry about his situation. Instead of dealing directly with his feelings, he is acting them out by getting into trouble.)

Do you think that Jack is aware of why he's getting into so much trouble? (Accept all answers, but give your opinion that Jack is probably not aware of why he's getting into so much trouble. He can't see the "big picture" of what he's doing.)

There are several issues that are common for teenagers in Jack's situation, living with a single parent, with little contact with the noncustodial parent.

OVERRESPONSIBILITY. Jack is the oldest child and has assumed responsibility for the family. He is also resentful that he doesn't have more time to do teen things, like band and sports.

Do you think overresponsibility is a common issue for teens?

ABANDONMENT. Jack feels abandoned by his father. He may idealize his father, and protect him by blaming his mother. He may protect his memory of his father and have a reunion fantasy: if he was just with his dad, everything would be okay. He may blame himself for his father's absence, which might result in very low self-esteem.

Do you think many teens feel abandoned by one or both of their parents?

FEWER RESOURCES. Because Jack's father sends little money, his mother has to work two jobs, which makes her less available to offer Jack emotional support, or to just take him places. There is less money in his family than in his friends' families. **Is the issue of fewer resources common for teens?**

MALE IDENTIFICATION. Because Jack's father is absent, there is no one for Jack to model after. He may be afraid that if he's too nice to his mom, he'll be a wimp or a sissy. He may feel like he has to prove he's male by getting into a lot of trouble.

How do other teenage boys deal with the issue of male identification?

Accept whatever ideas your group members come up with on these topics.

Now move on and ask a student to read Scenario 3.

Scenario 3

Mandy is a tenth grader who lives with her mother, her sister Robin, an eighth grader, and her brother Mark, a senior. Mandy's parents separated when she was in sixth grade; the divorce was not final for four years. During that time, the children lived with their mother in the beautiful big house on a lake that Mandy grew up in. Then, because of the divorce settlement, her mother had to move out and into a small townhouse, and her father moved into the big house. She had to choose whether to live with her mom or with her dad and his girlfriend. When Mandy started high school, she discovered that her

(Scenario 3 continued in next column.)

(Scenario 3 continued.)

parents got a divorce because her father had been having an affair with a woman 15 years younger than her mother, an affair that started when they were still married. Her father had even introduced Mandy to this woman. Mandy couldn't believe her father would betray her mother—and her—like that. She doesn't like the girlfriend, so she's staying with her mother in the small townhouse; so is Robin. Her brother chose to live with their dad. She doesn't like to go back to her old house, and her father always insists on bringing his girlfriend when they go out, so Mandy really doesn't see him much at all. Her father is a lawyer and can afford a Mercedes, but he claims he can't afford to send her brother to college. Her parents still fight about how the jewelry, the furniture, and the property they bought in Florida was divided. Mandy's mother is often furious after she gets off the phone with Mandy's father. Since her mother is a secretary and doesn't make a lot of money, Mandy doesn't like to ask her for things. Her father seems to have more money, so she'd like to ask him for money for school pictures and for her cheerleading uniform. Instead of agreeing to pay for these things, her father accuses her of using him since she doesn't visit him often. Once she told her father he wasn't being fair to her mother. He got really mad at her and didn't talk to her for several weeks. Once, he told her she was just like her mother, and she knows that he's really mad at her mother. Sometimes Mandy wishes she could make things better for her mother.

Use the following questions to initiate discussion:

What kinds of *feelings* might Mandy be having? (Accept all answers, but expect feelings like hurt, anger, loss, guilt, loneliness, or betrayal.)

There are several *thoughts or beliefs* that Mandy might be having. Which do you think are true, or correct?

1. She might believe that she has to choose between her parents.
2. She might think that her father rejected her, as well as her mother, when he fell in love with another woman.
3. She might think the divorce will never be over.

4. She may feel that she's responsible for her parents continuing to fight.
5. She may believe that she should be able to get them to stop fighting.
6. Since her father insists that his girlfriend always be there when Mandy comes over, she may believe that her father prefers his girlfriend to Mandy.
7. She may believe that if she allows herself to be friendly with her father, it means she thinks his having an affair is okay.
8. She might also think being friendly with her father would be disloyal to her mother, who didn't do anything wrong.

What kinds of *behaviors* might Mandy be having? (She might try to be a therapist to her mother and help her solve her problems. She might try to change her father's behavior by telling him what he's doing wrong. She might try to be really good in school to make everybody happy. She might not ask for things to avoid causing a fight between her parents. She might just try to avoid her father.)

There are several major issues for teenagers in Mandy's situation, where there is ongoing parental conflict.

ONGOING PARENTAL CONFLICT. Teenagers often feel responsible for causing continued parental fighting. Sometimes they believe they can do something to make it better.

How do you think teens deal with the issue of ongoing parental conflict?

LOSS OF LIFESTYLE. Mandy had to move out of a big beautiful home into a small townhouse.

What effect does loss of lifestyle have on teens?

LOSS OF IDEALIZATION OF PARENT. Mandy used to respect her father. Once she found out that he had an affair, she judged his behavior as wrong, immoral, and unfair. She no longer had respect for him.

What happens to teens who lose their high opinion of their parents?

LOSS OF USUAL RELATIONSHIP WITH NONCUSTODIAL PARENT AND DEALING WITH A PARENT'S NEW GIRLFRIEND OR BOYFRIEND. Mandy sees less of her father since she's not living with him. Ever since he started living with his girlfriend, he has insisted that Mandy develop a relationship with her. He even introduced Mandy to her before the separation. He refuses to do anything with Mandy alone.

How does a changing relationship with a noncustodial parent affect teens? How do teens deal with a parent's boyfriend or girlfriend?

Accept whatever ideas your group members come up with on these topics.

Now, move on and ask a student to read Scenario 4.

Scenario 4

Adam and Allison are a freshman and sophomore in high school. Their parents are divorced. They used to live in another state, and they spent equal time with their mother and father. Then their mother married a man who lives here, and their mother moved to join him. Now, they live with their mother, stepfather, an older stepsister, and two stepbrothers who are in elementary school. (They are also real pests.) Their mother and stepfather are just getting used to living with each other. Their mom is having a hard time finding a job and is irritable: she's always telling them to be quiet so they don't disturb their stepfather. They don't think their stepfather likes them. He's always yelling at them because they are too messy and leave their things all over. He also gets mad at them because they load the dishwasher the wrong way. There are a lot of quarrels among the children in this family. Their two stepbrothers don't have to clean up their toys, and they come into Adam's room without knocking. They tease Allison because of her braces. Their stepsister dates a lot and never cleans up her dishes; their mother expects them to clean up after her. And not only that, her stepsister never lets Allison borrow her clothes, even though they are the same size. Adam and Allison hardly ever get to see their father. He writes once a week and sends them money, but he doesn't call very

(Scenario 4 continued on next page.)

(Scenario 4 continued.)

often. They also don't get to have as much time with their mother as they did before she got remarried. Now she and her new husband spend a lot of the evening by themselves. Allison is trying really hard to help out around the house as much as possible. She's also trying to get really good grades. She's having a hard time making friends because everybody else has known their friends since grade school. It seems like nothing is going right. Adam doesn't even want to try. He's spending all of his time playing Nintendo.

What *feelings* might Adam and Allison have? (Accept all answers, but expect feelings like anger, resentment, jealousy, hurt, loneliness, or sadness.)

There are several *thoughts or beliefs* that Adam and Allison might be having. Which do you think are true or correct?

1. They might believe that their mother loves their stepfather more than them.
2. They might believe that their stepfather lets his sons get away with more than them.
3. They might believe their mother did a terrible thing to their father by moving away.

What kinds of *behaviors* might Adam and Allison have?

(They might try to help out a lot, or to be perfect, in the hope of pleasing their mother. They might give up and be passive and just play Nintendo. They might fight a lot.)

There are several issues common for children who live in stepfamilies, like Adam and Allison.

LOYALTY. They may think they can't make friends with their stepfather because it would mean they were betraying their father.

How might teens deal with the loyalty issue?

LOSS OF RELATIONSHIP WITH THEIR FATHER. Since they're no longer living in the same town with their father, they don't see him as often. Letters and calls just aren't the same.

How might teens deal with this issue?

LOSS OF RELATIONSHIP WITH THEIR MOTHER. After the divorce, and before their mother got remarried, Adam and Allison were really close to her. She spent all her free time with them, and they really enjoyed it. Now, she wants to spend time with her new husband.

How common is this issue for teens?

DIFFERENT STYLES OF LIVING AND DISCIPLINE. Adam and Allison are adjusting to a new stepfather, who has a different style of discipline from their mother. He yells a lot, and expects much more from them. Their mother used to do their chores for them, and then yell.

How can teens deal with different styles of living and discipline?

RIVALRY AND JEALOUSY. Teenagers in stepfamilies and blended families often wonder whether the parents love one child or set of children more than another. Teens sometimes think that their stepparent is harder on them than on their natural children.

How do teens deal with the issues of rivalry and jealousy?

Summarize quickly by saying that the changing families of the 1990s present lots of issues for teens. We've talked about some of these families and the effects on teens of living in these families. We've also identified issues common to teens from these families. Next week we'll talk about the family patterns that can develop in these families, and we'll begin to help group members develop good coping strategies to deal with these patterns.

BASIC FACTS

Review the new basic facts for this session. Refer the students to the List of Basic Facts. Ask a group member to read the new basic facts.

5. A separation or divorce in a family is never the children's fault.

6. Children usually love both their mother and their father, even if the parents no longer live together.

Assignment

Have the group members take Assignment 3 out of their folders. Read the directions: "Over the next week, once each day, look at the issues for the teens described in the scenarios for Session 3. Jot down if any of these issues apply to you." Explain that the purpose of this exercise is to help them become aware of the issues they are dealing with. People need to be aware of their issues before they can begin to identify how they deal with them.

Wrapping Up

Centering Exercise

Settle the students and then repeat "The Pyramid."

Affirmation

Involve the group in an affirmation. Stand and join in a circle with the students, holding hands. Go around and have the students share an issue described in today's session that they have experienced. Start the affirmation yourself: "One issue that was described in today's session that I have experienced is. . . ."

Closing

Remain standing in a circle with the students, holding hands, and lead the group in the closing activity.

Tell the students that you're going to make a silent wish for the student on your right. Then, when you've made the wish, gently squeeze that student's hand. The student makes a silent wish for the person on his or her right, then gently squeezes the student's hand, and so on. Continue around the circle until a wish and squeeze come back to you. If necessary, the students can pass the wish in any appropriate way they choose.

Collect the folders. Fill out a copy of the Process and Progress Form (page 199) or, if you are an experienced leader, the Progress Notes (page 200) as soon as possible after leading the group.

Scenarios for Session 3

Scenario 1

Martha is a high school sophomore who lives with her parents and younger brother. She's on the school volleyball team, gets pretty good grades, fights with her brother, and has a best friend, Sharon. Her mother is an office manager for a group of doctors, and her father is an insurance salesman. Martha likes to sew with her mother, and she loves it when her father comes to her volleyball games. One morning before school, Martha's parents tell her and her younger brother, Thomas, that they are going to get a divorce. They say they don't want to be married any more, for adult reasons, but that they will always be parents to Martha and Thomas and will take good care of them. The kids will spend part of each week with their father, who will move to another house in a nearby neighborhood, and part of the week with their mother. Martha couldn't believe what her parents were telling her. It was true that her mother never seemed very happy and that her father didn't talk much; but her parents never fought like some of her friends' parents. She just couldn't believe it.

Scenario 2

Jack is a 14-year-old freshman in high school who lives with his mother and three younger brothers and sister. Jack's mother is a nurse's aide who works in a hospital. In order to make ends meet, she has a second job in a nursing home. Because his mother is working so much, Jack has to spend a lot of time taking care of his brothers and sister. He has to make sure they're up in the morning and ready to get on the bus, has to make lunches, and has to fix them something to eat for dinner. When they fight, he tries to get them to stop. Jack's father left his family several years ago and moved to New York. He married another woman, and they have two small children. Jack's father calls Jack and his brothers and sister about once a year. He comes to visit about once every other year. He only started sending child support after his mother went to court. Jack's grades are usually Cs and Ds. He's starting to hang around with the guys who are always getting into trouble at school. He's been sent to the office twice himself for talking back to a teacher. *(But Mr. Smith is so stupid!)* Last week, he was caught shoplifting. Whenever his mother tries to talk to him, he just yells at her. *(He's not going to let her tell him what to do!)*

Scenario 3

Mandy is a tenth grader who lives with her mother, her sister Robin, an eighth grader, and her brother Mark, a senior. Mandy's parents separated when she was in sixth grade; the divorce was not final for four years. During that time, the children lived with their mother in the beautiful big house on a lake that Mandy grew up in. Then, because of the divorce settlement, her mother had to move out and into a small townhouse, and her father moved into the big house. She had to choose whether to live with her mom or with her dad and his girlfriend. When Mandy started high school, she discovered that her parents got a divorce because her father had been having an affair with a woman 15 years younger than her mother, an affair that started when they were still married. Her father had even introduced Mandy to this woman. Mandy couldn't believe her father would betray her mother—and her—like that. She doesn't like the girlfriend, so she's staying with her mother in the small townhouse; so is Robin. Her brother chose to live with their dad. She doesn't like to go back to her old house, and her father always insists on bringing his girlfriend when they go out, so Mandy really doesn't see him much at all. Her father is a lawyer and can afford a Mercedes, but he claims he can't afford to send her brother to college. Her parents still fight about how the jewelry, the furniture, and the property they bought in Florida was divided. Mandy's mother is often furious after she gets off the phone with Mandy's father. Since her mother is a secretary and doesn't make a lot of money, Mandy doesn't like to ask her for things. Her father seems to have more money, so she'd like to ask him for money for school pictures and for her cheerleading uniform. Instead of agreeing to pay for these things, her father accuses her of using him since she doesn't visit him often. Once she told her father he wasn't being fair to her mother. He got really mad at her and didn't talk to her for several weeks. Once, he told her she was just like her mother, and she knows that he's really mad at her mother. Sometimes Mandy wishes she could make things better for her mother.

Scenario 4

Adam and Allison are a freshman and sophomore in high school. Their parents are divorced. They used to live in another state, and they spent equal time with their mother and father. Then their mother married a man who lives here, and their mother moved to join him. Now, they live with their mother, stepfather, an older stepsister, and two stepbrothers who are in elementary school. (They are also real pests.) Their mother and stepfather are just getting used to living with each other. Their mom is having a hard time finding a job and is irritable; she's always telling them to be quiet so they don't disturb their stepfather. They don't think their stepfather likes them. He's always yelling at them because they are too messy and leave their things all over. He also gets mad at them because they load the dishwasher the wrong way. There are a lot of quarrels among the children in this family. Their two stepbrothers don't have to clean up their toys, and they come into Adam's room without knocking. They tease Allison because of her braces. Their stepsister dates a lot and never cleans up her dishes; their mother expects them to clean up after her. And not only that, her stepsister never lets Allison borrow her clothes, even though they are the same size. Adam and Allison hardly ever get to see their father. He writes once a week and sends them money, but he doesn't call very often. They also don't get to have as much time with their mother as they did before she got remarried. Now she and her new husband spend a lot of the evening by themselves. Allison is trying really hard to help out around the house as much as possible. She's also trying to get really good grades. She's having a hard time making friends because everybody else has known their friends since grade school. It seems like nothing is going right. Adam doesn't even want to try. He's spending all of his time playing Nintendo.

Assignment 3

Over the next week, once each day, look at the issues for the teens described in the scenarios for Session 3. Jot down if any of these issues apply to you.

Immediate Crisis Stage
Loss
Change
The Reason for the Separation
Intense Feelings

Single-parent Family
Overresponsibility
Abandonment
Fewer Resources
Male Identification

Ongoing Parental Conflict
Loyalty Conflict
Loss of Lifestyle
Loss of Idealization of Parent
Loss of Usual Relationship with Noncustodial Parent
Dealing with a Parent's New Girlfriend or Boyfriend

Stepfamily
Loss of Relationship with Noncustodial Parent
Less Attention from Remarried Parent
Different Styles of Living and Discipline
Rivalry and Jealousy

Day one

Day two

Day three

Day four

Day five

Day six

Day seven

Other feelings or comments

SESSION • 4

The Effects of Divorce, Separation, and Other Nontraditional Lifestyles on Families: Family Sculptures

Objectives

To help the students:

- learn that children can't cause, change, or control their parents' separation or divorce
- discover four things teenagers from separated or divorced families can do to take care of themselves

Session at a Glance

1. Group Rules: review if necessary—1 minute
2. Centering Exercise: "The Meadow"—3 minutes
3. Feelings Check-in: look at Feeling Wheel—5 minutes
4. Basic Facts Review—4 minutes
5. Review Assignment —2 minutes
6. Mini-lecture and Discussion: Family Sculptures—18 minutes
7. Activity: Family Sculptures —2 minutes
8. Basic Facts: read Basic Facts 7 and 8; discuss—2 minutes
9. Assignment—2 minutes
10. Centering Exercise: "The Meadow"—3 minutes
11. Affirmation: share one thing you will remember from today's session—2 minutes
12. Closing: pass a silent wish—1 minute

Preparation

- Display the posterboard copy of the group rules.
- Have posters with Basic Facts 1-6 available, or the List of Basic Facts already in the folders, or index cards with a basic fact on each one.

- Add the following materials to each folder:

  —Handout 4 ("Family Sculptures")

  —Assignment 4.

- Place the each student's folder, a pencil, and crayons or markers at his or her place.
- Copy the "Three Cs" (Basic Fact 7) and the "Four Steps" (Basic Fact 8) onto a piece of posterboard or newsprint to display during the session. (Note: Save these posters to use again should you decide to do Session 10.)
- Have chalkboard and chalk or newsprint and a marker available.
- Read through the session plan before meeting.

Background and Guidelines

THE THREE CS

Because children usually don't possess the knowledge and perspective necessary to correctly identify the stresses in their family, they often try to create order out of the chaos that they do see. However, given their developmental levels, they generally do so in "childish," egocentric, and incorrect ways. They develop misconceptions typical of children living in at-risk families, thinking that they have caused, or can control or change, parental violence, chemical dependence, or separation or divorce. Although adolescents are sometimes able to correctly identify the family's problems, and are becoming less egocentric, they still hold on to the misconceptions typical of younger children.

For example, adolescents often believe that their family's problems are their fault, that they've *caused* a parental separation: "My parents are separating because I'm always getting into trouble." Or some teens try to *control* a parental separation by trying to intervene, telling the parents to get back together, or trying to be the parents' therapist. Unfortunately, although teens may believe that they have the power necessary to insist that a parent get help, they can't have such power. Thus, when teens are unsuccessful in their controlling efforts, they feel like failures and suffer low self-esteem.

When adolescents believe that they've caused a parental separation, they often think that they can *change* it as well. Teenagers try to effect change through a variety of means: by getting good grades in school, by doing all the chores around the home, or by finding another way to bring honor to the family (through their efforts in sports, dance, art, and so on). Again, these efforts won't be effective, and again the children will feel like failures.

Students who begin to trust and talk about family problems are beginning to get better. They often feel uncomfortable talking about their changing families, whether the situation is a separation or a divorce, a parental affair, or a stepfamily. But as they talk and the group leader normalizes their feelings, they begin the process of accepting their situations and learning to cope with their feelings.

The group leader corrects teens' misconceptions by teaching them the three Cs: *children* (1) *don't cause,* (2) *can't control,* and (3) *can't change a parent's separation or divorce.* Since this will be new information for many of the students, they may resist it. While respecting the students' feelings and opinions, you should be ready to help them understand that they really don't have the power to cause, control, or change parental behavior. Acknowledge to the students that it would be wonderful if teens could control or change another person's behavior. Unfortunately, teenagers don't have that kind of power. Point out that not even the spouse of a person who decides to divorce has such power. Help the students see that no one can control anyone else's behavior.

By teaching the students the three Cs, the session also helps them deal with the factors of *codependence, detachment,* and *empowerment.* It's important that you understand how each of these factors affects the teens.

CODEPENDENCE

Although the term codependence is not introduced to the students, the curriculum is designed to help them learn alternatives to codependent behavior. A person's behavior may be described as *codependent* when (1) the person feels responsible for another's feelings, problems, or behavior; or (2) the person doesn't take action on his or her own behalf but simply reacts to the behaviors or feelings of another. Codependent people may be very controlling of another, or they may worry so much about another that they don't pay attention to themselves, thus never fulfilling their own potential.

In Session 2, the students discovered that they can do some things to take care of themselves and to improve their relationships. Knowing this is the first step to learning alternatives to codependent behavior. As the group progresses, the students will learn that they don't have to depend on someone else for their feelings, but that they can be responsible for themselves, can learn how to deal effectively with feelings, and can choose to do things that they enjoy.

DETACHMENT

Learning the three Cs also helps the students begin the *detachment* process. This doesn't mean that children cut themselves off from their parents. Rather they give up believing that they are responsible for a parent's problem. The students discover that they can love and care for a parent and can express that love and concern without having to control a parent or fix his or her problem.

EMPOWERMENT

Finally, the three Cs *empower* the students. They help the teens begin to turn their focus away from their family's problems and to train it on themselves in positive and healthy ways. The session introduces four steps the students can take to empower themselves.

The four steps teens can take if they live in a changing family are:

1. **Accept what they can't change.**
2. **Ask for help for themselves.**
3. **Be friendly with both parents.**
4. **Learn to recognize, accept, and share their feelings.**

Since many students think that such empowerment is a form of selfishness, be ready to help them see the difference between selfishness and self-preservation. For example, you might ask a student to imagine that he or she is one of three people on an island, with only one piece of cake to eat. Eating the whole piece is selfishness; giving it to the other two people and having none yourself is being a martyr; dividing the cake into three pieces and claiming your share is self-preservation.

The students need to realize that self-preservation is a positive activity and means taking care of themselves in age-appropriate ways. The students can't do this if they're engaged in the futile and overwhelming task of trying to fix their parents' problems.

Throughout the session, use your knowledge of the group members' individual situations to tailor the activity and discussion to speak to those situations. If, for example, you find that the teens refuse to let go of the belief that they have to choose between parents, spend more time discussing that issue. Or if you have a student who is rejecting a stepparent because of a loyalty conflict, use the family sculpture of Divorce, which will be described shortly, to help the teen realize that he or she can have positive relationships with both sets of parents. In fact, if you feel that the students' needs dictate it, use two meeting times to present this session. For the sake of the students, this session's concepts and ideas deserve whatever time it takes to help the students understand them. Also remember that it takes time for students to change their belief system.

The Family Sculpture

Today's activity, "Family Sculpture" (adapted from a sculpture presented by Rokelle Lerner, a therapist who has worked with children from alcoholic families), is a form of role playing that demonstrates these concepts. As you involve the students in creating the five sculptures outlined in the session, recognize that there are five ideas or concepts that will be demonstrated. The sculptures will allow you to teach the students about enmeshment, boundaries, closed family systems, survival roles and intermittent reinforcement, and enabling, all of which are related to at-risk families and codependence. Understanding something about these concepts can help you explicate them when you coach the students in the sculptures.

Divorce

The first sculpture, *Divorce,* is a role play that is directed by you, with the scenes suggested by the students. They can role-play a divorce that is calm and peaceful or violent. The students can role-play a parental affair, or alcoholism, or violence. They can decide if the children will side with one parent, or be caught in the middle, or be neglected by both parents.

Enmeshment

The second sculpture, *Enmeshment,* shows extremely codependent behavior, where family members assume responsibility for the feelings of other family members. These children are unable to set boundaries between themselves and their parents. For example, enmeshed children might assume parental feelings ("If Mom is sad, I must be sad, too") or feel responsible for fixing parental problems ("I must try to do things to solve the problem or make my parents feel better"), or they might feel they have to conduct themselves in ways that will not disturb the other person ("I can't ask for the car tonight, or dad will explode").

Boundaries

Boundaries shows that when teens are enmeshed with one or both parents, they often fail to develop a separate identity, a sense of personal integrity, and the internal resources necessary to form relationships and deal with life's stresses. To be healthy, teens must develop a sense of separateness and individuality that allows for closeness when needed. It is also healthy for teens to develop a sense of personal space and integrity that allows them to set limits in a relationship when they don't desire closeness. The *kill-them-with-kindness sandwich, the three Cs, and the four steps* presented in this chapter will help the students escape enmeshment, set appropriate boundaries, and learn to take care of themselves. A kill-them-with-kindness sandwich is a technique that teens can learn to make it easier for them to set boundaries politely. In this technique, the teens learn to (1) say something nice; (2) set the limit or boundary; and (3) say something nice.

Scenarios are provided in this section that will help the students set boundaries in situations they may face. Girls are coached to set limits in situations where their boyfriends are beginning to use violent behavior or want sexual activity. Boys learn to set limits when their friends prod them to engage in vandalism, or some other acting-out behavior. Both boys and girls are coached to set limits with parents to avoid placing themselves in the middle between parents.

Closed Family System

The *Closed Family System* sculpture demonstrates a family living by the rules "Don't talk; don't trust; don't feel." In this sculpture students learn about these unwritten,unspoken rules. They also see the teen in the family begin to break the rules: she talks about the family's problems and the effects they have on her. As teens open up about family problems, they begin to feel a variety of feelings, including embarrassment, guilt, shame, anger, rage, hurt, and fear. During the activity, remind the group members that although breaking the rules of the closed family system is uncomfortable, it's also the beginning of getting better. Teens who open up the closed family system by seeking help may feel conflicted, uncomfortable, embarrassed, and guilty. Eventually, though, they'll feel better because they're beginning to recognize, accept, and share their feelings.

Survival Roles and Intermittent Reinforcement

Survival Roles

The next sculpture, *Survival Roles and Intermittent Reinforcement,* is divided into two parts. This first part introduces the familial "survival" roles adopted by children living under traumatic stress, first described in the chemical dependence literature. Children from families that experience separation and divorce may also suffer from traumatic shock and experience feelings of fear, anger, sadness, anxiety, loneliness, and hopelessness. They may take on the survival roles in order to make life less painful. The roles typically described for children in a dysfunctional family are superhero, lost child, scapegoat, and clown.

Superheroes (or "overachievers" or "too-good-to-be-true" children) generally—and mistakenly—believe that if they are only good enough, or perfect enough, their families' problems will be solved. These children try to help out at home, get good grades, and be therapists to their parents. They do anything and everything they can to help parents solve their problems. These children live under the misconception that their behavior (if it's good enough) can control or cure parental behavior (such as getting a parent to stop using violence). Superhero children generally end up feeling like failures, because no matter how good they are, their "perfect" behavior can never be good enough to make their parents stop fighting.

Superheroes are outwardly successful; the family can point to them, feel proud, and say, "We're okay." Superheroes pay a price, however. Generally, they experience feelings of hurt, inadequacy, confusion, guilt, fear, and low self-esteem. Living with the misconception that if they are only "perfect" enough they can change parental behavior, superheroes may become rigid and perfectionistic. They may overreact and become unduly upset over the slightest criticism from an authority figure (teacher, coach, clergyperson). Superheroes seem to be able to do anything, except what they want to do most—make their family well.

Lost children may feel personally responsible for the parental chaos in an unhappy home. Rather than trying to control that chaos, however, lost children try becoming invisible. Invisible, they won't be held accountable for parental stress or family distress. These children might spend a lot of time by themselves, away from other family members, "lost" in their own worlds. They may become overeaters or underachievers in school, or they may become isolated and withdrawn, seeing themselves as alone, helpless, vulnerable, and powerless. Lost children give a family in crisis some relief. Pointing to the quiet, lost child, a family can think that everything's all right in the family. On the inside, lost children feel unimportant, lonely, hurt, abandoned, fearful, and defeated.

Scapegoats tend to be the lightning rods for anger in a family. These children may act out their own anger by fighting or yelling at home or at school. They tend to get themselves in trouble and, in this way, focus attention away from the parental problems by drawing parental attention to themselves in a self-sacrificing rescue attempt. Scapegoats feel hurt and abandoned, angry and rejected, and totally inadequate; they possess little or no self-esteem.

Clowns provide comic relief for family members by making them laugh. Like scapegoats, they focus attention away from parental problems. These children generally see themselves as "jokes." Thus, they have low self-esteem and feel frightened, lonely, anxious, inadequate, and unimportant. Clowns may be diagnosed as having attention-deficit hyperactivity disorder, or they may have learning disabilities in school.

These survival roles aren't meant to be labels or rigid categories. In fact, children in troubled families may exhibit characteristics of several different roles at the same time; or, over time, they may adopt different roles. For instance, a younger child who acts as a scapegoat may become a superhero after an older sibling, who has played the role until then, leaves home. Likewise, children from families in crisis may exhibit other traits that don't necessarily lend themselves to the roles identified here. These roles are stressed to alert you to behaviors typically found in children from troubled families, behaviors you might find in the members of your group.

INTERMITTENT REINFORCEMENT

The second part of the sculpture *Survival Roles and Intermittent Reinforcement* demonstrates how children in troubled families may sometimes be successful in their roles, thereby reinforcing the role behavior. Help the students understand the meaning of intermittent reinforcement: a pattern of rewarding behavior in sporadic, rather than consistent, ways. In the sculpture, you coach the students to play a superhero, a scapegoat, a lost child, and a clown, and then you set up a situation where they try to attract attention from a noncustodial parent or from an overworked single parent. Sometimes, the parent in the role-play rewards the children's behavior by being attentive. However, the attention is inconsistent and unpredictable. Sometimes the behavior draws no response at all. The children are likely to continue their behavior in the hope that the parent will reward it by giving them the attention they crave. This explains why some teens—and adults—keep behaving in ways that appear self-defeating.

ENABLING

The final sculpture is *Enabling.* This concept is generally used to demonstrate a family pattern that commonly develops in chemically dependent families. It is presented here to help the students understand the concept, which may also apply to their behavior with peers. As you help the students present this sculpture, make the point that people who enable have positive motives—they want to help the alcoholic or addict, they want to protect the person, they want to preserve the family name. However, their rescuing behavior actually prevents the chemically dependent person from getting the help he or she needs. When family members stop enabling, the chemically dependent member will have to face the consequences of his or her behavior. This, in turn, increases the chances that the person will admit that he or she has a problem and will decide to get better.

There may be enough material in this session for it to be given over two sessions. If you find that to be the case, present the sculptures on *Divorce, Enmeshment, Boundaries,* and *Closed Family System* the first week. Present *Survival Roles, Intermittent Reinforcement,* the *Three Cs,* the *Four Steps,* and *Enabling* the second week. Read over the section of the plan that describes the family sculpture activity, and decide how best to present it to the students.

Beginning the Session

GROUP RULES

Have the folders at the appropriate places. Welcome the students and, if necessary, begin with a quick review of the group rules. Draw attention to the poster listing the rules. Call on different students to read them one at a time.

Check for understanding before moving on.

CENTERING EXERCISE

Lead the students in a new centering exercise, "The Meadow."

THE MEADOW

Imagine that it's the month of April. You're in a meadow of soft green grass. The meadow is surrounded by beautiful dogwood trees in such full bloom that the blossoms look like a snowfall. You can smell the fresh scent of spring in the air and the smell of new spring grass. The sky above is bright blue and dotted with white fluffy clouds. You are there with a very good friend—somebody you really trust, like a mom or dad, a best friend, or maybe someone you were once close to who has died, like a grandparent or an aunt or uncle. You feel very safe and secure with this friend.

You begin to experience a difficult feeling—anger or sadness or even fear. Imagine that you are experiencing anger right now. Think of something that has happened that has made you very angry. Maybe you even feel rage. Feel how angry your body feels: maybe your muscles are tight, or maybe you feel very hot. You tell your friend how angry you are, and your friend is so understanding that it's okay for you to be very angry, and you know that you will be safe. You feel so safe that you beat the ground with your fists. Eventually, you don't feel so angry.

Now, imagine that you are feeling sad. Imagine some losses that you have had. Maybe someone close to you has died; maybe your parents split up; maybe your best friend has moved away. Maybe you feel so sad that it feels like grief. You trust your friend so much that you feel safe telling him or her about your losses. Your friend doesn't tell you to get over it; doesn't tell you not to feel that way. Instead, your friend just listens and understands how hard it is for you. You feel safe enough to cry, maybe even sob, with your friend. After you have cried for a while, you don't feel quite so sad.

Now, imagine that you are feeling some fear. Maybe your parents are getting a separation. Maybe someone close to you has a serious illness. Maybe you're worried about your future. You tell your friend how scared you are, that you even feel some panic. You may even begin to shake, you're so scared. Your friend helps you stay grounded and helps you remember that it's okay to feel this panic, but that it will pass. In a little while, the intense panic does pass.

Exercise continued in next column.

Exercise continued from previous column.

After you've finished telling your friend about the feeling, experienced it in your body, and maybe even pounded, cried, or shook, you begin to feel better. You experience a sense of release, a calmness and peacefulness you haven't felt for a long time. You begin to be aware of the meadow again. It's as if you're seeing the dogwoods, the sky, and the clouds for the first time. You feel a sense of thanks and appreciation for the beauty of the surroundings, and for your friend. You again feel in control, calm, and peaceful.

FEELINGS CHECK-IN

Do a feelings check-in with the students. Have them take out their Feeling Wheels. Ask the group members to decide how they are feeling today. Remind the students that if they want, they can color in the section on the Feeling Wheel that describes how they're feeling today. Also remind the teens that they might have more than one feeling, since it's possible to have more than one at a time. Tell the students that if they're having a feeling that is not named on the wheel, they can add a bubble to the outside of the wheel and name the feeling there.

When the students finish, have a go-around. Begin by sharing your own feelings. Then, invite each student to share his or her feelings. Teenagers often list many feelings. In the interest of time, you may need to ask them to name the feelings they have, but then pick only two to discuss. Be sure to accept each student's feeling(s) and to affirm each student. Ask the students to return the wheels to their folders.

BASIC FACTS REVIEW

Review Basic Facts 1-6. Use the posters, the List of Basic Facts, or index cards.

In a go-around, ask a student to read Basic Fact 1 aloud and to explain what it means. If the student has trouble explaining the fact, don't contradict or judge, simply clarify his or her explanation. Repeat the procedure for the next basic fact. This review ensures that the students understand and integrate the basic facts that have been taught. It is also easy preparation for the presentation and provides a lead-in for the session material.

ASSIGNMENT REVIEW

Ask the students to pull out their assignments from last week. Remind them that they were to observe themselves and to jot down any of the issues discussed last week that apply to them. In a go-around, ask each student what he or she found. If students have forgotten to do the assignment, ask them to think about which of the issues that apply to changing families have been significant for them.

Exploring the Material

MINI-LECTURE

The Effects of Divorce, Separation, and Nontraditional Family Styles on Families

The family sculptures are adapted from a sculpture by Rokelle Lerner, a therapist who has worked with children from alcoholic families. They show the patterns that some families affected by stresses such as chemical dependence, divorce, severe physical illness, or family violence might develop. You can use your knowledge of the group members' families and their patterns to personalize these sculptures in an anonymous way. For instance, you can make the enmeshed family a father and his children. If the students want to, let them demonstrate what their own family would look like in a sculpture.

To begin, tell the students that living in one of the changing families you have been discussing presents some special challenges. Like many other families with severe stresses, these families sometimes develop patterns of behavior for coping with these stresses or challenges. Tell the students that you will ask them to help you demonstrate some of these patterns through family sculptures, using them as the actors.

After each sculpture, write the words *Divorce, Enmeshment, Boundaries, Closed Family System, Survival Roles and Intermittent Reinforcement,* and *Enabling* on a chalkboard or newsprint.

Sculpture 1: Divorce.

The first sculpture shows what a separation or divorce looks like in a family. Ask two students to be the mom and dad, and two others to be the children. Have them act like a happy family, with the mom and dad spending time with each other. (Ask the students in the group what the mom and dad do when they are getting along well, and have them act it out.) Also have the whole family do something together, when everybody is getting along well. (Ask the students what the family does, and have them act it out.)

Now tell the parents to start having problems. Ask the students to suggest a conflict, such as fighting, an affair (have a third student be the "other person"), withdrawing from each other, alcoholism, family violence, and so on. Have the mom and dad act out the marital conflict.

Then ask the mom and dad to act out their version of a separation. This could be calm and peaceful, or angry and violent. Now, ask the two students portraying the children what happens to them as their parents are separating. Are they caught in the middle, or do they side with the mother or with the father, or are they abandoned by one or both parents? You might decide to have the students act out each of these possibilities.

Sculpture 2: Enmeshment.

Have the mom and two children stand next to each other and link arms closely. Link arms with the mom yourself, and push the family from one side to the other. As you move in one direction, say, "This family is enmeshed. When Mom feels happy, they all feel happy." Pull them to the other side, and say, "When Mom feels sad, they all feel sad." Now push them to the other side, and say, "When Mom has a headache, they all take aspirin. If Mom is angry about Dad's affair, they're all angry. This family is enmeshed, too close. They all react to Mom's moods and take on her moods. Teenagers in enmeshed families may be so close to one parent that they have mistaken beliefs that they can cause, control, or change a parental separation or divorce."

Sculpture 3: Boundaries.

Have mom and daughter stand next to one another and lock arms tightly. Point out how close the two are. Say, "Can you tell where mom ends and daughter begins? No, you can't tell, and sometimes neither can they." Point out that a teenager who has no boundaries has little sense of who he or she is, that is, as a separate person from mom. Suppose mom is really sad about the divorce. The daughter may feel very sad too and may feel that her father is divorcing her as well as her mom. If her mom is very angry at her dad and doesn't speak to him, the daughter may not speak to him either. Teenagers who have no boundaries have little sense of their own identity. They're not sure what they think or feel. They may not have much self-worth and may get into trouble because they can't say no to others. They can easily allow themselves to be abused or to cheat at school, shoplift or use alcohol or other drugs.

Explain to the group that it's good for people to develop a sense of themselves as individuals, and that one of their tasks as adolescents is to develop a sense of identity, of knowing who they are, what their values are, and how they want to live. Another way to think of boundaries is to think of a sense of personal space. Most of us like to have our own space and to know that other people won't come into our space if we don't want them to—this is a boundary. Now direct two students to stand at opposite sides of the room. Tell them that you will walk toward each, one at a time. Explain that they should call out "Stop!" when you get too close. Walk toward one and stop when told. Ask the student how he or she knew to say stop. Accept the student's reply. Repeat for the other student. Point out that everybody has his or her own sense of territory and personal space—their boundaries.

Then, tell the students that sometimes boundaries can change, depending on the emotion of the person approaching. Tell the students that you're going to approach them, and they can say stop whenever they want. Put an angry look on your face and walk toward one student saying how angry you feel. Stop when told. Ask the student how he or she knew when to say stop. Repeat with the other student. Then, announce you'll try it again. This time, put a sad look on your face, and turn and walk toward the first student while describing how sad you feel. Stop when told. Ask the student how he or she knew when to say stop. Point out that boundaries are very individual and can depend on a person's emotions. Usually people want more space if someone approaching them seems angry, but often they're willing to let a sad person come a little closer. Some people are willing to let the angry person get right in their face, but they want the sad person to stay far away.

Point out that some teenagers don't have a clear sense of their own boundaries. They don't realize that they can set limits. Tell the students that they will act out four different ways teens can set boundaries. The concept of boundaries can help teenage girls realize that they have the right not to allow even minor incidents of violence in their relationships. They also have the right to set limits regarding sexual activity, so they don't go further than they want to or are ready to. Teenage boys need to understand the concept of boundaries so they can say no to friends who might be prodding them to do something they really don't want to do, whether it's vandalism or using alcohol or other drugs. Both boys and girls need to be able to set limits to avoid being placed in the middle between their parents. Point out that kill-them-with-kindness sandwiches are very effective ways to set boundaries. In a *kill-them-with-kindness sandwich,* you (1) say something nice; (2) set the limit or boundary; and (3) say something nice.

Minor violence. Direct two students to act out a scenario about a teenage girl and her boyfriend. Tell the students that domestic violence often starts with very minor incidents, sometimes with the man being controlling, jealous, and possessive. The violence becomes more severe and more frequent. Explain that research shows that one major way of stopping the man's violence is for the woman to calmly and firmly set limits, telling him with conviction and determination that violence will not be part of their relationship.

Set up a situation where the boy pushes the girl against the wall. Coach the girl to say to him: "I really like you, and I'm glad we're dating. But I need to let you know that it's not okay for you to push me against the wall when you get angry. I'm not going to allow violence, no matter how small, in any relationship that I'm in. We're going to have to find some other way to solve problems that we have besides you pushing me. I hope that we can, because I really enjoy spending time with you."

Sexual limits. Set up a situation where the boy is saying, "Come on, let's do it. You would if you really loved me." Coach the girl to say to him: "I really care about you, but I don't want to make love to (or French kiss, depending on age level) you right now; I'm just not ready for that. But I would like to keep going out with you."

Turning friends down. Set up a situation where a boy's friends are encouraging him to join them in delinquent behavior. Have the boy say to his friends: "I really like having you guys for friends, and I like hanging around together. But I just can't go around breaking windows with you. With my luck, we'd be caught, and then I'd have to spend the rest of my life mowing lawns to pay it off. Why don't we shoot baskets instead?"

Parental conflict. Set up a situation where the two parents are divorced and are continuing to fight. Direct the teenagers to stand between the parents. Have the dad order the teenager to tell the mom that the child support check will be late this week. After the teens pass the message, have the mom respond in an angry way, and tell the teen to tell the dad he'd "better have it on time, or else." Ask the teens to describe their feelings when they're in the middle. Then tell them you'll help them set limits. Repeat the scene. Have the dad order the teen to tell the mom her child support check will be late again this week. Now, coach the mom to get angry and tell the teen to tell the dad, "He'd better have it on time, or else." Coach the teen to say to Dad, "Dad, I really would like to do what you say, but I can't pass messages about child support to mom. You're going to have to get that message to her yourself. But I'd really like to spend time with you." Coach the teen to say to Mom, "Mom, I'm sorry you're upset about what Dad did. But I care for both of you, and I can't listen to you say bad things about Dad. I want to be close to both of you." Ask the teens to describe their feelings when they set limits.

Conclude by pointing out that it's healthy to have and know our boundaries and to set limits so that others don't cross our boundaries without our permission. It's especially important for teenagers to have a good sense of personal identity and boundaries.

Sculpture 4: Closed Family System.

Have the children join arms to form a tight circle around the parents, who are fighting in the middle. Then ask the children to move the circle slowly. Ask the parents to demonstrate their fight. Explain that this family is very private and secretive.

Ask the group:

Are these children going to let any outsiders in? (No.)

Will the children tell anyone at school that their parents are having terrible fights? (No.)

Suppose the parents are fighting so much that they break promises that they make to the children. Are these children going to trust what their parents say? (No.)

Suppose the kids tell the parents that they're scared there's going to be a divorce, or that they're angry because the parents are always fighting. Do you think these parents are going to be able to accept their kids' feelings? (No.)

So the children learn "don't talk, don't trust, and don't feel." These are unwritten rules in some families.

Now, pull one child out of the circle, and say: "Maybe this teenager is beginning to talk to the people at school about what's going on at home. She or he might feel conflicted, uncomfortable, and guilty because she or he is breaking the family rules. But breaking the family rules of 'Don't talk, don't trust, don't feel' is the only way she or he can take care of herself or himself and start to get better."

Sculpture 5: Survival Roles and Intermittent Reinforcement.

Point out that the children in the family are probably worried about their parents and will try to keep them calm so they won't be angry or depressed or decide to separate. Ask the group members playing the children how they might try to keep their parents happy and together. Accept all replies.

Point out that in many troubled families, the children adopt ways of behaving that have been called survival roles. You will help the students play four of the roles here.

Superheroes. Tell the students that one of the teenagers may get good grades and do chores around the house, like mowing the lawn. Kids who try to be perfect are sometimes called Superheroes. Ask which group member wants to be the superhero, and then have him or her stand next to Mom and Dad. What would he or she do to please the parents and to keep them calm? After the superhero acts out what he or she would do, say, "Sometimes the parents will be pleased and compliment the superhero and even spend time with him or her." Ask the student what else the superhero would do, and have them act it out. This time, coach the dad to explode and to fight with the mother. Say, "But sometimes the parents might be in a bad mood and explode about the chores not being done well enough, or the grades not being all A-pluses."

Scapegoats. Tell the students that another role is that of the teen who might act up in school or around the neighborhood. Teens who get in a lot of trouble are sometimes called Scapegoats. Ask who would like to play the scapegoat, and what kind of trouble he or she would like to get into. Coach Mom and Dad to respond appropriately when the teen gets into trouble, by consulting with a school counselor and by stopping their fighting with each other. Ask the student what else a scapegoat might do. This time, have Mom and Dad ignore the scapegoat and continue to fight with each other, and maybe even fight with the teenager.

Lost Children. Say that other teens in such families might isolate themselves, spending most of their time in their bedrooms by themselves, sometimes overeating. They may be trying to avoid causing any trouble, as well as to avoid the fighting. A teen who isolates himself or herself is called the Lost Child. Ask for a volunteer to play the lost child, and ask where he or she would like to hide. Coach Mom and Dad to quietly do what they would usually do. Then, have the lost child come home from school and go back to his or her room. This time, suggest Mom and Dad start a fight.

Clown. Point out that other teens might be the family clowns, trying to keep everybody happy by keeping them laughing, even if it is at their expense. These teens are called the Family Clowns. Call for a volunteer to play the clown and have the student say or do something funny. Coach the parents to respond favorably and to laugh. Ask the clown to do something else, and this time, coach the parents to argue.

Intermittent Reinforcement. Point out that, in most families, if the teens act in a certain way to help the parents to get along, sometimes it might work, but sometimes it won't. Sometimes the parents will reinforce the teen's behavior by being pleasant and getting along, and sometimes they won't—this is called intermittent reinforcement. When behavior is rewarded by intermittent reinforcement, it is usually very hard to extinguish. For instance, the superhero will continue to struggle to be perfect, even if it doesn't work every time, because maybe the next time it will work. Children of troubled parents often act in a self-defeating way, as long as it will occasionally get their dad to calm down or their mom to smile. For the scapegoat, the attention might be negative, but for some teens, negative attention is better than none.

Inattention from parents. Tell the group members that children use survival roles not only to stop their parents from fighting, but, if there has already been a divorce, to get attention from an absent parent.

Have the parents stand together, then separate. Ask the group which parent should leave the family altogether. Instruct that parent to go and stand in a corner. Then ask the group how the other parent should act (yelling at the kids, overworking, crying, etc.), and have that parent act accordingly.

Tell the group that it is the parents' responsibility to love the children, to support them, to teach them, to spend time with them, to have fun with them, to let them make mistakes that they can learn from, to help them develop their own individual sense of spirituality. Some parents don't do a good job of meeting these responsibilities: they don't provide adequate support; they don't spend time with the child, teaching or having fun; they don't let the children make mistakes. When parents don't do a good job of meeting parental responsibilities, it is never, ever the child's fault; it's because of some problem the parent has. Maybe the parent grew up in a home where their parents did not do a good job of meeting parental responsibilities.

Now ask the group what might happen to children whose parents have problems that make them unable to do a good job of parenting. What might the children in this role play do to get attention, either from the parent who is still there, although unavailable, or from the parent who has left the family? Accept all replies. (Some teens try to be perfect, to help around the house and get good grades. Some teens try to act out and get into a lot of trouble to get some attention. Some teens try to be therapists to their parents. Some teens try to be clowns to get attention. Some teens just give up trying to get any attention at all.)

Direct the parent who is still there but unavailable to act out an activity (yelling, overworking, crying), and have one of the children act out a way of getting attention. Have the parent stop the activity and give the child a hug. Say, "Sometimes the parent will give attention." Now repeat the scene, but have the parent ignore the child. "Sometimes the parent won't respond."

Have the child call (on an imaginary phone) the other parent, who is standing in the corner. Ask the group what the child should say ("Guess what, I got straight As!" or "Guess what, I got suspended!" or "How are you feeling? What can I do to help?" or "Let me tell you the latest joke I heard!") Have that parent respond by visiting the child. Say, "Sometimes the child's behavior succeeds in getting attention from the absent parent." Now have the parent refuse to come. "But sometimes it doesn't."

Point out that these roles are not necessarily rigid; say that sometimes teens show behavior common to all of these roles. Also note that the behaviors of some of these roles may not be completely harmful: It's okay to try to get good grades, if you're doing it for yourself. But if you get A's to get your parents to stay together, you'll never succeed, and you'll always feel like a failure. Humor is a very important skill to develop, but you have to be serious some of the time. And the behaviors of scapegoats and lost children may be harmful and self-defeating.

Mention that some teens may hold on to the wish of reuniting the parents and may think that their behavior will get the parents to end the separation or divorce, sometimes even if the parents have already married other partners.

Display the poster you have made.

The Three Cs and the Four Steps

Teens should learn the Three Cs and the Four Steps if they live in a changing family.

The *Three Cs* are:

1. Teens can't *cause* their parents to separate or divorce (even if they do argue or get bad grades).
2. Teens can't *control* a parental separation or divorce (even if they do try to get good grades or help around the house).
3. Teens can't *change* a parental separation or divorce (even if they do try to be therapists for their parents).

Since teens can't change a parental divorce, they can take *four steps* for themselves:

1. *Accept what they can't change.* (And maybe give up the reunion fantasy.)
2. *Ask for help for themselves.* (Maybe to establish boundaries and break up the enmeshment.)
3. *Be friendly with both parents.* (Don't take sides; set limits with parents who want you to take sides.)
4. *Learn to recognize, accept, and share feelings.* (We'll talk more about that next week.)

Sculpture 6: Enabling.

Tell the students that they are now going to demonstrate the concept of enabling. This pattern usually occurs in families where someone has a chemical dependence, but it can also occur in families where someone is violent, which is what they will demonstrate now.

Direct the students playing Mom and the children to form a tight V, with Mom at the point of the V. Say, "This family loves their Dad and tries to help him. When Dad is violent, they rescue him. Here's an example: 'Dad gives Mom a black eye. Mom doesn't tell anybody and skips work for a few days, until the swelling goes down.'" Ask the student playing Dad to stand with his back to the opening of the tight V. (Caution Mom and the kids to be ready to catch Dad.) Then gently push Dad so that he falls back into the V, where the family will catch him. Say, "Mom rescues Dad by letting him get away with hitting. She doesn't call the police; she doesn't tell her family or his family; she doesn't give any consequences; and she puts up with his inappropriate behavior. She may feel powerless and put up with his hitting, not because she likes it, but because she has no money, no job, and nowhere to go."

Explain to the group that every time Dad is violent and the family doesn't tell anyone, they are catching, or rescuing him. Ask the students, "Is Dad ever going to change his violent behavior if the family keeps on catching him?" (No.) Tell the students that rescuing behavior like this is called *enabling. Enabling* means protecting someone from the consequences of his or her actions. Dad won't change his violent behavior until his family stops catching him and he "falls," and hits the ground and experiences some pain. We call this a consequence. People who protect their friends from the consequences of their behavior, like drinking or vandalism, are enabling them to continue it. Teenagers are often put in the position where they are expected to enable their friends.

When all the sculptures have been formed, thank the students for their role-playing work.

ACTIVITY

Instruct the group members to take Handout 4 from their folders. Explain that there are six descriptions of family sculptures on the sheet, but none are labeled. Write the names of the family sculptures on the chalkboard or newsprint. Have the youngsters read each description on the sheet and write in the correct title. The students may complete the sheet individually or complete it as a group.

Afterward, have a brief go-around, asking the students to share their answers. If you wish, use the following questions to process the activity. You may need to ask the questions while the students are filling out their sheets.

- **What is enmeshment?** (Feeling so close to someone else that you don't know where he or she ends and you begin. Teens enmeshed with parents might assume parental feelings and try to solve parents' problems.)
- **What are boundaries?** (Having an identity of your own and the ability to keep people away or to let them in.)
- **Do adolescents who are enmeshed with or overly close to their parents have a good sense of boundaries?** (No, they usually don't see themselves as separate or complete, and they often have a hard time saying no.)
- **Is it good to have boundaries?** (Yes, teens need to be able to decide if they want people to come in close or stay away. Teens also need to respect other people's boundaries.)
- **What is a kill-them-with-kindness sandwich?** (A good, polite way to set limits or boundaries. You say something nice, set the boundary or limit, and say something nice again. For example: "I really like hanging around with you guys, but I don't want to drink any beer. Why don't we shoot baskets?")
- **What is a closed family system?** (A closed family system enforces the rules "Don't talk; don't trust; don't feel.")
- **How do teens feel when they begin to break these rules?** (They often feel uncomfortable, anxious, or guilty. But breaking these rules helps teens get better. Eventually, teens will feel better as they begin to talk about their problems, trust a little at a time, and learn to recognize, accept, and share their feelings.)
- **What is intermittent reinforcement?** (It means that teens will keep on acting in a way that may not really help them, as long as it will sometimes get them some attention—no matter what kind—from a parent who is unavailable or absent. Sometimes these parents will pay attention to their children, and sometimes they won't.)
- **What is enabling?** (Rescuing people from the consequences of their behavior.)
- **Will people who drink too much, or who are violent, change their behavior if they are rescued all the time?** (Probably not. They need to experience the consequences of what they're doing before they can admit they have a problem and decide they want to get better.)

Even if you decide not to use these questions, make sure that you highlight the concepts, ensuring that the students understand them.

BASIC FACTS

Review the new basic facts for this session. Refer the students to the List of Basic Facts. Ask two group members to read Basic Facts 7 and 8.

7. The three Cs are:
    1. Children never cause their parents to separate or divorce.
    2. Children can't control a separation or divorce.
    3. Children can't change a separation or divorce.
8. The four steps children can take are:
    1. Accept what they can't change.
    2. Ask for help for themselves.
    3. Be friendly with both parents.
    4. Learn to recognize, accept, and share their feelings.

Briefly discuss each, checking for understanding.

ASSIGNMENT

Have the group members take Assignment 4 out of their folders. Read the directions: "Each day this week observe yourself, your family members, and your friends. Each day look for an example of one of the family patterns described today: enmeshment; the survival roles of superhero, scapegoat, lost child, or clown; intermittent reinforcement; boundaries, a closed family system; or enabling. Write it down." Remind the students that the purpose of this assignment is to help them become aware of patterns many families have.

Wrapping Up

Centering Exercise

Settle the students and then repeat "The Meadow" (page 97).

Affirmation

Involve the group in an affirmation. Stand and join in a circle with the students, holding hands. Going around the circle, have each student share something that he or she will remember from today's session. Start the affirmation yourself: "One fact or idea that I'll remember from today is. . . ."

Closing

Remain standing in a circle with the students, holding hands, and lead the group in the closing activity. Tell the students that you're going to make a silent wish for the student on your right. Then, when you've made the wish, gently squeeze that student's hand. The student makes a silent wish for the person on his or her right, then gently squeezes that student's hand, and so on. Continue around the circle until a wish and squeeze come back to you. If necessary, the students can pass the wish in any appropriate way they choose.

Collect the folders. Fill out a copy of the Process and Progress Form (page 199) or, if you are an experienced leader, the Progress Notes (page 200) as soon as possible after leading the group.

Family Sculptures

1. Everyone in the family is happy. They are a traditional family, with a mom and a dad and two perfect children. Then the parents decide to split up and they are not a traditional family any longer.

2. The people in this family are so tightly connected to one parent and his or her behavior that when that parent feels happy, they all feel happy. When that parent feels angry, they all feel angry. When that parent has a headache, they all take aspirin.

3. The mom and the child in this family are so close, you can't tell where one begins and the other leaves off.

4. This family is like a tiny, tight football huddle or a circle guarding some dark secret inside.

5. Some teens try to be perfect; some act out; some go to their rooms and hide; some act like clowns.

6. Sometimes the parent pays attention to the teens, and sometimes the parent doesn't.

7. This family does everything it can to make sure the violent parent doesn't slip up and have to face the consequences.

ASSIGNMENT 4

Each day this week observe yourself, your family members, and your friends. Look for an example of one of the family patterns described today:

- the survival roles of superhero, scapegoat, lost child, or clown
- intermittent reinforcement
- enmeshment
- boundaries
- a closed family system
- enabling

Write down what you observe.

Day one

Day two

Day three

Day four

Day five

Day six

Day seven

Other feelings or comments

SESSION • 5

Feelings

Objectives

To help the students:

- identify a variety of feelings
- realize that feelings aren't good or bad, or right or wrong; they just are
- learn to put thinking between feeling and behavior

Session at a Glance

1. Group Rules: review if necessary—1 minute
2. Centering Exercise: "The Clouds"—3 minutes
3. Feelings Check-in: look at Feeling Wheel—4 minutes
4. Basic Facts Review—5 minutes
5. Assignment Review—3 minutes
6. Mini-lecture and Discussion—10 minutes
7. Activity: brainstorm feelings; describe examples of feeling, negative and positive thinking, behaving, and changed feeling for each—8 minutes
8. Basic Facts: read Basic Facts 9 and 10; discuss—3 minutes
9. Assignment—1 minute
10. Centering Exercise: repeat "The Clouds"—3 minutes
11. Affirmation: share a negative or incorrect self-talk, how you can change it from negative or incorrect to positive and correct, and how that will influence your feelings and your behavior—3 minutes
12. Closing: pass a silent wish—1 minute

Preparation

- Display the posterboard copy of the group rules.
- Have posters with Basic Facts 1-8 available, or the List of Basic Facts, or index cards with a basic fact on each one.

- Have chalkboard and chalk or newsprint and a marker available.
- Add the following materials to each folder:

  —Handout 5 ("Three Components of Emotions: Feeling, Thinking, and Behavior")

  —Assignment 5.
- Place each student's folder, a pencil, and crayons or markers at his or her place.
- Read through the session plan before meeting.

Background and Guidelines

In the last session, the students discovered four things teenagers in changing families can do to take care of themselves: (1) accept what they can't change; (2) ask for help for themselves; (3) be friendly with both parents; and (4) learn to recognize, accept, and share their feelings. This session helps the students learn what recognizing, accepting, and sharing feelings mean.

Regulating Emotions and Swallowing Feelings

As discussed in the section on adolescent development, one of the tasks of childhood is emotion regulation. Putting emotions into words helps people to moderate feelings, both positive and negative. Many of the students in the group have not learned how to regulate their emotions; their parents may not have learned how to regulate their own emotions. Many people minimize or deny their feelings or pretend they are without feelings. Others fear feelings. They may fear pain, may fear that they will be overwhelmed by their feelings or lose control of themselves. These people may try to swallow their feelings. However, no matter how hard people try to hold feelings down, they don't go away. Sometimes feelings show themselves in physical aches and pains (somatizing). Other times they are expressed through external acting out (fighting, disrespect, delinquent behavior). Or they may be expressed internally (depression, suicidal thoughts).

Feelings Are Temporary

Many people who try to avoid feelings do so thinking that feelings are permanent. They are not. Unfortunately, many people often behave or take action based on this misconception. For instance, very depressed people may attempt suicide because they believe that their depression is a permanent condition. Very angry people may commit acts of violence, not realizing that their anger will eventually lessen. Feelings are not permanent; they are temporary. As part of mastering the task of emotion regulation, adolescents need to understand that they can learn to tolerate uncomfortable feelings until the feelings pass or until they can do something to make themselves feel better.

People Can Do Things to Feel Better

This session reinforces the concept, introduced in Session 2, that teens can be responsible for changing their feelings: if they wake up in an angry or down mood, they can do something to help themselves feel better. Be ready to share with the students the variety of behaviors and activities you use to feel better. Reinforce the concept that if they feel sad or angry, they can do something that will make them feel better. This is important to help teens gain a sense of control and mastery and to help them develop an internal locus of control.

Feelings Are Normal

In this session, the students learn that feelings are natural and normal, and that they shouldn't be judgmental about their feelings. They also discover that anger is a normal feeling that most people experience 12 to 14 times a day. The group members learn that, while they should not judge themselves as bad for being angry, they can make judgments about their behavior, which might be considered good or bad. At the same time, the students also begin to understand that they *can* be responsible for the way they express their feelings. They can use some feelings to work for them; they can express other feelings so they can let them go.

FEELINGS CAN BE INTENSE AND DIFFICULT

As a group leader, you should be ready for some intense feelings from the students throughout the 11 sessions of the group. For example, it's not uncommon to hear a teen from a divorced family vehemently say, "I hate my mom. She refuses to let me see my dad. I wish she were dead!" If you hear statements like this, don't succumb to the temptation to tell the student not to feel a certain way. Doing so discounts and invalidates his or her feelings. Never tell the students not to feel what they say they're feeling. Instead, help them see that they need to identify, validate, accept, tolerate, and express their feelings in helpful ways.

For example, if a student is angry about parental violence, and speaks of this anger in group, *identify* the feeling: "I can tell you're feeling angry." *Validate* it: "Most teens feel angry like you do if they have seen their father beat up their mother." *Tolerate* the anger: "Tell me more about how angry you felt when your dad lost his temper." *Encourage* the teen to express his or her anger in a helpful way: "Some teens in your situation write in their journal or paint a picture of how angry they feel," "Some teens go to the gym and work out when they're feeling angry," or "Some teens write their parents a letter, which they don't send, telling them exactly what they think." Leading the students through this process helps them let go of their anger.

This session simplifies the process (identification, validation, acceptance, toleration, and expression) for the students. They learn that instead of swallowing their feelings, it's better for them to recognize and accept them. They think about the best way to express their feelings, by sharing them with someone they trust, by writing or drawing, or by just sitting with the feelings until they pass. They also learn that there are some feelings they can *use*. For instance, adolescents who feel guilty about shoplifting can use their guilt productively, to help them change their behavior so they won't shoplift again. With your help, the students can discover (1) words to recognize and identify (name) their feelings; (2) ways to accept their feelings (remember, feelings aren't right or wrong—they just are); and (3) how to think of appropriate ways to express their feelings.

THREE COMPONENTS OF EMOTION: FEELINGS, THINKING OR SELF-TALK, AND BEHAVIOR

As you lead the students through this session, keep in mind that a particular emotion possesses three components: feeling, thinking, and behavior. People can't control the feelings they get, but they can control their behavior. Sometimes, examining their thinking can help people control their behavior. For example, teens may feel sad because their parents are sad. Seeing the sadness of their parents, the teens think (or "self-talk"): "I can't be happy if my parents are sad." Their behavior might include crying or withdrawing into inactivity. But adolescents can examine their thinking and change their self-talk: "I can't be responsible for the way my parents feel. My parents feel sad, but I don't have to feel sad. I'm different from my parents. I'm responsible for my feelings. If I do feel sad, I can choose to do something to help me feel better (call a friend, read, listen to music, exercise)."

The Mini-lecture in this session is relatively short to allow plenty of time for the activity, which focuses on the thinking, or self-talk, that accompanies feelings and leads to behavior. The scenarios give examples of both negative self-talk and positive self-talk, and the behaviors that follow each. Becoming aware of positive and negative thinking or self-talk is an important cognitive behavioral technique to help the students learn to choose their behavior. It will enhance their ability to control their behavior and help them feel that they can control what they do; both are self-esteem boosters.

For the most part, middle and secondary school students enjoy brainstorming feelings and are not threatened by doing so. Although students generally struggle with understanding the concept of negative and positive self-talk, and the different behaviors that follow from each, it is well worth the time to help them make this connection, so they can do it on their own in the future. You will need to be active in this session so encourage the students' participation and help them see how the three different components (feeling, thinking, and behaving) apply to each feeling. You will also need to be active to help the teens to identify negative, or incorrect thinking or self-talk; to understand how it can be replaced by positive, or correct, thinking or self-talk; and to examine how both positive and negative thinking affect feelings and behavior.

Beginning the Session

Group Rules

Have the folders at the appropriate places. Welcome the students and begin with a quick review of the group rules. Draw attention to the poster listing the group rules. If necessary, call on different students to read them one at a time.

Check for understanding before moving on.

Centering Exercise

Lead the students in a new centering exercise, "The Clouds."

THE CLOUDS

Close your eyes and relax. This centering exercise can help you learn how to handle your feelings.

Imagine that it's a warm sunny day and that you are on the beach. You have been riding a dune buggy on the sand dunes and have had a great time. Now, you sit on a beach chair and let the waves come up to your feet. Just relax and imagine how warm and sunny it is.

Now, look up and see a blue sky dotted with clouds. You remember the game you used to play when you were a kid, when you would try to see objects in the clouds. Today, you decide to pretend that you're the sky and that those clouds are like the feelings you have. Watch the clouds move across the sky. See how they come and go. They are like your feelings. They come and go, too, like clouds in the sky.

Look what's coming now. It's a big storm cloud, filling the sky. It's filled with thunder and lightning. Your feeling of anger is like that cloud. It's a loud, crashing, shocking, frightening feeling! You wonder if you will be struck by lightning. The roar of the thunder makes you feel small and vulnerable. Eventually, though, the big storm cloud goes away. The sun begins to shine, and the sky is bright blue again.

Slowly, a rain cloud approaches. Soon it's raining—just a few drops—then a steady sheet of rain falls on the water. The sky looks gray and sad. Before you know it, a heavy, steady rain is falling. You remember how you felt when your best friend moved away, or when you broke up with a boyfriend or a girlfriend, or maybe even when a close friend was killed in a car accident. You felt sad, just like the clouds in a rainy sky, and you felt that you would be sad forever, just like sometimes it seems that it will rain forever. But the rain cloud doesn't last forever, just like sadness doesn't last forever. Eventually, the rain stops. They sky turns from gray to blue once again.

Now imagine that you're spending the night on the beach. It's the middle of the night. The wind is blowing. The moon is shining. You feel very unprotected out on the beach. Lots of clouds fill the sky. These are frightening clouds. They make strange, monsterlike shapes against the moonlight. These clouds are like your feelings of being scared or worried or afraid. You worry about how strong the wind is. Eventually, the wind dies down. The frightening clouds go away. The moon is shining brightly, and you feel safe on the beach again. You fall back asleep.

Exercise continued on next page.

Exercise continued from previous page.

Now it's daytime again, and you're sitting on your beach chair. The sky above is blue and beautiful. The clouds in the sky are white and fluffy, like big marshmallows. They go dancing across the sky. These clouds are like feelings of happiness, cheerfulness, or even love. They make you feel warm and happy inside. They put a smile on your face. But these clouds drift away, too. Soon, the sky is blue and clear once more.

Your feelings are like clouds in the sky. They come, just like clouds do. Sooner or later, they go away, just like the clouds.

FEELINGS CHECK-IN

Do a feelings check-in with the students. Have them take out their Feeling Wheels. Ask the group members to decide how they are feeling today. Remind the students that if they want, they can color in the section on the Feeling Wheel that describes how they're feeling today. Also remind the teens that they might have more than one feeling, since it's possible to have more than one feeling at a time. Tell the students that if they're having a feeling that isn't named on the wheel, they can add a bubble to the outside of the wheel and name the feeling there.

When the students finish, have a go-around. Begin by sharing your own feelings. Then, invite each student to share his or her feelings. Teenagers often list many feelings. In the interest of time, ask them to name the feelings they have, but then to pick only two to discuss. Be sure to accept each student's feeling(s) and to affirm each student. Ask the students to return the wheels to their folders.

BASIC FACTS REVIEW

Review Basic Facts 1-8. Use posters, the List of Basic Facts, or index cards.

In a go-around, ask a student to read Basic Fact 1 aloud and explain what it means. If the student has trouble explaining the fact, don't contradict or judge, simply clarify his or her explanation. Repeat the procedure for the next basic fact. This review ensures that the students understand and integrate the basic facts that have been taught. It is also easy preparation for the presentation and provides a lead-in for the session material.

ASSIGNMENT REVIEW

Ask the students to pull out their assignments from last week. Remind them that they were to observe themselves, their family members, and their friends. They were supposed to look for an example of one of the family patterns: enmeshment; boundaries; a closed family system; survival roles (superhero, scapegoat, lost child, clown); intermittent reinforcement; or enabling. In a go-around, ask each student what he or she found. If students have forgotten to do the assignment, ask them to think about their families and friends, and see if they can recognize any of the family patterns.

Exploring the Material

MINI-LECTURE

Feelings

In the last session, the students discovered four steps teenagers in changing families can take to take care of themselves: (1) accept what they can't change; (2) ask for help for themselves; (3) be friendly with both parents; and (4) learn to recognize, accept, and share their feelings. This session helps the students learn what recognizing, accepting, and sharing feelings mean. They will learn the three components of emotions: feelings, thinking or self-talk, and behavior. You will help them see anger as a normal feeling; discuss how thinking, or self-talk, can be positive or negative; and look at how both kinds of thinking influence feelings and behavior.

One way to learn how to handle feelings is to put them into words. The feeling wheel is a short list of feelings that are common to teenagers. All of these feelings are normal, including anger. In order to handle feelings well, teens first have to be able to recognize their feelings and put them into words.

Swallowing Feelings

Many people do not put their feelings into words; they may not even admit to themselves that they are having a feeling. These people swallow feelings by minimizing, denying, or burying them. People who do this may get depressed, or they may get physically sick, or they may explode at something else.

Some people are afraid of feelings. They may fear the pain that accompanies feelings, especially feelings of sadness. Some people fear that they will be overwhelmed by their feelings or that they will lose control. They may fear that if they let themselves feel anger, they won't be able to control their behavior. However, no matter how afraid people are of their feelings, the feelings don't go away. Sometimes feelings show themselves in physical aches and pains. People may act out their feelings by fighting or using alcohol or other drugs. They may turn their feelings inward and become depressed.

Feelings Are Temporary

Many people think that when they get a feeling, they will have it forever. Some people make suicide attempts when they are very depressed and they think the depression will last forever. Very angry people may commit acts of violence, not realizing that eventually their anger will die down.

Feelings are really temporary and fleeting; they don't last forever. Feelings come, but then they go. So teenagers can just wait until a difficult feeling passes. Teens can also do something to make themselves feel better.

People Can Choose to Do Things To Feel Better

Some people don't understand that they can do something about some feelings they might have. For instance, teenagers who have fights with their parents often feel better when they call their friends and complain about their parents. Some days, people wake up in an"up" mood: they feel happy. But some days, people wake up in "down" moods: they feel angry or sad. It's important for teens to learn what they can do to help themselves feel better if they wake up in a sad or angry mood. Teens might play sports, listen to music, dance, call their friends, write a poem to help themselves feel better. It's important for adults to have fun things to do as well. This concept is similar to the idea discussed in Session 2, that teens can try to do things they enjoy with each parent.

Feelings Can Be Intense and Difficult; Anger Is a Normal Feeling

Adolescents may have intense feelings that can be very unpleasant. Some teens live in families where they feel intense anger, even hatred, for their parents; they often feel guilty and ashamed because they think they are bad to hate their parents. Anger is not a bad feeling; feelings are not good or bad; they just are. But feelings like anger, hate, rage, and even sadness, panic, and grief can be very difficult to have. They are normal feelings that most people have at least some of the time.

People can't control what feelings they get, so they have to learn to accept them. They are, however, responsible for their behavior, which they can and should control. So, it is okay for teens to feel anger, or even hate; but it is not okay for them to act in violent ways. It is okay for adolescents to feel very angry at their parents; but it is not okay for them to hit their parents.

Three Components of Emotion: Feelings, Thinking or Self-talk, and Behavior

Feelings have three components: feeling, thinking, and behaving. Teenagers who act out a lot in school—talk back to teachers, break school rules, fight with peers, skip school, don't do school work—are probably not putting thinking between their feeling of anger and their behavior. They may be feeling angry about something like a parent's divorce or alcoholism, but they may not be aware of the feeling. They might just be acting it out. Some teens may feel very sad or even depressed. Their behavior might be to feel exhausted and lie around and do nothing.

Sometimes teens need to look at their thinking before they can handle their feelings. They may need to check if their thinking is straight, or if it is incorrect. They may realize that they have negative thinking, for instance, always expecting the worst or putting themselves down. They may realize that their thinking is incorrect, or a false belief, or a misconception.

Ask the students to pull out their scenarios for Session 3. Instruct them to glance over Scenario 2, about Jack, the high school student whose mother works two jobs and whose father remarried and doesn't pay child support, call, or visit. Jack was helping around the house a lot, but he was also shoplifting and talking back to his mom.

Ask the students the following discussion questions:

1. **What were Jack's feelings?** (Anger, rejection, resentment.)
2. **What was his thinking, or "self-talk"?** (Maybe that it was his fault that his father wasn't paying attention to him. Maybe that he's the man of the house, so he should help his mom with the younger kids. Maybe that he's losing his childhood by being a parent. Maybe that he'll be a wimp or a sissy if he's nice to his mom.)
3. **What was his behavior?** (He helped at home, but he also shoplifted and talked back.)
4. **How could he change his thinking, or self-talk?** (He can change his belief that he's the man of the house and has to take over with his younger brothers and sisters. He can think that he doesn't have to choose between helping and still having a life of his own. He can think that he can help around the house some and be polite to his mother, but do "guy" things like play sports, date girls, and ride motorcycles. Then he can change his behavior so that he will still help some, but he'll start to do things that he likes, like playing basketball and going to the movies with his girlfriend. He can change his belief that it was his fault that his father doesn't pay any attention to him. He can believe that his father doesn't do a good job of parenting because of problems the father has, not because of Jack. Then his feelings of rejection and guilt and low self-esteem should improve a little.)

Remind the students of the three Cs: teenagers cannot cause, control, or change a parent's separation or divorce.

Teens who think they can *cause, control,* or *change* a divorce have a misconception—an incorrect belief. Their self-talk is wrong. Teens who *try to get their parents back together* are starting off with the false belief that they can control a parental separation; they are probably not going to be successful, and then they'll feel like failures. There are other issues for teens from changing families where the teens may have misconceptions. Teens who *feel they have to take sides with one parent against the other* don't realize that divorce is between parents, not between the parent and the teen. They may have the the misconception that they have to choose. *Teens whose parents don't spend time with them may believe it's their fault.* They may blame themselves and feel guilty and helpless. They don't realize that it's a parent's job to be a good parent, and if the parent isn't, it's because of some problem he or she has, not because of the teen.

How can these teens change their thinking or their self-talk?

- They can learn and begin to believe the three Cs.
- They can accept what they cannot change and give up the reunion fantasy.
- They can be friendly with both parents and realize they don't have to choose.
- They can realize that if a parent doesn't spend time with them, it's because of a problem the

parent has. It's not because of anything they've done.

How might their behavior change?

In order to learn how to deal with their feelings, teens have to learn to put thinking between their feelings and their behavior. It helps to learn how to *recognize* (identify or put a name to feelings), *accept* (tell yourself it's okay to have feelings), *tolerate* (just sit with the feeling because it will pass), and *share* (express them in a helpful way) all feelings, including anger. Teens may also need to look at their thinking. Sometimes they need to change their thinking in order to handle their feelings.

DISCUSSION

Lead a discussion to help the students better understand the key concepts presented. As the group discusses, remember to go around, making sure that each student has an opportunity to add to the discussion. Encourage participation, but don't force it. Remember the group rule that allows a student to pass. Accept all ideas and answers, explaining or clarifying information where necessary to reinforce learning or to correct misconceptions. Questions like the following will aid the discussion.

- **What does it mean to swallow a feeling?** (To pretend that you don't have it; to bury it inside; to try to hide the feeling.)
- **What happens when you swallow feelings?** (You might feel physically sick; you might feel sad; you might explode in anger at others.)
- **What does it mean to recognize feelings?** (To know what you're feeling and to put a name to the feeling.)
- **What are the names of some of the different feelings teens have?** (Accept all reasonable replies. If a student mentions "bad" or "good," however, point out that those are not feelings or feeling words—they're judgment words.)
- **What are the three components of an emotion?** (Feeling, thinking, and behaving.)
- **Give an example of how self-talk can change feelings and behavior.** (A teenage girl who thinks she has to keep going out with a boy just so she won't hurt his feelings has incorrect thinking. She can correct her thinking by realizing that she can decide whether she wants to date him; if she doesn't, she can tell him that politely.)
- **What does it mean to accept a feeling?** (To tell yourself that no matter what you're feeling, it's okay to have that feeling.)
- **What does it mean to tolerate a feeling?** (To sit with a feeling until it passes.)
- **What are some ways you can share feelings?** (Accept all reasonable replies. For example: talk to a friend; paint a picture; write a story; write a poem.)
- **Do feelings last forever?** (No, they're temporary. Sooner or later they pass. Or if the feeling is uncomfortable, you can do something to feel better.)
- **Can you control the feelings you get?** (No, feelings just come to you. You can look at your thinking—or "self-talk"—and change it from negative to positive; you can control your behavior or actions, but not your feelings.)
- **What are some things you can do to help yourself feel better?** (Help the students recall ideas from the brainstorming they did earlier—talk to friends, play games, read a good book, get some exercise.)

ACTIVITY

Ask the students to get out their copies of Handout 5 ("Three Components of Emotion: Feeling, Thinking, and Behavior"). Explain that the purpose of this activity is to help them become aware of positive and negative thinking and the effect of each on feelings and behavior. The activity will also show how to change negative thinking to positive. Ask the group members to look at the examples given. Explain that in the first example the teen thinks negatively or incorrectly that she is responsible for her friends: she feels guilty because she thinks the world is her fault; she then tries to take on her friends' problems. If she changes her thinking to positive and correct, she realizes that she can only control her own behavior and can only offer support to friends. Her behavior is to take care of herself. Her feeling changes from guilt to relief. Ask if a group member can explain the second and third examples.

Example 1:

Marcy is a good friend of Paula and Joanna. Paula is having real problems. Her mother smokes marijuana all the time; her brother is on probation; and Paula is beginning to try marijuana herself. Also, Joanna's boyfriend is pressuring her to have sex, and Marcy is afraid Joanna is going to get pregnant. Marcy spends most of her time worrying about Paula and Joanna.

NEGATIVE THINKING
Feeling: guilt
Negative thinking or self-talk: "The world is my fault."
Behavior: take on friends' problems

POSITIVE THINKING
Feeling: guilt
Positive thinking or self-talk: "I can only be responsible for myself. I can care for my friends, but I can't control them."
Changed behavior: talk to friends to help them, but don't take on their problems
Changed feeling: relief

Example 2:

Bill usually looks sad when he's walking to his classes. Bill's father is in a work-release program, after getting his fourth DWI. Bill is afraid his father is going to divorce his mother when he gets out.

NEGATIVE THINKING
Feeling: sadness
Negative thinking or self-talk: "The sun will never shine again."
Behavior: isolation

POSITIVE THINKING
Feeling: sadness
Positive thinking or self-talk: "I am sad, but I can do something about it."
Changed behavior: go shoot baskets
Changed feeling: acceptance

Example 3:

Phil is a freshman on the soccer team. He was a really good player in middle school, but now he spends a lot of time on the bench. The upperclassmen on the team are always putting the freshmen down. Phil is getting very tired of their insults.

NEGATIVE THINKING
Feeling: anger
Negative thinking or self-talk: "How dare they!"
Behavior: hurt someone or damage something

POSITIVE THINKING
Feeling: anger
Positive thinking or self-talk: "I can tell them how I feel" or "I can use my anger to improve my skills in soccer."
Changed behavior: share feelings of anger with the upperclassmen; work out every day
Changed feeling: confidence

Now ask the students to think of one or two feelings they have had, writing down their negative thinking or self-talk and their behavior. Ask them to change the negative thinking to positive thinking, and ask them to write it down, as well as the corresponding feeling and behavior. Give the students three minutes to do this activity, and help them during this period. Then have a go-around, allowing each student to report what he or she wrote. Point out that they can't control the feelings they get, but they can learn to control what they do with them, how they think about them, and how they behave or act on them.

Conclude the activity by asking the students to put their activity sheets away in their folders.

BASIC FACTS

Tell the students to look at the List of Basic Facts. Ask group members to read Basic Facts 9 and 10.

9. Feelings aren't good or bad, or right or wrong; they just are.

10. Putting thinking between your feeling and your behavior enables you to choose helpful ways to express feelings.

Briefly discuss each fact, checking for understanding.

GIVE ASSIGNMENT

Have the group members take Assignment 5 out of the folders. Read the directions: "Over the next week, once each day, observe your feelings, thinking or self-talk, and behavior, and write them down. Decide if your thinking is positive or negative, and write that down." Explain again that you don't want the students to spend too much time on this, but you do want them to observe their thinking, feeling, and behavior. You will ask them what they observed in themselves next week also.

Wrapping Up

CENTERING EXERCISE

Settle the students and then repeat "The Clouds" (page 112).

AFFIRMATION

Involve the group in an affirmation. Stand and join in a circle with the students, holding hands. Go around the circle and ask each group member to share a negative or incorrect belief or self-talk they have, how they can change it from negative or incorrect to positive and correct, and how that will influence their feelings or behavior. Start the affirmation yourself: "One negative or incorrect belief or self-talk that I have (or have had) is . . .I can change it from negative to positive and correct by saying to myself . . .This will influence my feelings or behavior by . . ." The students will need you to role-model this complicated but very effective affirmation. Each group member will probably also need your help to get all three parts as they go through it themselves.

CLOSING

Remain standing in a circle with the students, holding hands, and lead the group in the closing activity. Tell the students that you're going to make a silent wish for the student on your right. Then, when you've made the wish, gently squeeze that student's hand. The student makes a silent wish for the person on his or her right, then gently squeezes that student's hand, and so on. Continue around the circle until a wish and squeeze come back to you. If necessary, the students can pass the wish in any appropriate way they choose.

Collect the folders. Fill out a copy of the Process and Progress Form (page 199) or, if you are an experienced leader, the Progress Notes (page 200) as soon as you can.

Three Components of Emotion: Feeling, Thinking, and Behavior

HOW THINKING AFFECTS FEELINGS AND BEHAVIOR

EXAMPLE 1: Marcy is a good friend of Paula and Joanna. Paula is having real problems. Her mother smokes marijuana all the time; her brother is on probation; and Paula is beginning to try marijuana herself. Also, Joanna's boyfriend is pressuring her to have sex, and Marcy is afraid Joanna is going to get pregnant. Marcy spends most of her time worrying about Paula and Joanna.

Negative thinking
Feeling: guilt
Negative Thinking or self-talk: "The world is my fault."
Behavior: take on friends' problems

Positive thinking
Feeling: guilt
Positive thinking or self-talk: "I can only be responsible for myself. I can care for my friends, but I can't control them."
Changed behavior: talk to friends to help them, but don't take on their problems
Changed feeling: relief

EXAMPLE 2: Bill usually looks sad when he's walking to his classes. Bill's father is in a work-release program, after getting his fourth DWI. Bill is afraid his father is going to divorce his mother when he gets out.

Negative thinking
Feeling: sadness
Negative Thinking or self-talk: "The sun will never shine again."
Behavior: isolation

Positive thinking
Feeling: sadness
Positive thinking or self-talk: "I am sad, but I can do something about it."
Changed behavior: go shoot baskets
Changed feeling: acceptance

EXAMPLE 3: Phil is a freshman on the soccer team. He was a really good player in middle school, but now he spends a lot of time on the bench. The upperclassmen on the team are always putting the freshmen down. Phil is getting very tired of their insults.

Negative thinking
Feeling: anger
Negative Thinking or self-talk: "How dare they!"
Behavior: hurt someone or damage something

Positive thinking
Feeling: anger
Positive thinking or self-talk: "I can tell them how I feel" or "I can use my anger to improve my skills in soccer."
Changed behavior: share feelings of anger with upperclassmen; work out every day
Changed feeling: confidence

YOUR EXAMPLES

Think of one or two situations of your own or someone else's. Tell how you or another person could change negative thinking to positive thinking. Tell how that would affect feeling or behavior.

1. SITUATION: ____________________

Feeling: ____________________

Negative Thinking or self-talk: ____________________

Behavior: ____________________

Feeling: ____________________

Positive thinking or self-talk: ____________________

Changed behavior: ____________________

Changed feeling: ____________________

2. SITUATION: ____________________

Feeling: ____________________

Negative Thinking or self-talk: ____________________

Behavior: ____________________

Feeling: ____________________

Positive thinking or self-talk: ____________________

Changed behavior: ____________________

Changed feeling: ____________________

ASSIGNMENT 5

Over the next week, once each day, observe your feelings, thinking or self-talk, and behavior. Decide if your thinking is positive or negative, and write that down.

DAY ONE

Situation ______________________

Feelings ______________________

Thinking or Self-talk ______________________

Behavior ______________________

DAY TWO

Situation ______________________

Feelings ______________________

Thinking or Self-talk ______________________

Behavior ______________________

DAY THREE

Situation ______________________

Feelings ______________________

Thinking or Self-talk ______________________

Behavior ______________________

DAY FOUR

Situation ______________________

Feelings ______________________

Thinking or Self-talk ______________________

Behavior ______________________

DAY FIVE

Situation ______________________

Feelings ______________________

Thinking or Self-talk ______________________

Behavior ______________________

DAY SIX

Situation ______________________

Feelings ______________________

Thinking or Self-talk ______________________

Behavior ______________________

DAY SEVEN

Situation ______________________

Feelings ______________________

Thinking or Self-talk ______________________

Behavior ______________________

SESSION • 6

Skills To Problem-Solve Anger Situations

Objectives

To help the students:

- realize the difference between problems they can change and problems they can't change
- learn three things they can do about problems they can't change
- learn the differences between passive, aggressive, and assertive behaviors
- learn five skills for problem-solving

Session at a Glance

1. Group Rules: review if necessary—1 minute
2. Centering Exercise: "The Space Shuttle"—2 minutes
3. Feelings Check-in: look at Feeling Wheel—4 minutes
4. Basic Facts Review—4 minutes
5. Assignment Review —4 minutes
6. Mini-lecture, Role Plays, and Discussion—20 minutes
7. Basic Facts: read Basic Facts 11, 12, 13, and 14 aloud; discuss—2 minutes
8. Assignment—2 minutes
9. Centering Exercise: repeat "The Space Shuttle"—2 minutes
10. Affirmation: share one time you got angry and a problem-solving skill you could have used—3 minutes
11. Closing: pass a silent wish—1 minute

Preparation

- Display the posterboard copy of the group rules.
- Have posters with Basic Facts 1-10 available, or the List of Basic Facts, or index cards with a basic fact on each one.

- On a sheet of newsprint, list the steps in "chunking down" the problem-solving skills (page 132).
- Add the following materials to each folder:
  —Handout 6 ("Scenarios for Session 6")
  —Assignment 6.
- Place each student's folder, a pencil and crayons or markers at his or her place.
- Read through the session plan before meeting.

Background and Guidelines

PROBLEMS THAT STUDENTS *CAN'T* CHANGE

In this session, the students learn to look at why they are angry and to decide if they are angry about something they can change or about something they can't change. They learn that they can't control some things that make them angry, such as a parental divorce, chemical dependence, or violence; the death of a close friend; or school regulations. In such cases, your task is to help the students realize they can learn to cope with the problem by accepting what they can't change, by learning to express their anger so that they can let it go, and by doing something good for themselves.

For example, a teenager who is angry over his or her parents' divorce will be unable to do anything to change the divorce. To such a student you might say: "Remember the three Cs: Children can't cause, control, or change a parent's separation or divorce. Divorce is something children, even if they are teenagers, just have to accept. It's an adult decision that children can't change. But let's talk about some helpful ways to express anger so you can let it go. Many teens in your situation write a letter to their parents—one they don't send—that tells them how angry they feel. Other teens whose parents are divorcing use a pillow or a punching bag and punch it until they don't feel so angry. Now let's talk about how you can do something good for yourself. Remember what we talked about in Session 5? You could visit your best friend and listen to music, or you could play your favorite sport." Help the students see that they can use their anger to take care of themselves, rather than remaining angry, powerless, and helpless.

PROBLEMS THAT STUDENTS *CAN* CHANGE

In this session, the students also begin to see anger as an energy or power that they can use to work positively for them. They discover that they can use their anger to solve problems or to make powerful changes in themselves. The students begin to see that they can change some problems by looking at their own behavior and changing it. This session builds on Session 5, where the students learned to look at their thinking and to see how it influenced their feelings and their behavior. In this session, the students learn alternative behaviors that they can use to deal with their anger. Putting thinking between their feeling and behavior will help them to do this.

PASSIVE, ASSERTIVE, AND AGGRESSIVE BEHAVIOR

The students learn the difference between passive, assertive, and aggressive behaviors. Much assertive behavior is mistakenly called aggressive. People with *passive behavior* handle conflict by doing nothing. Persons who have *aggressive behavior* handle conflict by trying to harm another person, either in words or action. People with *assertive behavior* use problem-solving skills to stand up for themselves. A lot of your work with students will help them develop assertive skills, especially as you teach them five problem-solving skills.

FIVE PROBLEM-SOLVING SKILLS

These five easy-to-remember skills will help the students solve problems, especially in relationships. The five skills will allow them to handle their anger in a problem-solving way, and will improve their assertive skills.

I statements. These three-part statements describe how a person feels. The three parts are: "I feel _______ when you _____because ________." For example, take a scenario typical for teens in a changing family. Kimberly is a tenth grader who is very upset because her parents are separating. If she were to use an *I statement,* Kimberly might say: "Mom, I feel really hurt and lonely when I think that we won't be living as a family any more." In comparison, if Kimberly were to use a *you statement,* she might say something accusing: "Mom, you are really selfish. Why are you getting a separation? Don't you know how much it will hurt everyone?" A person who hears a you statement is likely to feel attacked and may want to fight back. A person who hears an I statement is less likely to feel attacked.

Reflective listening. This refers to the ability to listen to what someone else says. When you teach this, you help the students realize that they can accept what others feel without reacting to them or feeling responsible for their feelings. For instance, using the same scenario, Kimberly might complain to her mother, saying "I'm really mad at you. You are so selfish. You're putting yourself ahead of our family." If Kimberly's mother is using reflective listening, she will say something like: "It sounds like you're pretty angry with me. It must feel pretty bad. Tell me some more about what's going on and what you're feeling about the separation." But if Kimberly's mother is not using reflective listening, she might simply react to Kimberly's anger and get angry back. Then they will both be angry. Or if Kimberly's mother feels responsible for fixing Kimberly's feelings, she might decide to go back to Kimberly's father just to make her happy. That might be a mistake for Kimberly's mother. Reflective listening allows Kimberly's mother to accept Kim's feelings, without taking the responsibility of making them better.

Kill-them-with-kindness sandwiches. This technique comes from Russell Barkley, author of a training program for parents of attention-deficit children. A kill-them-with-kindness sandwich is a three-part statement: (1) say something nice, (2) set the limit or boundary, or state your position, and (3) say something nice. In our scenario, let's imagine that Kimberly's parents are very angry with each other, and frequently comment about how bad the other parent is. Kimberly could listen to her mom's comments for a short time and then could say: "Mom, I really love you a lot, and I'm glad you're my parent. But I really love Dad too, and I get very sad and hurt when you say bad things about him. From now on, if you start putting him down, I'm just going to leave the room. I'd rather talk about how you are doing when I'm with you." In this statement Kimberly states her position clearly; she does not criticize her mother, but she doesn't agree with her either. She states that she loves both parents and doesn't want to hear one criticize the other. She doesn't demand that they stop, but she sets limits by saying she won't listen to the negative comments.

Apologizing. Research about violence shows that acts of aggression are more likely to occur in situations where there are threats and counterthreats. A simple apology can prevent a situation from escalating into a violent one. Suppose Kimberly has used you statements with her mother, accusing her of being selfish and mean. Kimberly could later say to her mother: "I'm sorry that I called you names and yelled at you last night. I was feeling upset about the divorce, and I was blaming you. I'm sorry." Kimberly may need to practice using I statements more to help her deal with her feelings.

Negotiating a compromise. Negotiating compromises is an important skill in a relationship. The process will be more successful if the two parties make a commitment to come to an agreement they can both live with. Each states his or her position, and they keep brainstorming ideas for solutions. Having time to think of different solutions often helps the process of negotiation. In the scenario, Kimberly and her mother could keep talking about how they can solve the problem of expressing their feelings. Kimberly's mom might say that instead of discussing her feelings about her ex-husband with Kimberly, she will talk about her feelings with one of her adult friends. Kimberly might say that she will try harder not to use you statements and will learn to express her feelings in I statements.

Chunking It Down

It takes people time to change how they deal with anger. People often want instant progress; school administrators often want instant improvement when students are in groups. Unfortunately, behavioral change takes time. The students won't be able to use these new skills immediately; it will take time for the students to develop the ability to use them. It helps to think of "chunking it down"—of looking at the process of behavioral change as requiring small steps that happen in stages (Gravitz and Bowden, 1985). Thus, group members will probably go through several steps before they develop the ability to use the problem-solving skills:

1. The teens observe their current behavior in anger situations.
2. The teens learn problem-solving skills to use in anger situations.
3. If the teens happen to express anger aggressively, they process how they could have used the problem-solving skills in each particular situation. They may need the help of an adult to do this processing.
4. Then the teens might begin to use some of the problem-solving skills in some anger situations; it may take two or three months for this to happen.

The Scenarios

The scenarios in this session are common situations for teens in changing families. The first scenario demonstrates the difference between passive, aggressive, and assertive behavior. The subject is a teenage girl who lives with her single mother and is overresponsible. The second scenario describes a girl whose parents are just separating. The third scenario addresses issues common for children in stepfamilies: (1) the loyalty conflict, when a teen feels that he will betray his father if he allows himself to like his stepfather, (2) the teen's anger over his stepfather trying to discipline him, and (3) his sense of loss of closeness with his mother. The last scenario addresses issues around parental dating and blended families.

The idea that anger can be used as a positive force will be a new one for most of the students. Expect some misunderstanding and resistance, especially as you introduce the problem-solving skills. If the group members make fun of the scenarios, ask them to help you make up scenarios that use the kind of language that they would use. Be very active and accepting during the session's discussion and activity. Acknowledge the students' ideas about ways to express anger, but gently correct and redirect any harmful ideas about expressing it. Help them tell the difference between problems they cannot change (such as parental divorce) and problems they can change (such as having too much homework to do). Offer specific suggestions geared to the age and personalities of the students. For example: "Use your anger to give you power to control yourself when someone gets in your face and to use an I statement with them;" "Use your anger to play football with more determination;" "Use your anger to get that social studies project started;" or "Use your anger to use a kill-them-with-kindness sandwich with your date if you don't want to kiss him."

Leaders who have themselves mastered the ability to use anger to make positive changes will be better equipped to present the concepts in this session. For example, leaders who are angry about their professional standing might use that anger to take classes to improve advancement opportunities, and leaders who tend to be passive with their spouses might use their anger to acquire the power to speak clearly for themselves. Leaders who practice what they preach will find themselves more effective in helping the youngsters understand this concept.

Remember, many of your group members are amply supplied with anger. Teaching them how to use their anger—and giving them alternative behaviors to aggression to use when angry—is a great act of empowerment. This session begins the process of tapping into the power of anger. Session 7 gives the students a structured plan for choosing helpful ways to problem-solve or to express their anger so they can let it go.

Beginning the Session

Group Rules

Have the folders at the appropriate places. Welcome the students and begin with a quick review of the group rules. Draw attention to the poster listing the group rules. If necessary, call on different students to read them one at a time.

Check for understanding before moving on.

Centering Exercise

Lead the students in a new centering exercise, "The Space Shuttle."

This exercise will help you learn how to use your anger.

THE SPACE SHUTTLE

Close your eyes and relax. Imagine that you work for the people who send the space shuttle into outer space. You have an important job: to put fuel into the space shuttle. The shuttle is parked on the launching pad and ready to go. It's going on a mission to help people in the world live peacefully together. All it needs is fuel—plenty of fuel—to get going. But the fuel that this shuttle uses is your anger. The shuttle will only be successful if you get in touch with your anger and put it in the shuttle.

So think of all the things that have happened to you today that might have made you angry. *(Give specific examples appropriate to the group.)* Feel how angry

Exercise continued on next column.

Exercise continued from previous column.

those things made you. Now, pump all that anger into the space shuttle tank.

Now think of all the things that you might have felt angry about over the past week. *(Give a few more examples.)* Imagine what that anger felt like, and pump it all into the shuttle.

Now think of all the things that you've felt angry about for the past year. Pump all that anger in.

By now you've been able to feel a lot of the anger you've felt in the past, and you've pumped all of it into the shuttle. It's loaded with fuel. It's ready to blast off into outer space.

You go back to the control tower to watch the launch. The countdown is beginning: 5, 4, 3, 2, 1: blastoff! The shuttle takes off! The launch is successful. You feel great because you've used your anger in a very positive way. You feel free because you've been able to let go of your anger. You feel peaceful. You feel calmer and more relaxed than you've felt in a long, long, time. You also feel proud because you used your anger to work for you.

Feelings Check-In

Do a feelings check-in with the students. Have them take out their Feeling Wheels. Ask the group members to decide how they are feeling today. Remind them that if they want, they can color in the section on the Feeling Wheel that describes how they're feeling. Also remind the teens that they might have more than one feeling, since it's possible to experience more than one feeling at a time. Tell the students that if they're having a feeling not named on the wheel, they can add a bubble to the outside of the wheel, and name the feeling there.

When the students finish, start a go-around. Begin by sharing your own feelings, then, invite each student to share his or her feelings. Teenagers often list many feelings. In the interest of time, ask them to name the feelings they have, but then pick only two to discuss. Be sure to accept each student's feeling(s) and to affirm each student. Ask the students to return the wheels to their folders.

Basic Facts Review

Review the basic facts learned so far. Use posters with Basic Facts 1-10, the List of Basic Facts, or index cards.

In a go-around, ask a student to read Basic Fact 1 aloud and explain what it means. If the student has trouble explaining the fact, don't contradict or judge, simply clarify his or her explanation. Repeat the procedure for the next basic fact. This review ensures that the students understand and integrate the basic facts that have been taught. It is also easy preparation for the presentation and provides a lead-in for the session material.

Assignment Review

Ask the students to pull out their assignments from last week. Remind them that they were supposed to observe their feelings, thinking, and behavior and decide if their thinking was positive or negative. In a go-around, ask each student to share what he or she learned about his or her feelings, thinking, and behavior. If the students have forgotten to do the assignment, ask them to try to remember one feeling that they had in the past week, what their thinking was, whether it was positive or negative, and what their behavior was. Remind the group members that putting thinking between feelings and behavior is a good way to handle feelings.

Exploring the Material

Mini-lecture

Skills to Problem-solve Anger Situations

Tell the group members that their goal today is to learn to be problem solvers who can deal with their anger in healthy, productive ways. Today they will

- look at two kinds of problems, those that they can change (such as feeling overwhelmed by too much homework or problems with getting along with peers), and those that they can't change (such as a parental divorce, chemical dependence, or violence).
- examine the differences between passive, assertive, and aggressive behavior.
- learn five easy-to-remember problem-solving skills that they can use instead of aggressive behavior.
- look at how teens develop problem-solving skills slowly.
- look at how they can use their anger as power to help them learn these skills.

Present the following information to the students in your own words.

Problems You Cannot Change

When you're angry, the first thing to do is to see if it's a problem you can change, or one that you can't. If you're angry about a problem you can't change, you should:

1. **Accept what you can't change.**
2. **Express your anger (in a safe and helpful way) so you can let it go.**
3. **Do something good for yourself.**

For instance, if your parents have separated or divorced, are violent, or are chemically dependent, you can't change these problems, so you will have to accept what you can't change. You need to express your anger so you can let it go: punch a pillow, exercise, clean, prune hedges, draw a picture, or write a letter. Then do something good for yourself, like calling a friend, applying to college, getting your homework done, playing Nintendo. If you're angry because your parents are nicer to a stepsister than to you, accept that you can't change their feelings. Then write a letter about how angry you are (but don't send it). Study to get good grades so you can make something of yourself.

Continue with the following information.

Problems You Can Change

If you're angry about a problem you can change, you can use your anger to work for you—to give you the power, or energy, to make changes in yourself by learning problem-solving skills.

For instance:

- You might be angry because you're caught in the middle between your divorced parents, who use you to send messages back and forth, like "Where's the child support?" Use your anger to give yourself the power to set limits with them. For instance, use a *kill-them-with-kindness sandwich* and say, "Dad, I'm really glad you're my father, but I won't be able to pass messages between you and Mom because it makes me too uncomfortable. Maybe you need to talk to a counselor to figure out the best way to approach Mom. In the meantime, would you like to go to the movies with me?"
- You might be angry about a big homework project. Use your anger to get started on a small piece of it.
- You might be angry when your friends get into your face because you've made a mistake. Use your anger to control yourself and give them an apology: "You know, I'm sorry. You're right; I messed up."

There is a lot of power and energy in anger, and it can be used as a very positive force.

Passive, Assertive, and Aggressive Behaviors

It's important to learn the difference between behaviors that are passive, assertive, and aggressive. Imagine that you're about to leave your home to go to a concert by your favorite rock star. You get a phone call just as you're walking out the door. It's an old friend who lives out of state. The friend wants to discuss a big problem. If you really want to get to the concert but you stay on the phone and help the friend, you're being *passive.* If you start yelling at the friend, saying, "How dare you call me now. Don't you know I'm going to a really important concert? You are really rude to call me! Don't ever call me again!" you're being *aggressive.* If you say to the friend, "I'd really like to talk to you about your problem, but I have tickets for a great concert, and I need to leave now to be on time. I'm sorry I can't talk now, but how about if I call you tomorrow?" you're being *assertive.* To be able to manage your anger and solve problems, you need to be assertive, not passive or aggressive.

Role Play of Passive, Aggressive, and Assertive Behavior

To help the students understand the differences between passive, aggressive, and assertive behaviors, ask them to pull Handout 6 out of their folders. Ask a student to read Scenario 1.

Scenario 1

Janine is a high school sophomore whose parents are divorced. She lives with her mother and her 5-year-old sister, Cheryl, and she never sees her father. Janine's mother works two jobs, and Janine has to baby-sit Cheryl every day after school. She also has to do the cleaning and the laundry, and has to cook dinner and do the dishes every night. Janine would really like to join the school choir, but she can't because she has too many responsibilities at home.

Tell the students that the group will have a role play to demonstrate the differences between passive, aggressive, and assertive behavior in this situation. Ask the group for three volunteers to play Janine, Cheryl, and Mom. Draft three students if no one volunteers. Assure them that you will coach them about what to do. Tell the students that the girl who is playing Janine will first act out a passive behavior. Have Janine ask Mom if she can join the school choir. Coach Mom to tell Janine she can't because she has to baby-sit Cheryl. Ask Janine and the group for ideas on how she should respond if she is passive. If they don't come up with any ideas, coach Janine to act out coming home from school and taking care of Cheryl. Coach Janine to cry silently as she does her chores.

Ask these questions:

1. **What will happen if Janine is passive?** (She will do what her mother asks without asking for things for herself.)
2. **What will Janine be likely to feel?** (Probably she'll feel overworked, lonely, hurt, and very powerless.)

Now, ask Janine to act out an aggressive behavior. Janine again asks Mom if she can join the school choir. Mom again tells Janine she can't because she has to baby-sit Cheryl. Ask Janine and the group for ideas on how she should respond if she is aggressive. If they don't come up with any ideas, coach Janine to act out having a temper tantrum when her Mom says no, throwing plates and yelling at Mom.

Ask the students these questions:

1. **What is likely to happen if Janine is aggressive?** (It's likely that her Mom will get angry with her. Her mother probably won't let her join the choir.)

2. **How are Janine and Mom likely to feel?** (Angry and resentful.)

Now, ask Janine to act out an assertive behavior. Janine asks Mom if she can join the school choir. Mom tells Janine she can't because she has to baby-sit Cheryl. Ask Janine and the group for ideas on how she should respond if she is assertive. If they don't come up with any ideas, coach Janine and Mom to say the following.

Janine: " Mom, I want to join the school choir. You know I'm a good singer, and I really love music."

Mom: "Janine, you can't join the choir because I need you to take care of Cheryl."

Janine: "Mom, I wonder if we can talk about this and find a way that I can join the choir because it's so important to me. Maybe we can find someone else to take care of Cheryl when I have choir practice. I feel left out when I don't get to be in any school activities."

Mom: "Well, let's talk about it some more. I can see that choir is important to you."

Ask the students these questions:

1. **What do you think will happen next for Janine?** (Probably Janine will be able to join choir; her Mom will find childcare for Cheryl.)

2. **How is Janine feeling after being assertive?** (Probably a little scared after standing up for herself and a little afraid that her Mom might be angry. But she is probably glad that she stood up for herself about the choir and very glad that she'll be able to join it.)

Five Problem-solving Skills

Now introduce the five easy-to-remember skills that will help the students solve problems, especially in relationships. The five skills will allow them to handle their anger well and will improve their assertive skills.

1. **I statements:** These statements describe how you feel.

2. **Reflective listening:** This skill helps you accept someone else's feelings, without reacting to them or feeling responsible for them.

3. **Kill-them-with-kindness sandwiches:** This technique lets you set limits, or tell someone no, politely.

4. **Apologizing:** If you see that you have made a mistake, admit it and say you're sorry.

5. **Negotiating a compromise:** Learn how to discuss the problem with the other person until you arrive at a decision you can both live with.

If you want, use a role play to demonstrate how teens can use these skills in a relationship. Ask a student to read Scenario 2.

Scenario 2

Kimberly is a tenth grader who is very upset because her parents are separating.

I statements are three-part statements that describe how a person feels. The three parts are: "I feel ________ when you ______because ________". Suppose that Kimberly blames her mother for making the decision to divorce. If she uses an **I statement,** Kimberly might say: "Mom, I feel really hurt and lonely when I think that we won't be living as a family any more." In comparison, if Kimberly uses a **You statement,** she might say something accusing: "Mom, you are really selfish. Why are you getting a separation? Don't you know how much it will hurt everyone?" A person who hears a you statement is likely to feel attacked and may want to fight back. A person who hears an I statement is less likely to feel attacked.

Reflective listening refers to the ability to listen to what someone else says. When teaching this, you are helping the students to realize that they can accept what someone else is feeling without reacting to that person, or feeling responsible for their feeling. For instance, using the same scenario, Kimberly might complain to her mother, saying "I'm really mad at you. You are so selfish. You're putting yourself ahead of our family." If Kimberly's mother is using reflective listening, she will say something like: "It sounds like you're pretty angry with me. It must feel pretty bad. Tell me some more about what's going on, and what you're feeling about the separation." But, if Kimberly's mother is not using reflective listening, she might simply react to Kimberly's anger and get angry back. Then, they will both be angry. Or, if Kimberly's mother feels responsible for fixing Kimberly's feelings, she might decide to go back to Kimberly's father just to make her happy. That might be a mistake for Kimberly's mother. Reflective listening allows Kimberly's mother to accept Kim's feelings, without taking the responsibility of making them better.

Kill-them-with-kindness sandwiches is an idea that comes from Russell Barkley, author of a training program for parents of attention deficit children. A Kill them with kindness sandwich is a three part statement: 1) say something nice, 2) set the limit or boundary, or state your position, and 3) say something nice. In our scenario, let's imagine that Kimberly's parents are very angry with each other, and are frequently making comments about how bad the other parent is. Kimberly could listen to a parent's comments for a short time, and then could say: "Mom, I really love you a lot, and I'm glad you're my parent. But, I really love Dad too, and I get very sad and hurt when you say bad things about him. From now on, if you start putting him down, I'm just going to leave the room. I'd rather talk about how you are doing when I'm with you." In this statement Kimberly states her position clearly; she does not criticize her mother, but she doesn't agree with her either. She states that she loves both parents and doesn't want to hear one criticize the other. She doesn't demand that they stop, but she sets limits by saying she won't listen to the negative comments.

Apologizing. Research about violence shows that acts of aggression are more likely to occur in situations where there are threats and counterthreats. A simple apology can prevent a situation from escalating into a violent one. Suppose Kimberly has used You statements with her mother, accusing her of being selfish and mean. Kimberly could later say to her mother: "I'm sorry that I called you names and yelled at you last night. I was feeling upset about the divorce, and I was blaming you. I'm sorry." Kimberly may need to practice using I statements more to help her deal with her feelings.

Negotiating a compromise. The art of negotiating compromises is an important skill in a relationship. The process of negotiating a compromise will be more successful if the two parties make a commitment to come to an agreement they can both live with. Each states his or her position, and they keep brainstorming ideas for solutions. Having time to think of different solutions often helps the process of negotiation. In the scenario, Kimberly and her mother could keep talking about how they can solve the problem of expressing their feelings. Kimberly's mom might say that instead of discussing her feelings about her ex-husband with Kimberly, she will talk about her feelings with one of her adult friends. Kimberly might say that she will try harder not to use You statements, and will learn to express her feelings in I statements.

Now have the students process how these five skills could be used in Scenario 3. Scenario 3 is an anger situation that is common for teens in stepfamilies.

Ask a student to read Scenario 3.

Scenario 3

Adam is a freshman in high school. He just moved to a new state because his mother remarried. Now he hardly ever gets to see his father or any of his old friends. He has to make new ones. Adam doesn't get to spend much time with his mother because she's always doing things with her new husband, stupid things like country dancing. *(Yuck, what awful music!)* Worst of all, his stepfather is a stupid idiot who makes dumb jokes. Michael can't stand anything about him.

Ask three students to role play Adam, Mom, and the stepdad, whose name is Mike. Ask the students to imagine what dinner is like with Adam, Mom, and Mike. If they can't come up with any ideas, coach Mom to try to create conversation by asking Adam and Mike how their days went. Direct Adam to give very short, non-responsive answers. Coach Mike to get angry with Adam, yelling at him to answer his mother politely and tell her how school went. Also tell Mike to criticize Adam for eating like a pig.

Coach the students to show how the problem-solving skills could work for Adam and for his mom and step-dad. If the students complain that real teenagers would never say the things that appear in the following examples, encourage them to figure out how to use the skills in their own way and language. Point out that these are ways Adam can deal with his feelings about (1) the move; (2) his loyalty conflict—feeling that he will betray his father if he allows himself to like his stepfather; (3) his anger over his stepfather trying to discipline him; and (4) his sense of loss of closeness with his mother.

1. ***I statement.*** Coach Adam to say to Mom: "It really hurts me to think of moving away from home and from Dad. I'm really angry that I had to move here. And I really don't like it that Mike is so critical of how I act at dinner and is always telling me what to do."

2. ***Reflective listening.*** Coach Mom to say to Adam: "I can tell that you're very angry about having to move. I can understand why. It's really hard to get used to a new place and to a new school. I also know that it's hard to get used to a new stepfather."

3. ***Kill-them-with-kindness sandwich.*** Coach Adam to say to his stepdad: "Mike, I know you're my stepfather, and we're supposed to be a family here. But I already have a father and I don't want you to replace him. But I will try to be friends with you."

4. ***Apologizing.*** Coach Adam to say to Mom and Mike: "I'm sorry I was rude at dinner. I know you're trying to be nice, but I don't feel like talking about school. But I'll try to be more polite."

5. ***Negotiating a compromise.*** Coach Adam to say to Mom: "I know you want to spend time with Mike, but it seems that you never have time for me. You don't watch my baseball games anymore and don't have time to take me to the mall. Do you think you could spend a little more time with me?"

Ask the students which of the problem-solving skills seems to apply the best to this situation. Ask Adam, Mom, and Mike how each felt when they were using the problem-solving skills.

Point out that practicing these skills will enable the students to start using them in real life.

Now ask a student to read Scenario 4.

Scenario 4

Susan, Michelle, and Ralph are George and Martha's three children. George and Martha have had a bitter divorce. George has remarried, and his new wife has three daughters. Martha has had a couple of different boyfriends and often gets depressed after they break up. George and Martha seem to hate each other. George often makes plans to come and get the children for the weekend but never shows up. He complains that when he calls to talk to the kids, Martha won't let him speak to them. George got his children a stereo for Christmas, but he won't let them take it to Martha's home, where they live. Instead, his new wife's three daughters get to use it.

Ask six teens to role play Susan, Michelle, Ralph, George, his new wife, and Martha. Have Susan, Michelle, and Ralph act out waiting for George to come and get them for the weekend, but instruct him not to show up.

1. *I statement.* Ask Ralph, Susan, and Michelle to demonstrate an I statement that they could give their father. Ask the group for an I statement if Ralph, Susan, or Michelle don't come up with one. If the group doesn't come up with any ideas, coach the actors to say: "Dad, we feel hurt and disappointed when you say you're going to come to get us for the weekend, and then you don't show up. We never know when we can count on you."

2. *Reflective listening.* Ask Michelle to demonstrate how she could use reflective listening if their mother has just broken up with a boyfriend. Coach Martha to say, "I just broke up with Pete. I enjoyed his company so much. I wonder if I'll ever find anybody." Ask the group for ideas if Michelle doesn't come up with one. If they don't come up with any ideas, coach Michelle to say, "It sounds like you're hurt and upset. I can see how you would be upset because I know you were really close to him."

3. *Kill-them-with-kindness sandwich.* Ask Ralph, Susan, and Michelle to demonstrate how they could use a kill-them-with-kindness sandwich with their mother. Have Martha tell the children that she just broke up with her boyfriend, and she's really feeling down. Ask the group for ideas if Ralph, Susan, and Michelle don't come up with any. If the group doesn't come up with any ideas, coach Susan to say, "Mom, I'm really sorry that you're sad over the breakup. But I'm not going to be able to help you decide what to do, or make you feel better. You may need to talk to one of your friends. But I'm really sorry you're feeling down."

4. *Apologizing.* Have Ralph, Susan, and Michelle wait for their dad to come, and have him not show up. Coach the teens to start fighting among themselves, by having Susan and Michelle blame Ralph for their dad not coming because he was rude to Dad's new wife. Then ask Susan and Michelle to demonstrate how they could apologize to Ralph for blaming him for their dad not coming. Ask the group for ideas if Susan and Michelle don't come up with one. If the group doesn't come up with any ideas, coach Susan and Michelle to say, "Ralph, we're sorry we blamed you for Dad not coming. He didn't come because of some problem he had, not because of anything you did. We're sorry we blamed you for what Dad did."

5. *Negotiating a compromise.* Ask Ralph, Susan, and Michelle to demonstrate how to negotiate a compromise about where the stereo will live. Ask the group for ideas if Ralph, Susan, and Michelle don't come up with any. If the group doesn't come up with any ideas, coach one of the children to say, "Dad, we want to thank you for buying us a stereo. We know you want to keep it at your house since you bought it. But then we hardly ever get to use it. We were wondering if we could keep it at Mom's house at least some of the time."

Chunking It Down

Tell the group members that it takes people a great deal of time to make changes in how they deal with anger. The students won't be able to use these new skills immediately; it will take time for them to develop the ability to use these skills. Introduce the concept of "chunking it down"—of looking at the process of behavioral change as requiring small steps that happen in stages. Display the newsprint on which you've listed the steps in chunking down the problem-solving skills. Read through them with the group:

1. Observe your current behavior in anger situations.
2. Learn problem-solving skills to use in anger situations.
3. If you express anger aggressively, process how you could have used the problem-solving skills in each particular situation. You may need the help of an adult to do this processing.

4. Begin to use the problem-solving skills in some anger situations. It may take two or three months for this to happen.

DISCUSSION

Lead a discussion to help group members better understand the key concepts presented. As the group discusses, remember to go around, making sure that each student has an opportunity to add to the discussion. Encourage participation, but don't force it. Remember the group rule that allows a student to pass. Accept all ideas and answers, explaining or clarifying information where necessary. To aid the discussion, you may wish to use questions like the following:

- **Is anger a normal feeling?** (Yes, people get angry as often as 12 to 14 times a day.)
- **What should you do when you feel angry?** (Look at why you're feeling angry and decide if it's a problem you can change or one you can't.)
- **What should you do if you're feeling angry because of a problem you can't change?** (1. Accept what you cannot change. 2. Express your anger so you can let it go. 3. Do something good for yourself.)
- **What should you do if it is a problem you can change?** (Use anger to work for you—to give you energy or power to make changes in your-self, or to use problem-solving skills in the anger situation.)
- **What are the differences between passive, aggressive, and assertive behaviors?** (A person with passive behavior handles conflict by doing nothing. A person with aggressive behavior handles conflict by trying to harm the other person, either through words or action. A person with assertive behavior uses problem-solving skills to stand up for himself or herself.)
- **What are problem-solving skills?** (I statements, reflective listening, kill-them-with-kindness sandwiches, apologizing, and negotiating a compromise).
- **What's an example of an I statement?** (Accept any appropriate response.)
- **What's an example of reflective listening?** (Accept any appropriate response.)
- **What's an example of a kill-them-with-kind ness sandwich?** (Accept any appropriate response.)
- **What's an example of apologizing?** (Accept any appropriate response.)
- **What's an example of negotiating a compromise?** (Accept any appropriate response.)
- **What are the steps of chunking down learning problem-solving skills?** (1. Observe your current behavior in anger situations. 2. Learn problem-solving skills to use in anger situations. 3. If you express anger aggressively, process how you could have used the problem-solving skills in each particular situation. You may need the help of an adult to do this processing. 4. Begin to use problem-solving skills in some anger situations. It may take two or three months for this to happen.)

Even if you choose not to use the above questions, make sure the discussion underscores these concepts.

BASIC FACTS

Review the new basic facts for this session. Refer the students to the List of Basic Facts. Ask four group members to read Basic Facts 11, 12, 13, and 14.

11. When teens are angry about a problem they can't change, they should:

    1. Accept what they can't change.
    2. Express their anger so they can let it go.
    3. Do something good for themselves.

12. When teens are angry about a problem they can change, they should use their anger to give them the power to make changes in themselves.

13. Five good problem-solving skills to use in anger situations are: I statements, reflective listening, kill-them-with-kindness sandwiches, apologizing, and negotiating a compromise.

14. Chunking it down is a good way to start on a long-term goal.

Briefly discuss each fact, checking for understanding.

GIVE ASSIGNMENT

Have the group members take Assignment 6 out of their folders. Read the directions: "Over the next week, once each day try to use problem-solving skills in an anger situation. Try to use an *I statement, reflective listening, kill-them with kindness sandwich, apologizing,* or *negotiating a compromise.* If you don't remember to use one of these skills, afterward jot down what you could have said." Remind them that changing passive or aggressive behavior takes chunking it down. This assignment is to help them see how they could have used the new skills they have learned.

Wrapping Up

CENTERING EXERCISE

Settle the students and then repeat "The Space Shuttle" (page 125).

AFFIRMATION

Involve the group in an affirmation. Stand and join in a circle with the students holding hands. Go around and have each student share a time he or she got angry and how he or she could have used a problem-solving skill. Begin the affirmation yourself: "One time that I got angry was . . . A problem-solving skill I could have used is. . . ." The students will need you to role model this affirmation. They will probably also need your help to see which skill they could have used when they were angry.

CLOSING

Remain standing in a circle with the students, holding hands, and lead the group in the closing activity.

Tell the students that you're going to make a silent wish for the student on your right. Then, when you've made the wish, gently squeeze that student's hand. The student makes a silent wish for the person on his or her right, then gently squeezes that student's hand, and so on. Continue around the circle until a wish and squeeze come back to you. If necessary, the students can pass the wish in any appropriate way they choose.

Collect the folders. Fill out a copy of the Process and Progress Form (page 199) or if you are an experienced leader, the Progress Notes (page 201), as soon as possible after leading the group.

Scenarios for Session 6

Scenario 1

Janine is a high school sophomore whose parents are divorced. She lives with her mother and her 5-year-old sister, Cheryl, and she never sees her father. Janine's mother works two jobs, and Janine has to baby-sit Cheryl every day after school. She also has to do the cleaning and the laundry, and has to cook dinner and do the dishes every night. Janine would really like to join the school choir, but she can't because she has too many responsibilities at home.

Scenario 2

Kimberly is a tenth grader who is very upset because her parents are separating.

Scenario 3

Adam is a freshman in high school. He just moved to a new state because his mother remarried. Now he hardly ever gets to see his father or any of his old friends. He has to make new ones. Adam doesn't get to spend much time with his mother because she's always doing things with her new husband, stupid things like country dancing. *(Yuck, what awful music!)* Worst of all, his stepfather is a stupid idiot who makes dumb jokes. Michael can't stand anything about him.

Scenario 4

Susan, Michelle, and Ralph are George and Martha's three children. George and Martha have had a bitter divorce. George has remarried, and his new wife has three daughters. Martha has had a couple of different boyfriends and often gets depressed after they break up. George and Martha seem to hate each other. George often makes plans to come and get the children for the weekend but never shows up. He complains that when he calls to talk to the kids, Martha won't let him speak to them. George got his children a stereo for Christmas, but he won't let them take it to Martha's home, where they live. Instead, his new wife's three daughters get to use it.

Over the next week, once each day, try to use problem-solving skills in an anger situation. Try to use an *I statement, reflective listening, kill-them-with-kindness sandwich, apologizing,* or *negotiating a compromise.* If you don't remember to use one of these skills, jot down afterward what you could have said.

PROBLEM-SOLVING SKILLS

Day one

Day two

Day three

Day four

Day five

Day six

Day seven

Other comments or observations

SESSION • 7

Anger Management Steps

Objectives

To help the students:

- learn a seven-step plan for managing anger
- understand that the anger management steps help teens put thinking between their feelings of anger and their behavior of anger
- practice ways to problem-solve anger situations

Session at a Glance

1. Group Rules: review if necessary—1 minute
2. Centering Exercise: "The Mountaintop"—2 minutes
3. Feelings Check-in: look at Feelings Wheel—4 minutes
4. Basic Facts Review—4 minutes
5. Assignment Review—5 minutes
6. Mini-lecture, Scenarios, and Discussion—20 minutes
7. Basic Facts: read Basic Facts 15 and 16; discuss—2 minutes
8. Assignment—1 minute
9. Centering Exercise: repeat "The Mountaintop"—2 minutes
10. Affirmation: share a time when you were angry and a helpful way you could have used to express that anger—3 minutes
11. Closing: pass a silent wish—1 minute

Preparation

- Display the posterboard copy of the group rules.
- Have posters with Basic Facts 1-14 available, or the List of Basic Facts, or index cards with a basic fact on each one.

- Prior to the session make a poster. Title it "Anger Management Steps." List the anger management steps. (See Basic Fact 16.) Save this poster to use again should you decide to do Session 10.
- Add the following materials to each folder:
  —Handout 7A ("Scenarios for Session 7")
  —Handout 7B ("Anger Management Steps")
  —a 3" x 5" index card
  —Assignment 7
- Place each student's folder, a pencil, and crayons or markers at his or her place.
- Have a chalkboard and chalk or newsprint and a marker available.
- Read through the session plan before meeting.

Background and Guidelines

Session 5 explored the cognitive behavioral technique of putting thinking between feelings and behavior. Session 6 taught problem-solving skills. This session helps students create a proactive plan to pull their learning together. It presents anger management steps that encourage the students to **think** first and then express their anger in positive ways or problem-solve the anger situation. The scenarios in this session allow the students (1) to practice the steps of anger management and (2) to practice using the problem-solving skills. The plan shows the students how to put thinking between feeling anger and expressing anger.

As you lead the students through the session, help them become aware of the many different ways they can express anger: in helpful ways, like problem solving, or in harmful ways, like blaming or exploding. Specific examples will be of great help: "One student I knew was angry about his parents' divorce and the way they each put the other down. He used a kill-them-with-kindness sandwich to say to each parent that he loved both of them, and could not listen to either one say bad things about the other." Or "One time when I felt angry, I cleaned the bathroom, top to bottom; then I went out and jogged. While I was jogging, I thought of different problem-solving skills to use, and I decided negotiating a compromise was the best solution." To help the group members evaluate the consequences of their expressions of anger, teach them to ask themselves: "Will this particular method of expressing anger or particular problem-solving skill be helpful or harmful?" During the session, you may notice that some students will describe harmful ways to express anger. Don't accept these harmful ways. Rather, gently encourage and redirect the students to find a positive way to express their anger.

Emphasize that the anger management steps are something the students can use in real life: at home, on the game field, on the bus, and in the classroom. Let the students know that it's hard to change behavior right away. In fact, most people change their behavior quite slowly. Tell the students that they can help themselves change their behavior by going through the anger management steps retroactively, even after they've chosen a harmful way to express anger. Doing so can help them figure out what would have been a more helpful choice to express their anger so they could let it go. It often takes people two to three months of processing the steps retroactively before they form the habit of using the plan at the time of anger.

Since students with behavioral problems may have difficulty remembering the anger management steps and the problem-solving skills, and won't be able to change their behavior immediately, it's helpful to engage their teachers, principals, and student assistance teams in using the plan. Work with teachers and students to set up a plan so that the students will know exactly what choices they have with regard to expressing their anger. Explosive students may benefit from a plan that includes helpful choices such as journal writing, drawing a picture, or sitting in a time-out chair in the office or with a guidance counselor. Help teachers choose behaviors that will work in a particular classroom and encourage them to help the students implement their plans when they feel angry. For instance, one teacher made files for all students, where they could keep letters they had written about their anger. It's also a good idea to teach the appropriate school personnel the anger management steps and the problem-solving skills so they can help the students use them in each anger situation they encounter. As a matter of fact, an in-service on this information will prepare school personnel to help all the students practice problem-solving skills on a daily basis.

Beginning the Session

GROUP RULES

Have the folders at the appropriate places. Welcome the students and if necessary, begin with a quick review of the group rules. Draw attention to the poster listing the group rules. Call on different students to read them one at a time.

Check for understanding before moving on.

CENTERING EXERCISE

Lead the students in a new centering exercise, "The Mountaintop."

THE MOUNTAINTOP

Imagine that you're walking in the dark along a mountain trail. You feel very angry. Someone has told you that your best friend gave away a secret you had told him or her. You just can't believe that your friend would do that. You're just furious. You're breathing fast, and your heart is pumping loudly. As you walk up the trail, it's so dark you can barely see anything except the trail's outline. You feel like you could walk forever. You keep walking up the trail until you finally arrive at the top of the mountain. At least you think it's the top of the mountain, because the trail seems to come to a level place.

Exercise continued next column.

Exercise continued from previous column.

Soon you can tell that you really are at the mountaintop, because it's beginning to get a little lighter. You're able to look out over the valleys and beyond to other mountaintops. Actually, it's quite pretty up there as dawn begins. You see more and more. You can see many mountaintops off in the distance. You sit down. Your heart isn't pumping as loudly, and your breathing calms. You sit for a long time. In the light, you're beginning to see things from a new perspective, and you begin to think about what it is you are feeling so angry about, also in a new light.

You think about whether it's true that your friend would give away such a secret. You think about how you can find out if it's true. You think about maybe asking your friend directly. You think if it is true, maybe you can't rely on that friend so much, and you won't confide in that friend so much. You realize that nobody's perfect, not even your friends. Sometimes friends come through for you, but sometimes they don't. You plan how you're going to deal with the possibility that your friend gave away an important secret.

Daylight finally breaks, and you watch as the sun rises. In the light, you see forests and rocks and mountains and valleys. You see things much more clearly than you could in the dark. You feel much calmer, now that you've made a plan for what to do with your anger at your friend. You head back down the mountain trail. Even though it's the same trail, it looks completely different to you. Now you can see the tall trees and the beautiful green bushes that surround it. You're feeling very calm and peaceful now.

Point out to the students that when someone is really angry, often they can't see the situation clearly. If they wait a little while until the anger dies down, they can see different aspects of the situation more clearly.

FEELINGS CHECK-IN

Do a feelings check-in with the students. Have them take out their Feeling Wheels. Ask the group members to decide how they are feeling today. Remind the students that if they want, they can color in the section on the Feeling Wheel that describes how they're feeling today. Also remind the teens that they might have more than one feeling, since it's possible to experience more than one feeling at a time. Tell the students that if they're having a feeling that isn't named on the wheel, they can add a bubble to the outside of the wheel, and name the feeling there.

When the students finish, have a go-around. Begin by sharing your own feelings. Then, invite each student to share his or her feelings. Teenagers often list many feelings. In the interest of time, you may need to ask them to name the feelings they have, but then pick only two to discuss. Be sure to accept each student's feeling(s) and to affirm each student. Ask the students to return the wheels to their folders.

Basic Facts Review

Review the basic facts learned so far. Use posters with Basic Facts 1-14, the List of Basic Facts, or index cards.

In a go-around, ask a student to read Basic Fact 1 aloud and explain what it means. If the student has trouble explaining the fact, don't contradict or judge, simply clarify his or her explanation. Repeat the procedure for the next basic fact. This review ensures that the students understand and integrate the basic facts that have been taught. It is also easy preparation for the presentation and provides a lead-in for the session material.

Assignment Review

Ask the students to pull out their assignments from last week. Remind them that each day they were supposed to use assertive behavior in an anger situation, such as an I statement, reflective listening, a kill-them-with-kindness sandwich, apologizing, or negotiating a compromise. In a go-around, ask the students to share the skills they used. If students forgot to do the assignment, ask them to remember one time that they were angry and to think about what problem-solving skill they could have used.

Exploring the Material

Mini-Lecture

Anger Management Plan

Remind the students that the goal of this group is to help them learn how to deal with the stresses of changing families. Anger is a feeling that is common for teens in changing families; in Sessions 6 and 7 the students are learning how to handle anger in positive ways, ways that aren't aggressive. They're also learning how to use problem-solving skills in anger situations. This session will focus on a specific plan that they can create to help them know what to do when they get angry.

Write *feeling, thinking,* and *behaving* on the chalkboard. Present the following information.

Anger Management Steps

Remember that anger is a normal feeling; it consists of feeling, thinking, and behaving. There is a difference between feeling angry, which is okay, and behavior—such as blaming, letting your grades drop, or exploding—which may not be okay.

You can't control what feelings you get, but you can control your behavior. You may need to look at your thinking, or self-talk, and see if it is positive or negative. You may need to change your thinking to help you change your behavior. You are responsible for your behavior when you are angry. No matter what problems or stresses have caused you to be angry, it is still your responsibility to choose nonviolent and helpful ways to express that anger. Each person is accountable for his or her behavior. You always have the choice to express your anger in a helpful or harmful way.

Some teenagers rush right from feeling to behaving. They get mad and hit someone, or put someone down, or yell. *(Depending on the age and developmental level of the group, you can call this minimal cognitive engagement.)* So teenagers need to learn how to put thinking between their feelings of being angry and their behavior.

The **anger management steps** are a plan to help you put thinking between your feelings of anger and your behavior.

Continued on next page.

Display the poster you made, "Anger Management Steps." Refer to the poster as you introduce and explain the steps.

Continued from previous page.

1. **Recognize that you're angry.**
2. **Accept your anger.**
3. **Practice relaxation.**
4. **Decide if it's a problem you can't change or a problem you can change.**
5. **Think about helpful and harmful ways to express the anger.**
6. **Evaluate the consequences.**
7. **Choose a best way.**
8. **Problem-solve or express your anger in a helpful way.**

Tell the students that these steps are listed on Handout 7B in their folders.

Practicing the Anger Management Steps

Have the students take out Handout 7A ("Scenarios"). Tell them that they will read and discuss some scenarios on how to put the anger management steps into practice in an anger situation. Ask a student to read Scenario 1.

Scenario 1

Mark is a freshman at Cornfield High School. His girlfriend, Betsy, goes to the same school and is on the softball team. He likes to talk to her on the phone all evening. Mark's mom is only 34. She has been divorced from Mark's father for several years. At first, her boyfriend, Ron, moved in, but after a year they broke up and he moved out. Now Mark's mom is going out with a lot of different guys. She says she is giving herself time to be independent before she gets really involved again. When Mom comes home from work, she wants to relax, listen to her answering machine, and then call all the guys back who have called her. If Mark is talking to Betsy, he has to hang up if his mom wants to use the phone. When this happens, Mark is so angry that he

(Scenario continues in next column.)

(Continued from previous column.)

can't see straight. He gets red and breathes fast. He gets upset because he wants to talk to Betsy, but he's also upset since it seems his mother finds her dates more important than her son. Sometimes he gets so angry he wants to throw the phone out the window or even punch his mom.

Use the following questions to process the anger management steps.

1. **How can Mark *recognize* that he is angry?** (He can look at the signals his body gives him: he can't see straight; he gets red; he breathes fast.)
2. **How can Mark *accept* his anger?** (He can admit that he's angry; he can decide that his feeling of anger is normal.)
3. **What can Mark do to *practice* relaxation?** (He can use a centering exercise, like "Breathing Through Your Feet," "The Icicle," "The Clouds.")
4. **Is this a problem he *can change,* or a problem he *can't change?*** (Mark can't change his mother wanting to use the phone; he can't change that it is a time in her life when she is dating, just as he is. He can change how he deals with the phone problem.)
5. **If Mark *thinks about helpful and harmful ways to express his anger,* what might he think about?** (He might think of harmful ways he can express his anger, like blaming his mom, or yelling at her, or exploding by being violent; he might think of using problem-solving skills. In this case, Mark can think of a lot of different things he can do in this anger situation.)

   a. He might do some *stuffing*— swallow his anger and pretend he's not angry.

   b. He might do some *withdrawing* and stop talking to his mom or doing his chores.

   c. He might do some *blaming* and yell at Mom: "You're just interested in yourself.

You're selfish. You don't have the right to tell me when I can talk to Betsy and when I can't. You're just interested in dating."

d. He might do some *triangling* and complain about his mom to his dad; maybe his dad will try to get custody.

e. He might do some *exploding* and try to punch his mom or destroy the phone.

f. He might *express his anger by getting into fights* with other students, or his sister and brother.

g. He might use a *problem-solving skill,* like an I statement, reflective listening, a kill-them-with-kindness sandwich, apologizing, or negotiating a compromise. *(Have the students role-play each skill.)*

I statement: "Mom, I feel angry when you interrupt my phone call to Betsy so you can talk on the phone. My talking to Betsy is important."

Reflective listening: "Mom, I can tell that it's important for you to return your phone calls, and I know that you want to make your calls as soon as you get home."

Kill-them-with-kindness sandwich: "Mom, I think you're a great Mom, and I'm glad you're popular and have lots of phone calls. But I'm a teenager, and it's important for me to get to know people too. It's important for me to talk to Betsy. She really helps me a lot. So I hope you will start letting me spend more time on the phone with her."

Apologizing: "Mom, I'm sorry for hogging the phone all evening long."

Negotiating a compromise: "Mom, I think we can solve the problem of the telephone. Why don't we think of setting times that I can use the phone to call Betsy, and times that you can use it to call your friends?"

6. **How could Mark *evaluate the consequences* of each of these actions?** (Mark could take each action, think of what will happen if he does it, and decide if it would be *helpful* or *harmful.*)

If he *stuffs* —that is, holds his anger in or denies that he feels it—he might get depressed and feel helpless; he might explode with other students. That would be *harmful.*

If he *withdraws*—cuts himself off emotionally—and stops talking to his mom and doing chores, she will probably get angry with him. Tension in the home will increase. It won't solve the phone problem. It would probably be *harmful.*

If he *blames*—that is, holds his mom responsible for his feelings—his mom might get angry with him. She might get defensive and stronger in her position and not allow him to use the phone at all. That would be *harmful.*

If he does *triangling*—that is, involves another person—he can complain a lot and maybe get his dad involved. Maybe if he moves in with his dad, he'll get unlimited phone use. But it won't solve the problem. It *won't be helpful.*

If he *explodes* and destroys the phone or punches his mom, he'll probably get into worse trouble. He also won't have a phone at all. That would be *harmful.*

If he uses an *I statement,* he gets a chance to express how he feels. It *might be helpful.*

If he uses *reflective listening,* he lets his mom know that he understands how she feels. It *might be helpful.*

If he uses a *kill-them-with-kindness sandwich,* his mom will probably say, "I know you want to use the phone to talk to Betsy. I just don't want to have to wait to use the phone after I've been working all day." It *might be helpful.*

If he *apologizes,* his mom might accept the apology, and let him use the phone when she's not using it. It would be *helpful.*

If he tries to *negotiate a compromise,* it might work. His mom might say, "You can use the phone all you want when you get home from school, and before I get home from work, and when I'm not talking at night. That should give you plenty of time. It *might be helpful.*

7. **How could Mark *choose a best way?*** (After he has a chance to calm down and think, and look at the consequences, he might decide the best thing to do is try to negotiate a compromise with his mom.)

8. **How could Mark problem solve or express his anger in a helpful way?** (He might say, "Mom, I think we can solve the problem of the telephone. Why don't we think of setting times that I can use the phone to call Betsy and times that you can use it to call your friends.")

If you have time, use the rest of the scenarios to demonstrate further how to process the anger management steps. You might have the students role-play each step. Another possibility would be to ask the students for examples of anger situations common for students in their school. Have the group members apply the anger management steps to these situations.

Scenario 2

Marcie is a 17-year-old senior who lives with her grandparents. Her father is in jail, and her mother moved to Australia. Marcie's grandparents won't let her do anything. She can't stay after school to be in any activities because she has to come home and help her grandmother clean. They don't want her to date

(Scenario continues in next column.)

(Continued from previous column.)

because they're afraid she'll turn out like her mother, who was 16 when she got pregnant. They even get upset if she talks on the phone with friends. Her grandparents don't want her to mention either her father or her mother. Marcie sometimes talks to a neat guy who is in her Spanish class. He has asked her to the senior prom, but her grandmother says she can't go. Marcie gets really depressed and spends a lot of time in her bedroom by herself.

1. **How can Marcie *recognize* that she's angry?**

2. **How can Marcie *accept* her anger?**

3. **How can Marcie *practice relaxation?***

4. **Is this a problem Marcie *can change?*** (She can't change her parents or her grandparents. She can change how she responds.)

5. **How can Marcie *express her anger* in helpful or harmful ways?** (She can use harmful ways, like stuffing, withdrawing, blaming, triangling, or exploding.)

   a. What would Marcie do if she used *stuffing?*

   b. *Withdrawing?*

   c. *Blaming?*

   d. *Triangling?*

   e. *Exploding?*

   (Marcie can use problem-solving skills like an I statement, reflective listening, a kill-them-with-kindness sandwich, apologizing, or negotiating a compromise.)

   a. How could Marcie use an *I statement?*

   b. *Reflective listening?*

   c. *Kill-them-with-kindness sandwich?*

   d. *An Apology?*

   e. *Negotiating a compromise?*

6. **How could Marcie evaluate the consequences of each method? Which would be helpful? Harmful?**

    a. *Stuffing*

    b. *Withdrawing*

    c. *Blaming*

    d. *Triangling*

    e. *Exploding*

    f. *An I statement*

    g. *Reflective listening*

    h. *A kill-them-with-kindness sandwich*

    i. *An apology*

    j. *Negotiating a compromise*

7. **What might Marcie *choose as a best way?***

8. **Then, how could Marcie *problem-solve* or *express her anger?***

Scenario 3

Corey lives with his father and his stepmother. Corey's father spends a lot of time lying on the couch, watching TV, and drinking 40-ounce bottles of beer. Corey's father and stepmother fight a lot. His older sister, Tina, is always getting into trouble. Corey would like to play on the basketball team, but his father won't pick him up from practices. Corey spends a lot of his time being angry. He doesn't try very hard in school and isn't very polite to the teachers.

1. **What style is Corey using to express his anger?** (Withdrawing.)

2. **What is Corey's anger situation?** (His father's chemical dependence.)

3. **Can Corey change this problem?** (No.)

4. **What should Corey do?** (Accept what he cannot change: realize that he can't cause, control, or change his dad's chemical dependence. Express his anger so he can let it go: write a letter about how angry he is; shoot baskets; paint a picture of his anger. Do something good for himself: ask a friend's dad to pick him up after practice so he can be on the team; study so he can go to college; attend a group to learn how to cope with a parent's chemical dependence.)

Take Corey through the anger management steps:

1. **How can Corey *realize* that he's angry?**

2. **How can Corey *accept* his anger?**

3. **How can Corey *practice relaxation?***

4. **Is this a problem Corey *can change?*** (Yes.)

5. **How can Corey *express his anger,* or *problem solve?*** (He can use harmful ways, like stuffing, withdrawing, blaming, triangling, or exploding.)

    a. What would Corey do if he used *stuffing?*

    b. *Withdrawing?*

    c. *Blaming?*

    d. *Triangling?*

    e. *Exploding?*

    (Corey can use problem-solving skills like an I statement, reflective listening, a kill-them-with-kindness sandwich, apologizing, or negotiating a compromise.)

    a. How could Corey use an *I statement?*

    b. *Reflective listening?*

    c. *A kill-them-with-kindness sandwich?*

    d. *An apology?*

    e. *Negotiating a compromise?*

6. **How could Corey *evaluate the consequences* of each method? Which would be helpful? Harmful?**

   a. *Stuffing*

   b. *Withdrawing*

   c. *Blaming*

   d. *Triangling*

   e. *Exploding*

   f. *An I statement*

   g. *Reflective listening*

   h. *A kill-them-with-kindness sandwich*

   i. *An apology*

   j. *Negotiating a compromise*

7. **What might Corey *choose* as a best way?**

8. **Then, how could Corey *problem solve* or *express his anger?***

   Tell the students that the anger management steps can be used in many situations common to teens, such as girls setting limits with boys and boys standing up for themselves with other boys who are annoying them.

Scenario 4

Annette, a high school student, is dating Anthony. Anthony is putting a lot of pressure on her to be sexually active. Annette really likes Anthony and is flattered that he wants to go out with her, but she doesn't feel ready to be sexually active. It's also against her religious beliefs. She's angry that Anthony is putting such pressure on her. Annette doesn't say anything to Anthony, but she's getting more and more nervous.

1. **How can Annette *realize* that she's angry?**

2. **How can Annette *accept* her anger?**

3. **How can Annette *practice relaxation?***

4. **Is this a problem Annette *can change?*** (Yes.)

5. **How can Annette *express her anger* in helpful or harmful ways?** (She can use harmful ways, like stuffing, withdrawing, blaming, triangling, or exploding.)

   a. What would Annette do if she used *stuffing?*

   b. *Withdrawing?*

   c. *Blaming?*

   d. *Triangling?*

   e. *Exploding?*

   (Annette can use problem-solving skills like an I statement, reflective listening, a kill-them-with-kindness sandwich, apologizing, or negotiating a compromise.)

   a. How could Annette use an *I statement?*

   b. *Reflective listening?*

   c. *A Kill them with kindness sandwich?*

   d. *An Apology?*

   e. *Negotiating a compromise?*

6. **How could Annette *evaluate the consequences* of each method? Which would be helpful? Harmful?**

   a. *Stuffing*

   b. *Withdrawing*

   c. *Blaming*

   d. *Triangling*

   e. *Exploding*

   f. *An I statement*

   g. *Reflective listening*

   h. *A kill-them-with-kindness sandwich*

   i. *An apology*

   j. *Negotiating a compromise*

7. **What might Annette *choose* as a best way?**

8. **Then, how could Annette *problem-solve* or *express her anger?***

Scenario 5

Derrick's locker is next to Reggie's. Reggie is pretty obnoxious and is always knocking things out of Derrick's hands, pulling books and papers out of his locker, and shutting the locker door on Derrick. Derrick tries to ignore Reggie, but finally he gets fed up and shuts the locker door on Reggie's arm.

1. **How can Derrick *realize* that he's angry?**
2. **How can Derrick *accept* his anger?**
3. **How can Derrick *practice relaxation?***
4. **Is this a problem Derrick *can change?*** (Yes.)
5. **How can Derrick *express his anger,* or *problem solve?*** (He can use harmful ways, like stuffing, withdrawing, blaming, triangling, or exploding.)

   a. What would Derrick do if he used *stuffing?*

   b. *Withdrawing?*

   c. *Blaming?*

   d. *Triangling?*

   e. *Exploding?*

   (Derrick can use problem-solving skills like an I statement, reflective listening, a kill-them-with-kindness sandwich, apologizing, or negotiating a compromise.)

   a. How could Derrick use an *I statement?*

   b. *Reflective listening?*

   c. *A kill-them-with-kindness sandwich?*

   d. *An apology?*

   e. *Negotiating a compromise?*

6. **How could Derrick *evaluate the consequences* of each method?** Which would be helpful? Harmful?

   a. *Stuffing*

   b. *Withdrawing*

   c. *Blaming*

   d. *Triangling*

   e. *Exploding*

   f. *An I statement*

   g. *Reflective listening*

   h. *A kill-them-with-kindness sandwich*

   i. *An apology*

   j. *Negotiating a compromise*

7. **What might Derrick c*hoose* as a best way?**
8. **Then, how could Derrick *problem-solve* or *express his anger?***

Remind the students not to expect to change their behavior right away: behavioral change often comes slowly and inconsistently. Remind them to chunk it down, and set very small, concrete goals if they want to change how they handle anger. Their first goal can be to observe how they deal with anger. Do they stuff, withdraw, blame, triangle, explode, or problem solve? If they don't usually problem solve, their second goal can be to think of how else they could have dealt with their anger. If they didn't use problem-solving skills, what skills could they have used? Could they have used their anger to give them the power to make changes in themselves; or could they have accepted what they couldn't change, expressed their anger in a helpful way so they could let it go, and then done something good for themselves? Tell them that sometimes people put the steps on index cards which they keep to remind themselves to use the steps.

Have the students take their index cards out of their folders, and look at their List of Basic Facts.

Ask them to copy Basic Fact 16—the anger management steps—onto an index card. Have them write Basic Fact 13—the five problem-solving skills—on the other side. Explain to the group members that they can fold their index card and carry it in their pocket to refer to for help whenever they find themselves feeling angry. Whenever they feel angry, they should look at the card to help them put thinking between feeling and action.

Tell the students that if they should express anger in a harmful way, they can then look at how they expressed anger, think about how else they could have dealt with it, and go through the steps of anger management. If they go through the steps often enough after they express their anger in a harmful way, then sooner or later, they will begin to use their anger to work for them, or express it in a helpful way, or use a problem-solving skill. It may take two or three months, so tell the students not to give up if they don't get the routine down quickly.

DISCUSSION

Lead a discussion to help the students better understand the key concepts presented. As the group discusses, remember to go around, making sure that each student has an opportunity to add to the discussion. Encourage participation, but don't force it. Remember the group rule that allows a student to pass. Accept all ideas and answers, explaining or clarifying information where necessary. To aid the discussion, you may wish to use questions like the following:

- **What does it mean to manage your anger?** (It means having a plan to help you put thinking between feeling angry and doing angry things.)
- **What are the steps of managing anger or anger management?** (Recognize that you are angry; accept your anger; practice some form of relaxing; decide if this is a problem you can change, or one you can't; think about helpful and harmful ways to express your anger; evaluate consequences; choose the best way; express the anger in a helpful way or problem solve.)
- **What are some ways you might *recognize* that you're feeling angry?** (Accept all responsible replies. Look for examples like the following: you might get hot, blush, sweat, feel tense, breathe hard, or feel your heart beating fast.)
- **How do you *accept* anger?** (Tell yourself it's okay to feel angry.)
- **What are some ways you can *relax?*** (Practice one of the centering exercises: "Breathing Through Your Feet," "The Icicle," "The Space Shuttle.")
- **How can you tell if it's a problem you *can change,* or one you *can't?*** (See if you can change your behavior.)
- **What are some ways to *express anger?* To tell if they are *helpful* or *harmful?*** (Accept all responsible replies.)
- **What does it mean to *problem solve? To choose a helpful way* to express your anger?** (To problem solve means to use one of the following: an I statement, reflective listening, a kill-them-with-kindness sandwich, apologizing, or negotiating a compromise. To choose a helpful way to express your anger means to pick a way that doesn't harm yourself or anyone or anything else.)
- **What does it mean to *express* your anger in a helpful way?** (To go ahead and act on your best choice of action.)
- **Why should you always try to problem-solve or to express your anger in a helpful way?** (So you can either solve the anger situation or let go of your anger without hurting yourself or anyone else.)
- **Do you think it will be easy to use these steps right away?** (No. It's hard to change behavior. But even if you choose a harmful way to express anger, it will help you to think back over the steps. Doing so often enough will help you use the steps when you're actually angry. The steps will help you put thinking between feeling and your behavior. It may take two or three months of practice, so be patient.)

Even if you choose not to use the suggested questions, make sure the discussion underscores these concepts.

BASIC FACTS

Review the new basic facts for this session. Refer the students to the List of Basic Facts. Ask two group members to read Basic Facts 15 and 16.

15. The anger management steps help teens put thinking between the feeling of anger and the behavior of anger.

16. The anger management steps are:

    1. Recognize that you're angry.
    2. Accept your anger.
    3. Practice relaxation.
    4. Decide if it's a problem you can change or a problem you can't change.
    5. Think about helpful and harmful ways to express the anger.
    6. Evaluate the consequences.
    7. Choose a best way.
    8. Problem-solve or express your anger in a helpful way.

By this time, the students should be very familiar with these facts. Even so, spend some time going through them, briefly discussing each and checking for understanding.

GIVE ASSIGNMENT

Have the group members take Assignment 7 out of their folders. Read the directions: "Over the next week, once each day, when you get angry, go through the anger management steps. Write down what would be the best way for you to problem solve or to express your anger." Remind the students that using the anger management steps after they get angry will eventually help them to problem solve or to express their anger in a helpful way when they are in an anger situation in the future.

Wrapping Up

CENTERING EXERCISE

Settle the students and then repeat "The Mountaintop" (page 139).

AFFIRMATION

Involve the group in an affirmation. Stand and join in a circle with the students, holding hands. Go around the circle and have each student share both a time they felt angry and a helpful way they expressed—or could have expressed—their anger. Begin the affirmation yourself: "One time that I got angry was . . . A helpful way to express my anger would have been. . . ." The students will need you to role-model this affirmation. They will probably also need your help to see what would have been a helpful way to express anger.

CLOSING

Remain standing in a circle with the students, holding hands, and lead the group in the closing activity.

Tell the students that you're going to make a silent wish for the student on your right. Then, when you've made the wish, gently squeeze that student's hand. The student makes a silent wish for the person on his or her right, then gently squeezes that student's hand, and so on. Continue around the circle until a wish and squeeze come back to you. If necessary, the students can pass the wish in any appropriate way they choose.

Collect the folders. Fill out a copy of the Process and Progress Form (page 199), if you are an experienced leader, or the Progress Notes (page 201) as soon as possible after leading the group.

Scenarios for Session 7

Scenario 1

Mark is a freshman at Cornfield High School. His girlfriend, Betsy, goes to the same school and is on the softball team. He likes to talk to her on the phone all evening. Mark's mom is only 34. She has been divorced from Mark's father for several years. At first, her boyfriend, Ron, moved in, but after a year they broke up and he moved out. Now Mark's mom is going out with a lot of different guys. She says she is giving herself time to be independent before she gets really involved again. When Mom comes home from work, she wants to relax, listen to her answering machine, and then call all the guys back who have called her. If Mark is talking to Betsy, he has to hang up if his mom wants to use the phone. When this happens, Mark is so angry that he can't see straight. He gets red and breathes fast. He gets upset because he wants to talk to Betsy, but he's also upset since it seems his mother finds her dates more important than her son. Sometimes he gets so angry he wants to throw the phone out the window, or even punch his mom.

Scenario 2

Marcie is a 17-year-old senior who lives with her grandparents. Her father is in jail, and her mother moved to Australia. Marcie's grandparents won't let her do anything. She can't stay after school to be in any activities because she has to come home and help her grandmother clean. They don't want her to date because they're afraid she'll turn out like her mother, who was 16 when she got pregnant. They even get upset if she talks on the phone with friends. Her grandparents don't want her to mention either her father or her mother. Marcie sometimes talks to a neat guy who is in her Spanish class. He has asked her to the senior prom, but her grandmother says she can't go. Marcie gets really depressed and spends a lot of time in her bedroom by herself.

Scenario 3

Corey lives with his father and his stepmother. Corey's father spends a lot of time lying on the couch, watching TV, and drinking 40-ounce bottles of beer. Corey's father and stepmother fight a lot. His older sister, Tina, is always getting into trouble. Corey would like to play on the basketball team, but his father won't pick him up from practices. Corey spends a lot of his time being angry. He doesn't try very hard in school and isn't very polite to the teachers.

Scenario 4

Annette, a high school student, is dating Anthony. Anthony is putting a lot of pressure on her to be sexually active. Annette really likes Anthony and is flattered that he wants to go out with her, but she doesn't feel ready to be sexually active. It's also against her religious beliefs. She's angry that Anthony is putting such pressure on her. Annette doesn't say anything to Anthony, but she's getting more and more nervous.

Scenario 5

Derrick's locker is next to Reggie's. Reggie is pretty obnoxious and is always knocking things out of Derrick's hands, pulling books and papers out of his locker, and shutting the locker door on Derrick. Derrick tries to ignore Reggie, but finally he gets fed up and shuts the locker door on Reggie's arm.

Anger Management Steps

Remember that anger is a normal feeling. It consists of feeling, thinking, and behaving. There is a difference between feeling angry, which is okay, and behavior—such as stuffing, withdrawing, blaming, triangling, or exploding—which may not be okay. These anger styles are usually not effective in helping you solve the problem that made you angry or in helping you get along with people and get what you want.

You can't control the feelings you get, but you can control your behavior. You may need to look at your thinking, or self-talk, and see if it is positive or negative. You may need to change your thinking to help you change behavior. You are responsible for your behavior when you are angry. No matter what might influence someone to use violent or aggressive behavior, it is still his or her responsibility to choose nonviolent and helpful ways to express anger. Each person is accountable for his or her behavior. You always have the choice to express your anger in a helpful or harmful way.

Some teens rush right from feeling to behaving. They get mad and hit someone, or put someone down, or yell. So teenagers need to learn how to put thinking between their feelings of being angry and their behavior.

The **anger management steps** are a plan to help you put thinking between feeling angry and your behavior.

1. **Recognize that you're angry.**
2. **Accept your anger.**
3. **Practice relaxation.**
4. **Decide if it's a problem you can change or a problem you can't change.**
5. **Think about helpful and harmful ways to express the anger.**
6. **Evaluate the consequences.**
7. **Choose a best way.**
8. **Problem-solve or express your anger in a helpful way.**

Remember the principle of chunking it down. You will probably not be able to change your behavior right away. Behavioral change often comes slowly and inconsistently. Remember to set small, concrete goals if you want to change how you handle anger. For instance, a first goal can be to look at how you deal with anger. Do you stuff, withdraw, blame, triangle someone else in, explode, or problem-solve? Each time you notice how you deal with anger, think if you should have done it differently. If you didn't problem-solve, what could you have done to problem-solve? Could you have used your anger to give you the power to make changes in yourself? Or could you have accepted what you can't change, expressed your anger in a helpful way so you could let it go, and then done something good for yourself?

You can go through the steps of anger management even after you express your anger in a harmful way. Sooner or later, you will begin to use your anger to work for you, or you will express it in a helpful way, or you will use problem-solving skills. Changing your behavior may take two or three months, so don't give up if you don't use the steps right away.

Over the next week, once each day, when you get angry, go through the anger management steps. Write down what would be the best way for you to problem solve or to express your anger.

The **anger management steps** are a plan to help you put thinking between feeling angry and your behavior.

1. Recognize that you're angry.
2. Accept your anger.
3. Practice relaxation.
4. Decide if it's a problem you can change or one that you can't change.
5. Think about helpful and harmful ways to express the anger.
6. Evaluate the consequences.
7. Choose a best way.
8. Problem-solve, or express your anger in a helpful way.

Five good problem-solving skills to use in anger situations are: **I statements, reflective listening, kill-them-with-kindness sandwiches, apologizing,** and **negotiating a compromise.**

Day one

Day two

Day three

Day four

Day five

Day six

Day seven

Other comments or observations

SESSION • 8

Other Coping Strategies

Objectives

To help the students:

- discover 10 rules for developing coping strategies
- draw on the facts they have learned to help them cope in stressful situations
- understand that they can't fix their parents' problems, but they can take care of themselves

Session at a Glance

1. Group Rules: review if necessary—1 minute
2. Centering Exercise: "The Waterfall"—3 minutes
3. Feelings Check-in: look at Feelings Wheel—5 minutes
4. Basic Facts Review—6 minutes
5. Assignment Review—4 minutes
6. Mini-lecture and Discussion—8 minutes
7. Activity: write coping strategies—8 minutes
8. Basic Facts Review: read Basic Facts 17 and 18; discuss—2 minutes
9. Assignment—1 minute
10. Centering Exercise: repeat "The Waterfall"—3 minutes
11. Affirmation: share coping strategies—3 minutes
12. Closing: pass a silent wish—1 minute

Preparation

- Display the posterboard of the group rules.
- Have posters with Basic Facts 1-16 available, or the List of Basic Facts, or index cards with a basic fact on each one.
- Add the following materials to each folder:
  —Handout 8A ("Rules for Relationships")
  —Handout 8B ("Coping Strategy Situations")
  —Assignment 8
- Place each student's folder, a pencil, and crayons or markers at his or her place.
- Read through the session plan before meeting.

Background and Guidelines

One of the most difficult issues for students from at-risk families is learning to accept their inability to solve their families' problems—namely, to stop a parental divorce, a parent's chemical dependence or a parent's use of violence to express anger. Group leaders like you also face this issue: you cannot solve the students' family problems, or the problems of the students themselves. Accepting this is the beginning of detachment (see Background and Guidelines for Session 4).

In this session, the students begin to own the concepts and facts they've learned in previous sessions and begin to apply them to their lives. They will use the three Cs and the four steps in this session, as well as their problem-solving skills. You will need to draw on your understanding of codependence, detachment, and empowerment to help the students.

In this session, the students also draw on 10 simple rules for maintaining healthy relationships to help them own and apply the concepts and facts they've learned. To do this well, however, they must first detach themselves from their family problems. Because children love their parents, this is no simple task. They will need your understanding, encouragement, and reassurance that they aren't acting selfishly. They can care about others, their parents included, but they can't fix other people's problems. Many at-risk adolescents, however, really believe they can fix their parents' problems. And parents of at-risk teens frequently, and misguidedly, seek help, emotional and otherwise, from their children. Such teens need your help to see that only an adult can fix adult problems, and that although it's okay for their parents to need help, they should get it from another adult.

Therefore, when a school counselor teaches teens to take care of themselves, the counselor is not advising selfishness. Rather, the counselor is urging self-preservation. The students need to take responsibility for handling their feelings in helpful ways. Doing so frees them to solve problems and to cope with those problems they can't solve. Remember, living in at-risk families is often difficult, frustrating, and unfair. The students will feel deeply about their situations and want to change them. They can't. They can, however, refuse to accept the responsibility for the family's problems or for their effects on the family. This frees the young people of a terrible burden and lets them use their energy to achieve personal goals. They can begin to take care of themselves, to control their own behavior, to ask for help, to choose to do things that are good for them, and to be with people who are helpful to them.

It's important to help the students recognize that although they have no power over their parents' problems, they do have the power to make things better for themselves. They can decide what they want to achieve and feel good enough about themselves to take steps to attain their goals, which will be the subject of Session 9.

The main material for this session consists of the rules for relationships. You will use these and the role-playing scenarios to make sure the students understand the concepts and can apply what they have learned.

Beginning the Session

GROUP RULES

Have the folders at the appropriate places. Welcome the students and, if necessary, begin with a quick review of the group rules. Draw attention to the poster listing the rules. If necessary, call on different students to read them one at a time.

Check for understanding before moving on.

Centering Exercise

Lead the students in a new centering exercise, "The Waterfall."

THE WATERFALL

Close your eyes and relax. Pretend that you're walking on a beautiful path in the mountains. You're taking a hike down the mountain. It's October, and the sky is clear and a deep shade of blue. The air is cool, but the sun is warm. The leaves are beautiful shades of red and orange and yellow. Look up at the sky and see the orange and yellow leaves like lace against the sky. There are also green pine trees, so imagine what the green pine needles look like next to the orange and yellow leaves.

You keep walking down the mountain path until you come upon a waterfall, a beautiful cascading waterfall, a stream tumbling down over huge boulders. You sit on a boulder near the waterfall, and you empty your mind. You empty your mind by listening to the sound of the water as it rushes over the boulders and trickles down the stream. You imagine that the water is rushing over you and making you feel clean and refreshed. But you're not cold because you're drinking in the warmth of the sun.

As you sit quietly on the boulder, you see leaves floating down the stream, because, remember, it's October, and the leaves are falling. The leaves are floating like tiny boats on the bubbling water. You decide to put all your worries, problems, and frustrations on the leaves and let them all float away.

So if you're worried because (use appropriate examples specific to the students in your group, such as. . .) you don't think your boyfriend or girlfriend likes you anymore, let that worry float away on a leaf for right now. Or if you haven't gotten started on that big English paper, for right now put the English paper on a leaf and let it float away. Or if you had a fight in the hall this morning, and you're afraid you might get suspended, for right now put that worry on a leaf and let it float away. Or if you've had lots of fights with your parents lately, for right now put your anger on another leaf and watch it float away.

Put all of your worries and problems and frustrations on leaves, and let them all float away for right now. When you open your eyes, you'll be able to concentrate on the work we're going to do here, because all your problems have floated away. You can go back and work on those problems later.

Feelings Check-in

Do a feelings check-in with the students. Have them take out their Feeling Wheels. Ask the group members to decide how they are feeling today. Remind the students that if they want, they can color in the section on the Feeling Wheel that describes how they're feeling today. Remind them that they might experience more than one feeling, since it's possible to have more than one feeling at a time. Tell the students that if they're having a feeling that isn't named on the wheel, they can add a bubble to the outside of the wheel and name the feeling there.

When the students finish, have a go-around. Begin by sharing your own feelings. Then, invite each student to share his or her feelings. Teenagers often list many feelings. In the interest of time, ask them to name the feelings they have, but then to pick only two to discuss. Be sure to accept each student's feeling(s) and to affirm each student. Ask the students to return the wheels to their folders.

Basic Facts Review

Review the basic facts learned so far. Use posters with Basic Facts 1-16, the List of Basic Facts, or index cards.

In a go-around, ask a student to read Basic Fact 1 aloud and explain what it means. If the student has trouble explaining the fact, don't contradict or judge, simply clarify his or her explanation. Repeat the procedure for the next basic fact. This review ensures that the students understand and integrate the basic facts that have been taught. It is also easy preparation for the presentation and provides a lead-in for session material.

Assignment Review

Ask the students to pull out their assignments from last week. Remind them that each day they were to go through the anger management steps when they got angry, and write down what would be the best way for them to problem solve or to express their anger. In a go-around, ask each student to describe one incident when he or she got angry, and to share what would have been the best way to problem solve or to express that anger. If students have forgotten to do the assignment, ask them to remember one time that they were angry, and to think of a problem-solving skill they could have used, or what would have been a good way to express the anger. Remind the students that they can learn from each other by seeing how other group members are beginning to learn how to use the problem-solving skills. Also remind them about chunking it down. Just going over an anger situation after it happens and using the steps of anger management will help them choose a helpful way to express anger in the future.

Exploring the Material

MINI-LECTURE
Rules for Relationships

Remind the students that in the last session they learned a strategy—the anger management steps—for dealing with their anger. Have the students take Handout 8A ("Rules for Relationships") from their folders. Tell the students that these rules will help them develop strategies they can use for coping with their anger and with the stresses of a changing family. Emphasize that although teens can't solve a parent's problems, they can use a coping strategy to help themselves.

Ask a student to read Rule 1. Discuss the rule briefly. Repeat this procedure for each rule. Make sure the students understand the meaning of terms such as *I statements, self-talk, and affirmations.* Relate the rules to the basic facts the students have learned.

RULES FOR RELATIONSHIPS

1. It's always okay to ask for help.
2. You can only control your own behavior. You can't control anybody else's behavior.
3. Teenagers can't fix their parents' problems. Only parents can fix their own problems. The parents may need to ask for help, and it's okay for them to ask for help.
4. Kill-them-with-kindness sandwiches are great ways to set limits or boundaries.

   Example: "I'm really glad you're my father, Dad, and I want to do what you tell me. But I really can't give Mom that message because I feel too uncomfortable when I'm in the middle like that. So I have to take myself out of the middle. I love both of you, and I'm going to try to get along with both of you." Another example of a kill-them-with-kindness sandwich is a teenage girl setting limits against her boyfriend hitting her: "I'm really glad you're my boyfriend, Jack. But I'm just not going to let you hit me, shove me, or push me around. I'm just not going to let that be part of any relationship. I'm sure we can find a way to solve our disagreements without force, because I really care for you."
5. I statements are great ways to express feelings: "I feel __________ when you __________ because ____________________."

   Example: "I feel angry when you and Dad fight all the time because I'm afraid you're going to get a divorce."
6. You can experience feelings, share them, and let them go. You can tolerate (put up with) feelings because they will pass. You can also choose to do things that make you feel better.
7. You can't control the feelings you get. However, you can look at your thinking, or self-talk, and change it from negative to positive. You can control your behavior. You can use your feelings to give you the power to make changes. You can learn to use problem-solving skills.
8. You can take care of yourself. This is self-preservation, not selfishness.
9. It's always a good idea to repeat positive affirmations for yourself.

   Example: "I am lovable and capable."
10. It's good practice to share caring, positive feelings and thoughts. Remember the three Ps: Be pleasant, positive, and polite.

Continue the discussion by turning to Handout 8B ("Coping Strategies Situations"). Ask the students to retrieve their copies from their folders. Use the discussion questions to help the students use the rules for relationships and the problem-solving skills.

Have a student read Problem 1 and the strategy.

Problem Situation 1:

Your parents are having a terrible fight. They are even throwing things at each other.

Coping Strategies

1. You can realize and accept that you cannot make your parents stop fighting. It's not your job, and you wouldn't succeed anyway (Rules 2 and 3).
2. You can go to a safe place where you won't get hurt, like your bedroom (Rule 8).
3. You can listen to your favorite song to help you feel better (Rule 6).

DISCUSSION QUESTIONS

- **What are some problem situations involving anger that students might want to talk about?** (Parents fight and throw things at each other because they are angry about an affair, or the separation, or one parent not paying child support, etc.)
- **What rule helps students see that they can't get their parents to stop fighting?** (Rule 2: You can only control your own behavior. You can't control anybody else's.)
- **Even though students can't solve their parents' problems, can they do anything for themselves?** (Yes, they can think of a coping strategy.)
- **What is a coping strategy?** (A way or plan to handle a problem you cannot change or solve.)
- **What are some coping strategies students can use when their parents fight?** (1. Realize and accept that teenagers can't make their parents stop fighting. It's not a teen's job and they wouldn't succeed anyway. 2. Go to a safe place where they won't get hurt—like to their bedroom. Then, they can do something to help them feel better—like listen to their favorite songs; call a boyfriend or a girlfriend; do their homework so they can go to college.)
- **Do you think children are being selfish if they won't try to solve their parents' problems?** (Look for answers showing that the students understand that it's not being selfish to take care of themselves; that while they love their parents, they can't change them and have to work at handling their own feelings, solving their own problems, and finding strategies to cope with the problems they can't solve.)

Even if you choose not to use the above questions, make sure the discussion underscores these concepts. Affirm the students on the ways they've been putting the facts they've learned into action.

ACTIVITY

Divide the group into teams or pairs. If a student is left out, pair up with him or her yourself. Assign each pair one of the problems on Handout 8B. Explain that each pair is to come up with a coping strategy for dealing with its particular problem; they can use the sample strategy provided or make up their own. Direct the pair to base their strategies on the Rules for Relationships (Handout 8A). They should also use the problem-solving skills they have learned: *I statements, reflective listening, kill-them-with-kindness sandwiches, apologizing,* and *negotiating a compromise.* Tell the students that you will be asking them to share their coping strategies with the rest of the group and to explain which of the rules helped them come up with their solutions.

When the students complete their coping strategies, go through the problems one at a time. If the group members make up their own strategies, be sure they are feasible and that the students are able to explain which rules for relationships and problem-solving skills helped them arrive at the strategies. Whether the young people devise their own solutions or use the ones given on the handout, you can use the suggestions below to process each problem.

Problem Situation 2:

Your mom is crying because she just found out your dad has been having an affair.

Coping Strategies

1. Give your mom a hug and tell her you love her (Rule 10).
2. Do something you enjoy, like listening to rock music (Rule 6), or do something that is good for you, like gymnastics (Rule 8).
3. You can talk to someone you trust if you feel worried or scared (Rules 1 and 6).

DISCUSSION QUESTIONS

- **Can teens make their moms feel better when their dads are having an affair, or vice versa?** (No, only a mom or a dad can do what she or he needs to do to feel better, Rules 2 and 3.)
- **If a mom is feeling sad or angry, does the teen have to feel the same way?** (No. Remember enmeshment and boundaries? Teens are separate from their parents. They have different feelings and should handle their own feelings, Rule 6. Teens can share feelings, Rule 10, with their parents, but they aren't responsible for making their parents feel better.)

Problem Situation 3:

Your dad asks you if he should divorce your mom, who has been drinking a lot, is chemically dependent, and won't get help.

Coping Strategies

1. You can tell your dad that you're sorry he's having problems, but you can't tell him what to do because you love both your mom and dad; maybe he should find an adult to talk to for help (Rules 3 and 4).
2. You can do something that's good for you (Rules 6 and 8).

Expect some students to resist the sample solution. Many teenagers are their parents' confidants and will resist hearing that such a role belongs to another adult, not to them. They may resist giving up that role and will need encouragement to establish age-appropriate boundaries. Remind the students that teenagers can't solve adult problems, but that they can share feelings for their parents. Help the youngsters see that it is all right and healthy for them to set boundaries and to politely refuse to help their parents in cases like this one.

DISCUSSION QUESTIONS

- **Can teens solve adult problems or make decisions for adults?** (No. Teenagers don't have the wisdom or experience necessary to help adults solve problems. Parents can ask for help from other adults, Rule 3. Teens can share caring feelings for parents, Rule 10, but they can't fix their problems.)
- **Can teens tell their parents they can't help them?** (In a case like this, yes. Teens can very politely set boundaries. They can use a kill-them-with-kindness sandwich and say, "I'm sorry you're feeling bad, Dad, but I can't help you solve this problem. But maybe you'd like to shoot baskets?")

Problem Situation 4:

Instead of helping you with your science fair project as she promised, your mom, who has been very irritable since the divorce, came home, drank beer, and is now yelling at you and telling you that you're a lazy, worthless, good-for-nothing brat.

Coping Strategies

1. Remember your positive affirmation: "I am lovable and capable" (Rule 9). Write it on an index card and carry it in your pocket. You might write, "I'm energetic, worthwhile, and a good kid."
2. If you're feeling angry, manage it (Rule 7) and talk about your angry feelings with someone you trust (Rule 1).
3. The next day, when your mom is sober, tell her how hurt you felt when she called you names, because you know that you are a good person (Rule 5).

DISCUSSION QUESTIONS

- **What can teens do if their parents hurt their feelings?** (They can look at themselves and their thinking. They can choose to look at good things about themselves and to work on changing things that need changing.)
- **Should teens explode and yell if they feel angry?** (No, but they should follow their steps for anger management and put thinking between their feelings and their actions.)
- **Do teens have to figure out how to handle their anger on their own?** (No, they can ask someone they trust for help.)
- **Should teens talk to a parent about their feelings when the parent has been using alcohol or other drugs?** (No. Teens should wait until a chemically dependent parent is sober before talking about how they feel.)

Make sure the students understand anger management (Basic Fact 16), positive affirmation (Rule 9), and I statements (Rule 5). Point out that the students can make positive affirmation cards (like their anger management cards) to carry with them or to post where they can see them regularly: on the refrigerator, on the bathroom mirror, on a bedpost.

Problem Situation 5:

You have a good friend whose parents are going through a messy divorce. Your friend has a bad temper and is always arguing with people. You're afraid your friend will get into real trouble and get suspended.

Coping Strategies

1. You remember that you can't control anybody else's behavior (Rule 2). Tell your friend how you feel, using I statements (Rule 5), and how much you care (Rule 10).
2. You stop enabling; you don't cover up for him or her. Allow your friend to experience some negative consequences so he or she will have a reason to change.
3. Share your feelings by using I statements (Rule 5) with your friend. For example: "I feel afraid when I see you arguing all the time, because I'm afraid no one will be able to stand you" or "I felt angry when you got mad at me last week. You were putting me down."
4. Discuss your concerns with a caring adult (Rule 1).

Problem 5 is a common concern for middle and high school students. *Choices and Consequences* (Schaefer, 1987) is an excellent resource for learning how to stop enabling and to do an intervention with a teenager, although it applies to adolescents who use alcohol or other drugs. By using these concepts, you can reinforce the facts and give the students specific steps to take if they have a friend who is acting out or using alcohol or other drugs excessively. You can tie in Rules 2, 5, and 10 to help the students establish boundaries between their concern for their friend and their responsibility for them. Step 2 can be explained by telling the students that someone who is constantly being rescued will have no reason to change; it can be tied to the family sculpture in Session 4. Finally, Step 4 reinforces to students that they are not alone in their concern for a teenager who is violent.

DISCUSSION QUESTIONS

- **Can a friend make a friend stop arguing?** (No, you can't control another person's behavior—even if the person is a friend.)
- **Are you helping a friend if you rescue, protect, or cover up for mistakes he or she makes while arguing, even if you know they're reacting to a parental divorce?** (No. Rescuing, protecting, or covering up for mistakes is enabling. People don't change unless they experience the consequences of their behavior.)
- **Why are I statements important to help solve a problem like this?** (They can help you give consequences in a caring way. They help you tell the other person what effect their behavior has on you.)
- **Why is it a good idea to ask an adult for help?** (Because you don't have to solve a friend's problems all by yourself, and there are other people who are concerned about teens.)

After processing the problems, ask the students to place their handouts in their folders. Affirm the students on their growing ability to cope with difficult problems.

BASIC FACTS

Review the new basic facts for this session. Refer the students to the List of Basic Facts. Ask two group members to read Basic Facts 17 and 18.

17. Teens cannot fix their parents' problems.

18. Teens can take good care of themselves.

Point out that the students encountered these facts in the rules for relationships. Briefly discuss each fact, checking for understanding.

ASSIGNMENT

Have the group members take Assignment 8 out of their folders. Read the directions: "Each day this week, look at how you act with your friends or family members. Each day, see if you can use one of the rules for relationships or one of the problem-solving skills. Write it down."

Wrapping Up

CENTERING EXERCISE

Settle the students and then repeat "The Waterfall." (page 155).

AFFIRMATION

Involve the group in an affirmation. Stand and join in a circle with the students, holding hands. Go around the circle and have each student share a coping strategy he or she can use. Begin the affirmation yourself: "One coping strategy I can use is. . . ."

CLOSING

Remain standing in a circle with the students, holding hands, and lead the group in the closing activity. Tell the students that you're going to make a silent wish for the student on your right. Then, when you've made the wish, gently squeeze that student's hand. The student makes a silent wish for the person on his or her right, then gently squeezes that student's hand, and so on. Continue around the circle until a wish and squeeze come back to you. If necessary, the students can pass the wish in any appropriate way they choose.

Collect the folders. Fill out a copy of the Process and Progress Form (page 199) or, if you are an experienced leader, the Progress Notes (page 201) as soon as possible after leading the group.

Note: If you have decided to use the optional Session 10, look ahead now to make plans for the students' presentation. Check out school schedules and available audiences. Be ready to talk briefly about the presentation at the conclusion of Session 9. You will need to inform the students about the times for practicing and giving the presentation.

Rules for Relationships

1. It's always okay to ask for help.
2. You can only control your own behavior. You can't control anybody else's behavior.
3. Teenagers can't fix their parents' problems. Only parents can fix their own problems. The parents may need to ask for help, and it's okay for them to ask for help.
4. Kill-them-with-kindness sandwiches are great ways to set limits or boundaries. Example: "I'm really glad you're my boyfriend, Jack. But I'm just not going to let you hit me, shove me, or push me around. I'm just not going to let that be part of any relationship. I'm sure we can find a way to solve our disagreements without force, because I really care for you."
5. I statements are great ways to express feelings: "I feel ______________ when you __________________ because ____."

   For example: "I feel angry when you and Mom fight all the time because I'm afraid you're going to get a divorce."
6. You can experience feelings, share them, and let them go. You can tolerate (put up with) feelings because they will pass. You can also choose to do things that make you feel better.
7. You can't control the feelings you get. However, you can look at your thinking, or self-talk, and change it from negative to positive. You can control your behavior. You can use your feelings to give you the power to make changes. You can learn to use problem-solving skills.
8. You can take care of yourself. This is self-preservation, not selfishness.
9. It's always a good idea to repeat positive affirmations for yourself.

   Example: "I am lovable and capable."
10. It's good practice to share caring, positive feelings and thoughts. Remember the three Ps: Be pleasant, positive, and polite.

COPING STRATEGY SITUATIONS

Problem Situation 1

Your parents are having a terrible fight. They are even throwing things at each other.

Coping Strategies

1. You can realize and accept that you cannot make your parents stop fighting. It's not your job, and you wouldn't succeed anyway (Rules 2 and 3).
2. You can go to a safe place where you won't get hurt, like your bedroom (Rule 8).
3. You can listen to a favorite song to feel better (Rule 6).

Your Strategy

____

____

Problem Situation 2

Your mom is crying because she just found out your dad has been having an affair.

Coping Strategies

1. Give your mom a hug and tell her you love her (Rule 10).
2. Do something you enjoy, like listening to rock music (Rule 6), or do something that is good for you, like gymnastics (Rule 8).
3. You can talk to someone you trust if you feel worried or scared (Rules 1 and 6).

Your Strategy

____

____

Problem Situation 3

Your dad asks you if he should divorce your mom, who has been drinking a lot, is chemically dependent, and won't get help.

Coping Strategies

1. You can tell your dad that you're sorry he's having problems, but you can't tell him what to do because you love both your mom and dad; maybe he should find an adult to talk to for help (Rules 3 and 4).
2. You can do something that's good for you (Rules 6 and 8).

Your Strategy

____

____

Problem Situation 4

Instead of helping you with your science fair project as she promised, your mom, who has been very irritable since the divorce, came home, drank beer, and is now yelling at you and telling you that you're a lazy, worthless, good-for-nothing brat.

Coping Strategies

1. Remember your positive affirmation: "I am lovable and capable" (Rule 9). Write it on an index card and carry it in your pocket. You might write, "I'm energetic, worth while, and a good kid."
2. If you're feeling angry, manage it (Rule 7) and talk about your angry feelings with someone you trust (Rule 1).
3. The next day, when your mom is sober, tell her how hurt you felt when she called you names, because you know that you are a good person (Rule 5).

Your Strategy

____

____

____

Problem Situation 5

You have a good friend whose parents are going through a messy divorce. Your friend has a bad temper and is always arguing with people. You're afraid your friend will get into real trouble and get suspended.

Coping Strategies

1. You remember that you can't control anybody else's behavior (Rule 2). Tell your friend how you feel, using I statements (Rule 5), and how much you care (Rule 10).
2. You stop enabling; you don't cover up for him or her. Allow your friend to experience some negative consequences so he or she will have a reason to change.
3. Share your feelings, using I statements (Rule 5), with your friend. For example: "I feel afraid when I see you arguing all the time, because I'm afraid no one will be able to stand you" or "I felt angry when you got mad at me last week. You were putting me down."
4. Discuss your concerns with a caring adult (Rule 1).

Your Strategy

____

____

Each day this week, look at how you act with your friends or family members. Each day, see if you can use one of the rules for relationships or one of the problem-solving skills. Write it down.

Day one

Day two

Day three

Day four

Day five

Day six

Day seven

Other comments or observations

SESSION • 9

Setting Personal Goals

Objectives

To help the students:

- discover that they need to make good choices
- set goals to take care of their bodies, feelings, minds, and choices

Session at a Glance

1. Group Rules: review if necessary—1 minute
2. Centering Exercise: "White-Water Rafting"—3 minutes
3. Feelings Check-in: look at Feelings Wheel—4 minutes
4. Basic Facts Review—9 minutes
5. Assignment Review—4 minutes
6. Mini-lecture and Discussion—5 minutes
7. Activity: draw river picture and write personal goals —11 minutes
8. Basic Facts: read Basic Fact 19; discuss—1 minute
9. Assignment—1 minute
10. Centering Exercise: repeat "White-Water Rafting"—3 minutes
11. Affirmation: share a way you can take care of yourself—2 minutes
12. Closing: pass a silent wish—1 minute

Preparation

- Display the posterboard copy of the group rules.
- Have posters with Basic Facts 1-18 available, or the List of Basic Facts, or index cards with one basic fact on each one.
- Add the following materials to each folder:
  —Handout 9A ("River Picture")
  —Handout 9B ("My Personal Goals")
  —Assignment 9

- Place each student's folder, a pencil, and crayons or markers at his or her place.
- Read through the session plan before meeting

Background and Guidelines

In this session, the students learn how to give up responsibility for their families' problems. By setting personal goals, they learn how to assume age-appropriate responsibility for themselves. The students are encouraged to take good care of themselves and to make good decisions for themselves in the areas of body, mind, feelings, and choices.

As leader, you won't be recommending that the group members abandon their families, leave home, and get a job. Rather, you need to encourage them to set their sights on age-appropriate responsibilities. For example, they can decide to try to get on the honor roll or eat a balanced diet, or they can decide to use problem-solving skills when they get angry.

When you discuss goals regarding feelings, remember that teens can't control which feelings they get. Teens can be responsible , however, for what they do with their feelings. Teens can wallow in feelings and be overwhelmed by them, or they can decide to choose an appropriate coping strategy, such as talking about their feelings with someone they trust or doing something that will help them feel better. Emphasize again that although they can't fix their families' problems, they can do things to cope with them.

This session has two activities. In the first one, the students have an opportunity to step back, look at their lives so far, and imagine how they would like to proceed. They draw a "river picture" to represent their past, present, and future. Even students who are self-conscious about their drawing ability like this exercise.

In the second activity, the students set personal goals for themselves in four areas: their bodies, minds, feelings, and choices. Setting and sharing goals in these areas will enable the students to create the kind of future they would like. With positive feedback from you and other group members, sharing these goals helps the students assume ownership and empowers them to take the steps necessary to achieve their goals.

As the students set their goals, remind them of the chunking-it-down principle. Setting small, concrete steps that are easily accomplished is a good way to start to achieve a long-term goal. For instance, someone who decides to compete in a marathon doesn't begin training by running 26 miles the first day. Rather, the person plans a training program that starts small—such as running two miles a day—and slowly builds up enough endurance to compete in a marathon. Similarly, high school students may have the goal of becoming lawyers. As high school students, they can't apply to law school. But they can go to the library and look up the requirements for entrance into law school. They will see that a college degree is necessary. Next they can look up requirements for college entrance. Then they can make sure they are taking the appropriate courses in high school. The most basic, concrete step they can take is to get good grades in their academic classes. Toward that goal, they may decide to focus on their homework tonight instead of watching TV.

Beginning the Session

Group Rules

Have the folders at the appropriate places. Welcome the students and begin with a quick review of the group rules. Draw attention to the poster listing the rules. If necessary, call on different students to read them one at a time.

Check for understanding before moving on.

CENTERING EXERCISE

Lead the students in the centering exercise, "White-Water Rafting."

WHITE-WATER RAFTING

Okay, close your eyes. Imagine that you're floating down a river in a one-person boat, an inflatable kayak called a duck. You've been placed on the river by a guide, who has told you that this is a safe stretch of water. He's given you the equipment you need—a paddle, a helmet, and a life jacket—and has shown you how to use them. The guide has told you that he will meet you a few miles down the river and to enjoy yourself. When you first start paddling, you go around in circles, but soon you can make the kayak go in the right direction.

Right now, you're floating along in a long, calm pool of the river. No one else is around. The sky above is very clear and bright blue. The surrounding mountains are steep and green. It's a beautiful wilderness area. You feel very safe in the calm pool, so safe that you take off your life jacket and helmet. You lie back in the kayak and put your feet up, soaking up the sunshine and listening to the quietness. You feel very relaxed.

As you float along, you hear a noise. The sound is coming from around a bend in the river. You can't see what's around the bend. As you drift closer, the sound grows louder. It's the sound of rushing water. You begin to worry. You wonder if your guide has placed you in the wrong part of the river. As the sound gets even louder, you worry more, wondering if it's a waterfall. You feel your heart beating faster and faster.

You sit up at attention. You fasten your life jacket and buckle your helmet. You grab your paddle, and get yourself ready to go through whatever lies ahead. As the noise becomes even louder, you slip around the bend in the river. It's white water, all right!

The kayak leaps into the white water, giving you a great ride around the rocks and through the rushing water. Waves break over the top of the kayak, but they don't stop you. You're feeling strong and excited. In a moment, you've passed through the rapids and you're floating gently in another of the river's calm pools.

You feel excited, confident, satisfied. You feel.proud of yourself. You were able to get through something that was frightening because it was unknown. You got through very successfully, using the tools you'd been given and the skills you developed. You feel so good that you are sitting on top of the world! So let those feelings of excitement, pride, confidence, and satisfaction wash all over you right now.

FEELINGS CHECK-IN

Have the students take out their Feeling Wheels. Ask the group members to decide how they are feeling today. Remind the students that if they want, they can color in the section on the feeling wheel that describes how they're feeling today. Also remind them that they might have more than one feeling, since it's possible to have more than one feeling at a time. Tell the students that if they're having a feeling that isn't named on the wheel, they can add a bubble to the outside of the wheel and name the feeling there.

When the students finish, have a go-around. Begin by sharing your own feelings. Then, invite each student to share his or her feelings. Teenagers often list many feelings. In the interest of time, ask them to name the feelings they have, but then pick only two to discuss. Be sure to accept each student's feeling(s) and to affirm each student. Ask the students to return the wheels to their folders.

BASIC FACTS REVIEW

Review the basic facts learned so far. Use the posters with Basic Facts 1-18, the List of Basic Facts, or index cards.

In a go-around, ask a student to read Basic Fact 1 aloud and explain what it means. If the student has trouble explaining the fact, don't contradict or judge, simply clarify the explanation. Repeat the procedure for the next basic fact. This review ensures that the students understand and integrate the basic facts that have been taught. It is also easy preparation for the presentation and provides a lead-in for session material.

ASSIGNMENT REVIEW

Ask the students to pull out their assignments from last week. Remind them that they were supposed to observe how they act with family members and friends and to see if they could use the rules for relationships or the problem-solving skills. In a go-around, ask the students what they used. If they forgot to do the assignment, ask them to think about whether they used the rules or skills in the past week, or if they can think of a time when they could have used them.

Exploring the Material

Mini-lecture and Discussion

Setting Personal Goals

Tell the group members that now that they have learned the three Cs—they can't cause, control, or change a parent's decision to separate or divorce—and now that they know they can't fix a parent's problem, the students are ready to learn that they can take care of themselves.

Explain the difference between selfishness and self-preservation. Use this example: you are one of three people on a deserted island, with nothing to eat but a piece of chocolate cake. If you eat the entire piece by yourself, you are being selfish; if you take none, you are being a martyr; but if you divide the cake into thirds, and eat your share, you are practicing self-preservation.

Point out that teenagers can take care of themselves in different ways. Write *Body, Mind, Feelings,* and *Choices* on a big piece of newsprint, or on a chalkboard, if one's available. Ask the students for examples in each area.

Body: (eat nutritiously, exercise, get plenty of sleep.)

Mind: (read, do homework, review notes.)

Feelings: (have fun, find a friend to share your feelings with, put thinking between feelings and behaving.)

Choices: (decide not to use alcohol or other drugs, decide to follow the rules at school, go to college, or be sexually responsible.)

Point out that teenagers can set goals for taking care of their bodies, minds, feelings, and choices. Explain that goals are plans for good things you will do for yourself. The goals might be long-term—things you hope to achieve in the distant future—or short-term, things you plan to achieve in the immediate future. Relate the process of achieving long-term goals to the principle of chunking it down. It's often helpful to set long-term goals that you keep in mind, but it's best to start by setting small, tiny, concrete goals that are easy to attain. For example, you don't start out to run a marathon by running 26 miles. You start with smaller distances, then you train and build up strength and endurance.

Suppose you decide you want to go to law school. You can't go to Harvard Law School now, but you *can* look at what you can do now to achieve that goal. First, go to the library and look up the requirements for entrance into law school. You will see that a college degree is necessary. Next you can look up requirements for college entrance. Then make sure you're taking the appropriate courses in high school. The most basic, concrete step you can take is to get good grades in your academic classes. Maybe you need to focus on your homework instead of watching TV tonight.

The same process applies to how you handle the feeling of anger. It's hard to change behavior quickly, but you can start by observing what you do when you get angry. Then, you can look at what you could have done to make your anger work for you by using a problem-solving skill. If you practice the anger management steps regularly—even after you express anger in a harmful way—in two or three months, you'll start changing your behavior without even knowing it.

Discussion

Lead a discussion to help the students better understand the key concepts presented. As the group discusses, remember to make sure that each student has an opportunity to add to the discussion. Encourage participation, but don't force it. Remember the group rule that allows a student to pass. Explain or clarify information where necessary to reinforce learning and correct any misconceptions. To facilitate the discussion, you may use questions like the following:

- **Can teenagers fix their parents' problems?** (No.)
- **Who can teens take care of?** (Themselves.)
- **Does taking good care of yourself mean getting a job and an apartment and living on your own?** (No. It means doing things that are good for your body, mind, feelings, and choices.)
- **What are goals?** (Goals are plans for good things you will do for yourself.)
- **What does chunking it down mean?** (Chunking it down means to start to achieve a long-term goal by taking very small, concrete steps that are easy to attain.)

Even if you choose not to use the suggested questions, make sure the discussion underscores these concepts.

ACTIVITY

Tell the students that there are two activities today that will help them set personal goals.

River Picture

Have the students take Handout 9A ("River Picture") out of their folders. Explain that they will draw a river picture that can help them set personal goals. It will be a three-part picture that shows their past, present, and future and will include a river that will stand for, or symbolize, their present. The left bank, or side, of the river will stand for their past, and the right bank of the river will stand for their future. They can draw the river as stormy or calm, wide or narrow, and they can draw any objects, or people, or things and use any color they want to stand for their past, their present, and their future.

As an example, tell the students that one girl drew the river as very rocky and full of waves and white water because she was going through some rough times. On the bank representing her past, she drew a garden with a heavy rain falling on it because of the sad things that had happened to her. On the bank representing her future, she drew a house with trees, flowers, and a white picket fence, because that's what she wants when she grows up.

Tell the students to think about what their past and present look like and to imagine what they want their future to look like. Remind them that you aren't looking for artistic ability. If they don't want to draw, they can write in the names of things in their past, present, and futures. Give the students time to do their drawings. When they finish, have a go-around and ask each student to explain his or her picture to the group.

My Personal Goals

Then, have the students take out Handout 9B. Read aloud the title at the top of the sheet, "My Personal Goals." Tell the students that they've drawn a picture of what they want their future to look like. Now they can set goals that will help them achieve what they want in their future. They should have goals in four areas: body, mind, feelings, and choices. People need to take care of themselves in all four areas. You may need to repeat some of the ideas they came up with during the lecture on how teens can take care of those areas. Remind the students to chunk it down: they can reach goals that seem impossible by starting with small goals that are easy to attain. Ask them to label each goal "ST" for short-term or "LT" for long-term. When the students finish writing, have a go-around again. Invite each student to tell one or two personal goals to the group. Affirm the young people on their goal-setting and on their growing willingness and ability to take good care of themselves.

BASIC FACTS

Review the new basic fact for this session. Refer the students to the List of Basic Facts. Ask a group member to read Basic Fact 19.

19. Teens need to take care of their bodies, their feelings, their minds, and their choices.

Assignment

Have the group members take Assignment 9 out of their folders. Read the directions: "This week, set one goal for yourself, and practice chunking it down. Write the long-term goal, and then write the small, concrete steps that will help you achieve the goal." Remind the students that it is easier to work on something if they are able to put it into words.

Wrapping Up

Centering Exercise

Settle the students and then repeat "White-Water Rafting" (page 167).

Affirmation

Involve the group in an affirmation. Stand and join in a circle with the students, holding hands. Go around and let the students share one goal they have for themselves and what the first step will be. Begin the affirmation yourself: "One goal I have for myself is. . . . The first step I can take is. . . ." The students may again need your help to chunk down their goal and to decide on a small and easily obtainable first step.

Closing

Remain standing in a circle with the students, holding hands, and lead the group in the closing activity. Tell the students that you're going to make a silent wish for the student on your right. Then, when you've made the wish, gently squeeze that student's hand. The student makes a silent wish for the person on his or her right, then gently squeezes that student's hand, and so on. Continue around the circle until a wish and squeeze come back to you. If necessary, the students can pass the wish in any appropriate way they choose.

Collect the folders. Fill out a copy of the Process and Progress Form (page 199) or, if you are an experienced leader, the Progress Notes (page 201) as soon as possible after leading the group.

Note: If you have decided to use the optional Session 10, tell the students that they will be making a presentation of the material they have learned. Make arrangements to present the basic facts to a guidance counselor, principal, or administrator, to a class in the school, or to a class in another school. Tell the students how you plan to meet in order to rehearse. A script is provided in Session 10. If possible, make plans to videotape the presentation. The students will enjoy viewing the tape in Session 11.

As alternatives to the presentation in Session 10, you might have the students present the basic facts in a bulletin board display—perhaps including artwork—or you might have the students present the basic facts in a series of broadcasts over the school's public-address system.

River Picture

The river picture represents your life. Draw a river that symbolizes your present; the left bank symbolizes your past; the right bank symbolizes your future. You can create any kind of future for yourself that you want. Use words if you don't want to draw.

My Personal Goals

On the lines provided, write one or more goals you have for taking care of your body, mind, feelings, and choices. Indicate whether each goal is short-term (ST) or long-term (LT).

For My Body:

For My Mind:

For My Feelings:

For My Choices:

This week, set one goal for yourself, and practice chunking it down. Write the long-term goal, and then write the small, concrete steps that will help you achieve the goal.

My long-term goal:

Chunking it down:
The small, concrete steps I need to take to achieve this goal:

1.

2.

3.

4.

5.

SESSION • 10

Group Presentation

Optional

Objectives

To help the students:

- demonstrate their understanding of the basic facts about changing families
- grow in self-esteem

To help the students as a group:

- share feelings of cohesiveness
- successfully complete a project

To help members of the audience:

- learn about the changing families of today's world
- become aware of some of the issues that arise from living in a changing family
- recognize that help is available for those who live in a changing family

Session at a Glance

1. Group Rules: review—1 minute
2. Centering Exercise: an exercise chosen and led by the students—3 minutes
3. Feelings Check-in: look at Feelings Wheel—5 minutes
4. Presentation: present all the basic facts—25 minutes
5. Audience Evaluation—3 minutes
6. Centering Exercise: repeat the chosen exercise—3 minutes
7. Affirmation: share what you liked or appreciated about the presentation—4 minutes
8. Closing: pass a silent wish—1 minute

Preparation

- Since the structure of this session varies from that of the other sessions, you may wish to schedule two meeting times to present it. If you and the students have decided on a presentation to an audience, you can use the first time period as a rehearsal session for the students to practice delivering the basic facts and to make any other necessary preparations. Use the second time period to conduct the actual session, allowing the students to make their presentation. Depending on your group, you may want to invite the audience only for the presentation and audience evaluation part of the session.

- Decide in advance on an appropriate audience for the presentation. If this is the first time for such a presentation, you may wish to invite only the school principal or SAP staff. If you're an experienced leader, you may want to invite a whole grade level, a particularly effective prevention measure for middle or high school levels. You can also consider having group members make a bulletin board presentation of the basic facts for display in a school hallway or lunchroom, or having them read the basic facts over the PA system.
- Make suitable seating arrangements for the audience.
- If possible, videotape the students' presentation so you can play it for them in Session 11.
- Display the posterboard copy of the group rules.
- Clear a wall or bulletin board space in the meeting area where the students can post all 19 Basic Fact Posters. Have pins or tape available.
- Have available the "Three Cs" and the "Four Steps" posters (both from Session 4) and the "Anger Management Steps" poster (from Session 7).
- Make copies of the Audience Evaluation Form (page 196) and have pens or pencils available for audience members.
- Read through the session plan before meeting.

Background and Guidelines

This session provides guidelines for a presentation in which the students explain all the basic facts to an invited audience. Instead of having the students do a presentation, however, you might allow them to develop their own project. Such projects might include steering a schoolwide focus on facts about changing families, or teaching younger students how to cope with changing families. For instance, some teens have read the stories of *Thomas Barker Talks about Separation and Divorce* to younger groups as their group task. Creating their own project and carrying it through, although usually requiring a major commitment of time and energy, can be a great source of positive self-esteem for middle and high school students. And teaching someone else how to use the anger management steps and problem-solving skills will reinforce the learning for your group members.

If you decide to do the presentation, but are concerned about having members of a confidential group stand up in front of an audience, rest assured that the purpose of this session is not to break confidentiality; rather, it's to provide an effective prevention activity.

There's a lot to do for and in this session. Planning ahead, however, will make the task less daunting. The most effective way of guaranteeing the success of the students' presentation is advance planning and practice.

Arrange to have one of the teens lead the group and the audience in a centering exercise of the group's choice. The centering exercise will begin and help to conclude the session. If none of the students want to lead the exercise, plan on doing so yourself.

The students can take turns presenting the facts. During the practice session, assign the basic facts to each student. During the presentation, the students will display each assigned fact on a poster, read it aloud, and explain it. They then post the posters (in sequence) in the space provided in the meeting room.

After a student reads a basic fact and explains it to the audience, further the discussion by asking questions of the student or the audience. (The students can also role-play different scenarios to illustrate selected facts.) To help the presentation flow smoothly, have the students sit in a row in front of the room. Then, when you call on them to present their facts, all they need to do is stand, look at the audience, and speak slowly and distinctly. As you practice the presentation, the order and method should become clear to the teens. To make sure the presentation is nonthreatening to the students, tell them that you will further explain the basic fact if they don't want to.

At the conclusion of the presentation, if you have presented to students, ask audience members to fill out an Audience Evaluation Form. The forms will give you important feedback and can serve as a referral source for future groups. If audience members, including teachers, identify themselves as children from changing families, be ready to refer them to available help.

The overall goal of the presentation is not to showcase group members' talents or academic abilities. Rather, the goal is to reinforce learning, to allow the group members to reach out to others, to convey a sense of hope to the audience, and to assure all that help is available for students to learn good ways to deal with anger and the issues affecting changing families.

Beginning the Session

GROUP RULES

Welcome the students and guests and, if necessary, begin with a quick review of the group rules. Draw attention to the poster listing the group rules. If necessary, call on different students to read them one at a time.

Check for understanding before moving on.

CENTERING EXERCISE

Explain to your guests that every time the group meets, it always begins with a centering exercise, which teaches ways of relaxing and helps everyone get ready to work together. Then invite the designated teen to lead an exercise—for example—"Breathing Through Your Feet."

FEELINGS CHECK-IN

Have the students take out their Feeling Wheels. Ask the group members to decide how they are feeling today. Remind the students that if they want, they can color in the section on the feeling wheel that describes how they're feeling today. Also remind the teens that they might have more than one feeling, since it's possible to have more than one feeling at a time. Tell the students that if they're having a feeling that isn't named on the wheel, they can add a bubble to the outside of the wheel and name the feeling there.

When the students finish, have a go-around. Begin by sharing your own feelings. Then invite each student to share his or her feelings. Teenagers often list many feelings. In the interest of time, ask them to name the feelings they have, but then pick only two to discuss. Be sure to accept each student's feeling(s) and to affirm each student. Ask the students to return the wheels to their folders.

Presentation

INTRODUCTION

Introduce the presentation using the following: "We're part of the counseling program at (name of school). We've learned some important basic facts about family values and the changing families of today's world. We want to share some of what we've learned with you."

Presenting Basic Facts 1 and 2

Call on the students designated to present Basic Facts 1 and 2.

1. **There are many different kinds of families, and each kind is special.**
2. **There are traditional families, separated or divorced families, single-parent families, stepfamilies, and blended families.**

Have the students display a poster of each fact, read it aloud, explain it, and then post it.

Call on group and audience members to give examples of the different kinds of families that teens live in today.

Presenting Basic Facts 3 and 4

Move on to the next set of basic facts. Call on the students designated to present Basic Facts 3 and 4.

3. **People usually get married because they love each other and want to be together.**
4. **People usually get separated or divorced because they no longer want to share their lives.**

Have the students display a poster of each fact, read it aloud, explain it, and then post it.

Invite the audience to share reasons why people get married (they're in love; they want to get away from home; they're fearful of being alone; the woman is pregnant; they like being together). Ask the audience which of these reasons are positive and which are negative. Then, ask why people get divorced (they change; they no longer love each other; one spouse is an alcoholic or batterer; a partner has an affair; a partner gets bored.) Ask the audience which of these reasons to leave are positive and which are negative. Remind them that there are no right answers; you are just asking for their opinions.

Presenting Basic Facts 5 and 6

Call on the students designated to present Basic Facts 5 and 6.

5. **A separation or divorce in a family is never the children's fault.**
6. **Children usually love both their mother and their father, even if the parents no longer live together.**

Have the students display a poster of each fact, read it aloud, explain it, and then post it.

Explain to the students in the audience that if parents separate, it is never the child's fault. It's an adult decision. Also explain that people who are divorcing are often very angry and sometimes want their children to be as angry as they are at the other parent. It's important to remember that children don't have to take sides in a parental divorce, even if the parents want them to. It's better for the children to try to be friendly with both parents.

Presenting Basic Facts 7 and 8

Move on to the next set of basic facts. Call on the students designated to present Basic Facts 7 and 8.

7. **The three Cs are:**
    1. **Children never cause their parents to separate or divorce.**
    2. **Children can't control a separation or divorce.**
    3. **Children can't change a separation or divorce.**

8. **The four steps children in a changing family can take are:**

    1. **Accept what they can't change.**
    2. **Ask for help for themselves.**
    3. **Be friendly with both parents.**
    4. **Learn to recognize, accept, and share their feelings.**

Have the students display a poster of each fact, read it aloud, explain it, and then post it.

Display the poster with the three Cs. Point out to the audience that the three Cs are included in Basic Fact 7. Use the following questions to help the students explain the three Cs:

- **How might teens think they cause a parent to separate or divorce?** (Teens might think that parents separate because the teens misbehave in school, don't listen to parents, fight with their sisters and brothers, or drop out of school or get pregnant.)
- **Can behaviors like these make parents separate?** (No. Behaviors like these can make parents angry, but it's their choice to separate.)
- **How might teens think they control their parents' separation?** (The teens might try various methods to get the parents to stop fighting; they might tell the parents to stop fighting; they might try to be a therapist to the parent or tell the parent to get professional help.)
- **How might teens try to change a parent's choice to separate or divorce?** (They might try to be perfect and get good grades in school; they might try to stay out of the parent's way and not cause any trouble.)
- **Will these actions ever change a parental separation or divorce?** (Probably not.)

After the students respond to the questions, point out to the audience that the four steps help teens stop trying to control and change their parents. Instead, the steps help teens learn ways to take care of themselves.

Presenting Basic Facts 9 and 10

Call on the students designated to present Basic Facts 9 and 10.

9. **Feelings aren't good or bad, or right or wrong; they just are.**

10. **Putting thinking between your feeling and your behavior enables you to choose helpful ways to express feelings.**

Have the teens display a poster of each fact, read it aloud, explain it, and then post it.

Point out to the audience that all feelings are normal, and that teens can't control which feelings they get; however, they certainly can control their behavior. Sometimes they need to put positive thinking between their feelings and behavior to make sure they express their feelings in helpful ways.

If you wish, have the students retrieve their copies of Handout 5 ("Three Components of Emotions: Feeling, Thinking and Behavior: How Thinking Affects Feelings and Behavior") and have them share their examples of the three components and how they change due to negative or positive thinking.

Presenting Basic Facts 11, 12, 13, and 14

Move on to the next set of basic facts, and call on the students designated to present Basic Facts 11, 12, 13, and 14.

11. **When teens are angry about a problem they can't change, they should:**

    a. **Accept what they can't change.**

    b. **Express their anger so they can let it go.**

    c. **Do something good for themselves.**

12. **When teens are angry about a problem they can change, they should use their anger to give them the power to make changes in themselves.**

13. **Five good problem-solving skills to use in anger situations are: I statements, reflective listening, kill-them-with-kindness sandwiches, apologizing, and negotiating a compromise.**

14. **Chunking it down is a good way to start on a long-term goal.**

Have the teens display a poster of each fact, read it aloud, explain it, and then post it.

Have the students role-play the five problem-solving skills by using a scenario from Session 6. Scenario 2 is repeated here for convenience.

Scenario 2

Kimberly is a tenth grader who is very upset because her parents are separating.

I statements are three-part statements that describe how a person feels. The three parts are: "I feel _______ when you _____because ________." Suppose that Kimberly blames her mother for making the decision to divorce. If she uses an I statement, Kimberly might say: "Mom, I feel really hurt and lonely when I think that we won't be living as a family any more." In comparison, if Kimberly uses a **You statement,** she might say something accusing: "Mom, you are really selfish. Why are you getting a separation? Don't you know how much it will hurt everyone?" A person who hears a you statement is likely to feel attacked and may want to fight back. A person who hears an I statement is less likely to feel attacked.

Reflective listening refers to the ability to listen to what someone else says. For instance, using the same scenario, Kimberly might complain to her mother, saying, "I'm really mad at you. You are so selfish. You're putting yourself ahead of our family." If Kimberly's mother is using reflective listening, she will say something like: "It sounds like you're pretty angry with me. It must feel pretty bad. Tell me some more about what's going on, and what you're feeling about the separation." But if Kimberly's mother is not using reflective listening, she might simply react to Kimberly's anger and get angry back. Then they will both be angry. Or if Kimberly's mother feels responsible for fixing Kimberly's feelings, she might decide to go back to Kimberly's father just to make her happy, which might be a mistake for Kimberly's mother. Reflective listening allows Kimberly's mother to accept Kimberly's feelings, without taking the responsibility for making them better.

A kill-them-with-kindness sandwich is a three-part statement that 1) says something nice, 2) sets a limit or boundary or states your position, and 3) says something nice. In our scenario, let's imagine that Kimberly's parents are very angry with each other and frequently make comments about how bad the other parent is. Kimberly could listen to a parent's comments for a short time, and then say: "Mom, I really love you a lot, and I'm glad you're my parent. But I really love Dad too, and I get very sad and hurt when you say bad things about him. From now on, if you start putting him down, I'm just going to leave the room. I'd rather talk about how you are doing when I'm with you." In this statement Kimberly states her position clearly; she does not criticize her mother, but she doesn't agree with her either. She states that she loves both parents and doesn't want to hear one criticize the other. Kimberly doesn't demand that they stop, but she sets limits by saying she won't listen to the negative comments.

The third skill is **apologizing.** Research about violence shows that acts of aggression are more likely to occur in situations where there are threats and counterthreats. A simple apology can prevent a situation from escalating into a violent one. Suppose Kimberly has used You statements with her mother, accusing her of being selfish and mean. Kimberly could later say to her mother: "I'm sorry that I called you names and yelled at you last night. I was feeling upset about the divorce, and I was blaming you. I'm sorry." Kimberly may need to practice using I statements more to help her deal with her feelings.

The art of **negotiating a compromise** is an important skill in a relationship. The process will be more successful if the parties involved make a commitment to come to an agreement they can each live with. Each states his or her position, and they keep brainstorming ideas for solutions. Taking time to think of different solutions often helps the process of negotiation. In the scenario, Kimberly and her mother could continue talking about how they could solve the problem of expressing their feelings. Kimberly's mom might say that instead of discussing her feelings about her ex-husband with Kimberly, she will talk about her feelings with one of her adult friends. Kimberly might say that she will try harder not to use you statements and will learn to express her feelings in I statements.

Explain to the audience that chunking it down means setting a long-term goal and deciding on the small, concrete steps that help you achieve the goal. In learning how to use the problem-solving skills, it helps to start by observing what you do now when you're angry. It then helps to think of which problem-solving skill you could have used in the anger situation. Suggest that you would like everyone to learn how to use problem-solving skills when they are angry.

Presenting Basic Facts 15 and 16

Call on the students designated to present Basic Facts 15 and 16.

15. The anger management steps help teens put thinking between the feeling of anger and the behavior of anger.

16. The anger management steps are:

1. **Recognize that you're angry.**
2. **Accept your anger.**
3. **Practice relaxation.**
4. **Decide if it's a problem you can change or one you can't change.**
5. **Think about helpful and harmful ways to express the anger.**
6. **Evaluate the consequences.**
7. **Choose a best way.**
8. **Problem-solve, or express your anger in a helpful way.**

Have the students display a poster of each fact, read it aloud, explain it, and then post it.

Next, ask the students to display the poster titled "Steps to Managing Anger." For the benefit of the audience, briefly go through the steps, using an appropriate example (see the lecture in Session 7) and asking the students to differentiate between helpful and harmful ways of expressing anger.

Presenting Basic Facts 17, 18, and 19

Move on to the next set of basic facts, and call on the students designated to present Basic Facts 17, 18, and 19.

17. Teens cannot fix their parents' problems.

18. Teens can take good care of themselves.

19. Teens need to take care of their bodies, their feelings, their minds, and their choices.

Have the students display a poster of each fact, read it aloud, explain it, and then post it.

A good way to explain these facts to the audience is to have one of the students read the first problem situation on Handout 8B ("Your mom and dad are having a terrible fight. Dad is slapping Mom."). Then ask the students to read aloud a coping strategy from those outlined in Session 8. If time allows, have a few of the group members role-play the coping strategy, teaching the audience that although teens cannot control a parent's behavior, teens can choose to do things that are good for them and will make them feel better.

After discussing Basic Fact 17, move on to Basic Facts 18 and 19. Explain to the audience that children from the changing families of today's world can live good, healthy lives if they learn to make good decisions. If appropriate, the students may share some personal goals.

Concluding the Presentation

Conclude the presentation by having the group stand, face the audience, and bow. Lead the audience in applause.

Wrapping Up

Audience Evaluation

Pass out copies of the Audience Evaluation Form and pens or pencils to audience members. Encourage them to spend a moment completing the form. When the audience members finish writing, collect the forms, pens, or pencils.

Centering Exercise

Ask the student who led the centering exercise at the beginning of the session to repeat it.

Affirmation

Afterward, involve the group and audience members in an affirmation. Invite everyone to stand in a circle and hold hands. Going around the circle, encourage everyone to share something he or she liked or appreciated about the group's presentation. Begin the affirmation yourself: "One thing I really liked about the presentation was. . . ."

Closing

Depending on the size of the audience and whether it seems appropriate, include the audience in a closing activity. Otherwise, do the closing after audience members leave. Stand in a circle with the students, holding hands, and lead the group in the closing activity. Tell the students that you're going to make a silent wish for the student on your right. Then, when you've made the wish, gently squeeze that student's hand. The student makes a silent wish for the person on his or her right, then gently squeezes that student's hand, and so on. Continue around the circle until a wish and squeeze come back to you. If necessary, the students can pass the wish in any appropriate way they choose.

Collect the folders. Fill out a copy of the Process and Progress Form (page 199) or, if you are an experienced leader, the Progress Notes (page 201) as soon as possible after leading the group.

SESSION • 11

Developing A Support System

Objectives

To help the students:

- review all the basic facts about changing families
- create a personal support system
- close out their group experience

Session at a Glance

1. Group Rules: review if necessary—1 minute
2. Centering Exercise: "The Rainbow"—3 minutes
3. Feelings Check-in: look at Feeling Wheel—4 minutes
4. Basic Facts Review (Optional: process Session 10's presentation; view videotape)—8 minutes
5. Assignment Review from Session 9—5 minutes
6. Mini-lecture and Discussion—4 minutes
7. Activity: draw up a list of people who can offer support—5 minutes
8. Group Evaluation—4 minutes
9. Certificates and Refreshments—4 minutes
10. Centering Exercise: repeat "The Rainbow"—3 minutes
11. Affirmation: share what you liked best about the group—3 minutes
12. Closing: pass a silent wish—1 minute

Preparation

- Display the posterboard copy of the group rules.
- Have posters with Basic Facts 1-19 available, or the List of Basic Facts, or index cards with

a basic fact on each one.

- If you videotaped the presentation, arrange for equipment so the students can view themselves in the presentation.
- Add the following materials to each folder:
  —Handout 11A ("Scenario for Session 11")
  —Handout 11B ("Yellow Pages")
- To help the students complete their personal yellow pages, prepare your own, with emergency phone numbers and the numbers of local self-help or crisis agencies. Have several copies of the local phone book's yellow pages available.
- Make copies of the Group Evaluation Form (page 191).
- Make copies of the Certificate of Recognition (page 192). Complete a certificate for each group member. Fill in the student's name, sign your name, and fill in the date. Mount each certificate on construction paper.
- Make arrangements to serve refreshments (chips and sodas, etc.) during the wrapping-up activity.
- Place each student's folder, a pencil, and crayons or markers at his or her place.
- Read through the session plan before meeting.

Background and Guidelines

This session summarizes the themes of the *Changing Families* curriculum: education about the changing families of today's world, putting thinking between feelings and behavior, teaching problem-solving skills to use in anger situations, correcting misconceptions, and empowerment. The students review all the basic facts, and, if they took part in Session 10, they also evaluate their group presentation.

Over the course of the group process, the students have discovered that although they can't change the separation in their family, or fix family problems, they can do some crucial things to help themselves. In this session, the students realize something new: they don't have to be alone as they focus on their efforts to help themselves. They see that not only is it okay to ask for help, but also it's healthy and smart. Teens can ask for help to learn how to deal with their feelings, how to develop coping strategies, and how to learn new skills. Thus, although this session marks the end of their group experience, the teens see that their support system is not diminishing, but has grown and can continue to expand.

As leader, you can help the students see that the average person needs a support system of about 30 people, not just two or three. Teens need to understand that they can ask for help in many different areas of their lives, and that it's perfectly okay to have different people help in different ways at different times.

This session provides the students with opportunities to share what they have gained and will remember from their group experience. But, as the students leave the group, the session does more than give them an opportunity to review. Throughout the lecture, the students discover that despite all they've learned, things will happen in the future that will upset them; that's why a support system is so vital. Emphasize this important point, stressing that using their support system (their "personal yellow pages" and other sources of help) during upsetting times is a wonderful way for them to take good care of themselves.

Note that there is a small ceremony in which the students receive certificates for taking part in this group. Be sure to have the certificates ready for the students. Do your best to provide some refreshments: this not only helps the students feel self-worth, but also tells them that they should and can have some fun, that they should and can celebrate their learning.

Sometimes, the end of group sessions is a bittersweet time for the students. Be ready for such feelings, and don't be afraid to speak and show your own appreciation and feelings toward the young people.

Beginning the Session

Group Rules

Have the folders in the appropriate places. Welcome the students and, if necessary, begin with a quick review of the group rules. Draw attention to the poster listing the group rules. If necessary, call on different students to read them one at a time.

Check for understanding before moving on.

Centering Exercise

Lead the students in a new centering exercise, "The Rainbow."

THE RAINBOW

Close your eyes and imagine you're asleep. In your sleep, you're dreaming. In your dream, you can fly. You soar way, way up into the sky, and you decide to land on a fluffy cloud. You lie back and relax on that cloud as it floats lazily across the deep blue sky. You look down and see other clouds below you. Far beneath those clouds is the world. It looks very small.

You reach deep into your pocket and pull out all of your worries, and problems, and sadness, and frustrations. You drop them one at a time on the clouds that float below you, one worry, one sadness, one problem, or one frustration per cloud. Soon, the clouds change your worries and sadness into rain. The rain falls gently to the ground. It washes away all the dust and dirt and grime, and it helps the plants and trees to grow, and it helps make the rivers and lakes and oceans beautiful.

Eventually the rain stops, the sun comes out, and you see a beautiful rainbow. You float over on your cloud and sit on top of the rainbow. You smile to yourself because you know that you made that beautiful rainbow. You remember that before there can be a rainbow, first there must

Exercise continued in next column.

Exercise continued from previous column.

be a cloud and a storm. Without your worries and sadness, the clouds couldn't have made the rain, and there would be no beautiful rainbow now.

Because you like to have fun, you slide down the rainbow. At the bottom there is a big pot, full of happiness. You reach into the pot and fill your pockets with happiness.

Tell the students that you hope they will see their group experience as a big pot at the end of the rainbow. If they need to, in the future, you hope that they can reach into the pot and pull out what they learned with a smile.

Feelings Check-in

Have the students take out their Feeling Wheels. Ask the group members to decide how they are feeling today. Remind the students that if they want, they can color in the section on the feeling wheel that describes how they're feeling today. Also remind the teens that they might have more than one feeling, since it's possible to have more than one feeling at a time. Tell the students that if they're having a feeling that isn't named on the wheel, they can add a bubble to the outside of the wheel and name the feeling there.

When the students finish, have a go-around. Begin by sharing your own feelings. Then, invite each student to share his or her feelings. Teenagers often list many feelings. In the interest of time, ask them to name the feelings they have, but then pick only two to discuss. Be sure to accept each student's feeling(s) and to affirm each student. Ask the students to return the wheels to their folders.

Basic Facts Review

Review Basic Facts 1-19. Use posters, the List of Basic Facts, or index cards.

In a go-around, ask a student to read Basic Fact 1 aloud and explain what it means. If the student has trouble explaining the fact, don't contradict or judge, simply clarify his or her explanation. Repeat the procedure for the next basic fact. This review ensures that the students understand and integrate the basic facts that have been taught and provides a lead-in for the session material.

Optional: If the group took part in the presentation of Session 10, take a moment to process it with the students. If you were able to videotape the presentation, show the tape now. Students generally enjoy seeing themselves on tape. Ask them what was hard and easy about the presentation, what was the most fun, what could have made it better. Record the students' observations to use and consider when presenting Session 10 in the future.

Assignment Review

Ask the students to pull out their assignments from Session 9. Remind them that they were to set a goal and practice chunking it down. They were to write the long-term goal, and the small, concrete steps that will help them achieve the goal. In a go-around, ask the students about their long-term goal and the steps that they can use to help them achieve the goal. If students forgot to do the assignment, ask them to set a goal now and determine what small, concrete steps will help them get started.

Exploring the Material

Mini-lecture and Discussion

Developing a Support System

Since this is the last session, ask the group members to summarize what they've learned in group. In a go-around, ask each student to tell something he or she learned. Encourage the students to tell something not mentioned by another student.

At the conclusion of the go-around, point out that the students have learned much about the many kinds of families in today's world. The goal of the group was to help them identify stresses for teens in various kinds of families, to help them identify feelings common for teens in these families, to help them learn to put thinking between their feelings and their behavior for all emotions, and to help them develop coping strategies. They've learned problem-solving skills that teens can use in anger situations, and they've learned how to set goals for themselves.

Encourage the students to look at how they have changed. Have they set long-term goals and tiny, concrete goals to start with?

Tell the group members that they will continue to encounter problems as life goes on—that's the way life is. But they don't have to fix their problems all by themselves or even figure out what to do all by themselves. Remind them that it's always okay to ask for help—whether to share feelings, ask for help with a car repair, or request help on homework problems. Everyone needs a support system of many kinds of people to help in many kinds of areas. The activity today will help them realize who is in their support system.

To help the students see the importance of asking for help, ask them to take out Scenario 1. Ask for a volunteer to read the scenario.

Scenario 1

Fred, a high school student, tends to have a lot of anger. His parents are divorced. He lives with his father, because his mother moved out of state and doesn't have a job. His father and stepmother fight a lot, especially when she's been drinking. Fred used to hang out with his friends Chuck and Raymond; they've been friends for a long time. Lately, though, he doesn't want to see anybody or do anything. He didn't even try out for cross-country this year, even though he made it to state last year. He's thinking of dropping band too.

Ask the students to imagine whom Fred could ask for help. He has some people in his support system already, but he's not using them for support.

If you wish, use the following questions to help in discussion.

1. **Who are the people in Fred's support system?** (*Family members:* his father, possibly his mother; *Friends:* Chuck and Raymond; *Teachers, coaches, clergy:* his band teacher, his cross country coach.)
2. **What community agencies could help Fred?** (Al-Anon; his school guidance counselor.)
3. **What are some things Fred could do to help himself feel better?** (He could join the cross-country team; he could play in band; he could spend time with his old friends, Chuck and Raymond. If he is upset with his stepmother's drinking, he could ask if there is a group at school for concerned persons; he could go to Al-Anon or Alateen.)

ACTIVITY

Show the students the yellow pages from the local telephone book. Note that the yellow pages list names and numbers of people to call for help with various problems. Tell the students they are going to make their own yellow pages. The students' personal yellow pages will contain the names of caring people they can call when they feel angry or depressed, or when they are worried about family violence. These people will form their support system.

Ask the students to take Handout 11B from their folders. Show the sample yellow pages you made prior to the session. Note that the handout has space for the names of friends, family members, school personnel, and community agencies. The students might like to include your name and the names of other members of the group. Using the telephone book you brought, show the students how to locate emergency phone numbers and the numbers of local self-help or crisis agencies, such as teen hotlines, Alcoholics Anonymous, Al-Anon, and Alateen. Help them with office numbers of school personnel. The students may have to fill in the numbers of family and friends later.

Give the students time to complete their personal yellow pages. Then have them put their yellow pages in their folders. Tell the students they can take their folders home with them.

GROUP EVALUATION

Pass out copies of the Group Evaluation Form and ask the students to complete it. Explain to the group members that their honesty will help you make the group better for other students. Point out that they needn't put their names on the form. When the students finish, collect the forms to use when you evaluate the group program.

Wrapping Up

CERTIFICATES AND REFRESHMENTS

Thank the students for their hard work, sharing, and openness by calling each forward and presenting him or her with a Certificate of Recognition. As you present the certificates, offer a personal note of thanks, mentioning something special to each student about his or her unique contribution to the group. Surprise the students with refreshments, and allow yourselves to enjoy the progress that everyone has made.

AFFIRMATION

Involve the group in a final affirmation. Stand and join in a circle, with everyone holding hands. Go around and ask each student to share something he or she liked or appreciated the most about being in the group. Begin the affirmation yourself: "What I liked best about being in this group is. . . ."

CLOSING

Remain standing in a circle with the students, holding hands, and lead the group in the closing activity. Tell the students that you're going to make a silent wish for the student on your right. Then, when you've made the wish, gently squeeze that student's hand. The student makes a silent wish for the person on his or her right, then gently squeezes that student's hand, and so on. Continue around the circle until a wish and squeeze come back to you. The students can pass the wish in any appropriate way they choose.

Collect the folders. Fill out a copy of the Process and Progress Form (page 199) or, if you are an experienced leader, the Progress Notes (page 201), as soon as possible after leading the group.

Scenarios for Session 11

Scenario 1

Fred, a high school student, tends to have a lot of anger. His parents are divorced. He lives with his father, because his mother moved out of state, and doesn't have a job. His father and stepmother fight a lot, especially when she's been drinking. Fred used to hang out with his friends Chuck and Raymond; they've been friends for a long time. Lately, though, he doesn't want to see anybody or do anything. He didn't even try out for cross-country this year, even though he made it to state last year. He's thinking of dropping band too.

My Personal Yellow Pages

Write the names and the phone numbers of anyone you would like to be in your support system. Include people you can ask for help with schoolwork and people you can talk to if you're having trouble with parents or friends. You can find the numbers of Alcoholics Anonymous, Al-Anon, Alateen, and other community agencies in the phone book yellow pages.

Friends:

Family members:

School personnel:

Community agencies:

Coaches, clergy, and other supportive adults:

Important phone numbers:

Group Evaluation Form

1. What did you like best about this group?

2. What did you like least about this group?

3. What do you think should be done differently?

4. What would have made the group more helpful to you?

5. What do you think is the most important thing you learned from this group?

6. What is one good thing that's happened to you because you were in this group?

7. As a result of being in this group, how have you changed?

Certificate Of Recognition

This Certificate of Recognition is awarded to

____

who has participated in a

Changing Families Group.

Congratulations!

____

LEADER'S NAME

____

DATE

____

SCHOOL

Part Four

Support Materials

Support Materials

This section of the manual includes the tools you'll need to develop and support the group program in your school. Each of the following materials is printed in blackline master form and is suitable for copying on most photocopy machines.

Audience Evaluation Form. This form may be used to evaluate the optional presentation in Session 10. It is designed to provide important feedback about the presentation's effectiveness and to serve as a referral source for future groups (p. 196).

Certificate of Recognition. This certificate may be photocopied and given to each group member during Session 11 (p. 192).

Feeling Wheel. This sheet will aid you in doing a feelings check-in with the students. Each group member will need one copy. The students will use their copies of the Feeling Wheel in Sessions 2-11. (See Session 2, p. 72).

Group Rules Contract. Make a copy of this contract for every group member. You will review the contract with prospective group members in the screening interview and will have all group members sign one in Session 1 (p. 61).

Group Evaluation Form. This form is to be used in Session 11 by the students to evaluate their experience in the group (p. 191).

Handouts. There are handouts in each session chapter, containing the scenarios, activities, and assignments.

List of Basic Facts. The complete List of Basic Facts is to be copied and stapled to the left inside flap of each student's folder for easy reference (p. 197).

Parental Consent Letter. Once students have been referred or self-referred to a group, you should seek parental consent by sending parents a copy of a letter like the one provided here (p. 198).

Process and Progress Form. This form is for you, the group leader. Make 11 copies of the form. After each session, fill out a copy of the form in order to evaluate the session and keep timely notes on the progress of the group (p. 199).

Progress Notes. This two-page form is a more condensed version of the Process and Progress Form and is suitable for the more experienced group leader. Simply copy each page and fill out the appropriate section after each group session (pp. 200-201).

Screening Interview Outline. After referrals are obtained and categorized, the students need to be interviewed individually. The Screening Interview Outline will help you get necessary information about the students and their daily lives (p. 202).

Self-referral Group Survey Form. This form should be made available to students after they've heard about the purpose of the support groups. Use the form in conjunction with a presentation at which available groups are explained to the students (see pages 24-25). When the students fill out the form, explain that if they want to be in more than one group, they should number their choices in order of priority. Also, make sure the students know that not everyone may be in groups right away and that groups will be offered according to need and time (p. 203).

This section of the manual also includes a list of professional resources for your reference and the names and addresses of helping agencies.

Audience Evaluation Form

1. The most interesting thing I learned from this presentation was:

____

____

____

____

____

____

____

2. How much impact has this presentation had on your knowledge of the issues for students from changing families and how students can cope with the stresses of living in a changing family? (Circle one)

NONE SOME MUCH

In what way?

____

____

____

____

____

____

____

If you are interested in being in a group to learn how to cope with the stresses that arise when you live in a changing family, please sign here. We will keep your name confidential and will contact you about your concern soon.

Name:____

Homeroom number or teacher's name: _______________________________

List of Basic Facts

1. There are many different kinds of families, and each kind is special.

2. There are traditional families, separated or divorced families, single-parent families, stepfamilies, and blended families.

3. People usually get married because they love each other and want to be together.

4. People usually get separated or divorced because they no longer want to share their lives.

5. A separation or divorce in a family is never the children's fault.

6. Children usually love both their mother and their father, even if the parents no longer live together.

7. The three Cs are:
   1. Children never cause their parents to separate or divorce.
   2. Children can't control a separation or divorce..
   3. Children can't change a separation or divorce.

8. The four steps children in a changing family can take are:
   1. Accept what they can't change.
   2. Ask for help for themselves.
   3. Be friendly with both parents.
   4. Learn to recognize, accept, and share their feelings.

9. Feelings aren't good or bad, or right or wrong; they just are.

10. Putting thinking between your feeling and your behavior enables you to choose helpful ways to express feelings.

11. When teens are angry about a problem they can't change, they should:
    1. Accept what they can't change.
    2. Express their anger so they can let it go.
    3. Do something good for themselves.

12. When teens are angry about a problem they can change, they should use their anger to give them the power to make changes in themselves.

13. Five good problem-solving skills to use in anger situations are: I statements, reflective listening, kill-them-with-kindness sandwiches, apologizing, and negotiating a compromise.

14. Chunking it down is a good way to start on a long-term goal.

15. The anger management steps help teens put thinking between the feeling of anger and the behavior of anger.

16. The anger management steps are:
    1. Recognize that you're angry.
    2. Accept your anger.
    3. Practice relaxation.
    4. Decide if it's a problem you can change or a problem you can't change.
    5. Think about helpful and harmful ways to express the anger.
    6. Evaluate the consequences.
    7. Choose a best way.
    8. Problem-solve, or express your anger in a helpful way.

17. Teens cannot fix their parents' problems.

18. Teens can take good care of themselves.

19. Teens need to take care of their bodies, their feelings, their minds, and their choices.

Parental Consent Letter

School address
Date

Dear Parent:

The counseling staff of ________________________ School is happy to be offering several groups this year. One group that we will be offering is for students who live in a changing family, a family that is separated or divorced, a single-parent family, or a stepfamily.

In the group, we will be discussing family values, the reasons why people get married and why they get divorced, the stresses and issues for students from changing families, feelings, coping strategies to deal with common stresses, anger management, setting personal goals, and developing a support system.

The group will meet for 11 weeks, for one class period during the school day, rotating class periods. As a teaching technique, we like the students to present what they have learned in Session 10, and as a self-esteem booster, we like to videotape the presentation. We think that this group will be very beneficial in helping students cope with their stresses, and we are pleased to be able to offer it.

We would like your permission for your child, ____________________________, to participate in this group. If you do give permission, please sign the permission form below and return it to us. Please call us at ________________________ if you have any questions.

Sincerely,

____

____

- -

I give permission for my child, ____, to participate in the

Changing Families group to be held at ____ School.

____ ____________________________

Name *Date*

Process and Progress Form

Name:______________________________ Session #:_______________

Date:____________________

Students Present:______________________________________

Processing the Session

1. What were the objectives of this session? ____________________________

2. How were they met?______________________________________

3. What concepts must the leader understand to facilitate this session effectively?__________

4. What happened during the session?______________________________

Highs:____

Lows:____

5. What did you see as your strengths as you facilitated this session?_______________

6. What changes would you make for next time?__________________________

Noting Progress:

Progress Notes

Group:____

Members of Group:____________________________________

____

Session 1:____________________________ Date:__________

Notes:____

____

____

Session 2:____________________________ Date:__________

Notes:____

____

____

Session 3:____________________________ Date:__________

Notes:____

____

____

Session 4:____________________________ Date:__________

Notes:____

____

____

Session 5:____________________________ Date:__________

Notes:____

____

____

Session 6:______________________________ Date:__________

Notes:____

____

____

Session 7:______________________________ Date:__________

Notes:____

____

____

Session 8:______________________________ Date:__________

Notes:____

____

____

Session 9:______________________________ Date:__________

Notes:____

____

____

Session 10:_____________________________ Date:__________

Notes:____

____

____

Session 11:_____________________________ Date:__________

Notes:____

____

____

Screening Interview Outline

Group: ______________________________

Date: ______________________________

Name: ______________________________

Age: ______________________________

Date of birth: ______________________________

Grade: ______________________________

Do you like school? ______________________________

What kind of grades do you make? ______________________________

What is your behavior in school? ______________________________

Home address: ______________________________

____

____

Phone: ______________________________

Who lives in your house? ______________________________

If your parents are divorced, where do they live? ______________________________

Visitation? ______________________________

What do you do after school? ______________________________

____

____

Typical daily schedule: ______________________________

Hobbies, sports, clubs: ______________________________

____

What are your strengths? ______________________________

What are your weaknesses? ______________________________

What are the stresses in your life? ______________________________

____

____

Self-referral Group Survey Form

Dear Student:

The Pupil Services Staff of ______________________________ School is pleased to be able to offer groups to the students of ____.

These groups will meet for 5 to 11 weeks, for one class period, during the school day, rotating class periods. We offer groups on many different subjects and we hope you will be interested in joining.

Please put an "X" on the group or groups you would like to join. If you are interested in more than one group, please number them in order of priority, with one being the highest.

_____ **Changing Families Group** *(for students from separated, divorced, single-parent families, or stepfamilies)*

_____ **Loss Group** *(if someone close to you has died)*

_____ **Concerned Persons Group** *(if you have concerns about someone's use of alcohol or other drugs)*

_____ **Anger Management Group** *(if you or someone close to you uses harmful ways to express anger)*

Name____

Teacher or room number ____

We will meet with students individually before starting the groups.

____

Guidance Counselor or School Social Worker

References And Suggested Readings

Beattie, M. 1987. *Co-dependent No More.* San Francisco: Harper/Hazelden.

Berger, S. 1983. *Divorce Without Victims.* Boston: Houghton Mifflin.

Black, C. 1981. *It Will Never Happen to Me.* Newport Beach, Calif.: ACT.

Bradley, B. 1982. *Where Do I Belong?* Reading, Mass.: Addison Wesley.

Cicchetti, D., and V. Carlson, eds. 1989. *Child Maltreatment: Theory and Research on the Causes and Consequences of Child Abuse and Neglect.* New York: Cambridge University Press.

Cicchetti, D., and P. W. Howes. 1991. "Developmental psychopathology in the context of the family: Illustrations from the study of child maltreatment." *Canadian Journal of Behavioral Science,.* 23 (3), (July): 257-81.

Coleman, J. C., and L. Hendry. 1990. *The Nature of Adolescence.* New York: Routledge.

Crittenden, P. M., and M. D. S. Ainsworth. "Child maltreatment and attachment theory." In *Child Maltreatment: Theory and Research on the Causes and Consequences of Child Abuse and Neglect,* ed. D. Cicchetti and V. Carlson, 432-63. New York: Cambridge University Press.

Despert, L. 1953. *Children of Divorce.* New York: Doubleday.

Diamond, S. 1985. *Helping Children of Divorce: A Handbook for Parents and Teachers.* New York: Schocken Books.

Dolmetsch, P., and A. Shih. 1985. *The Kids' Book About Single-parent Families.* Garden City, N.Y.: Dolphin.

Erikson, E. H. 1968. *Identity: Youth and Crisis.* New York: W. W. Norton & Company, Inc.

Friel, J., and L. Friel. 1988. *Adult Children: The Secrets of Dysfunctional Families.* Deerfield Beach, Fla.: Health Communications, Inc.

Francke, L. 1981. *Growing Up Divorced.* New York: Linden Press/Simon and Schuster.

Gabarino, J. 1989. "Troubled youth, troubled families: The dynamics of adolescent maltreatment." In *Child Maltreatment: Theory and Research on the Causes and Consequences of Child Abuse and Neglect,* ed. D. Cicchetti and V. Carlson, 685-706. New York: Cambridge University Press.

Gardner, R. 1981. *The Boys and Girls Book About Divorce.* New York: Bantam Books.

_____ 1981. *The Parents Book About Divorce.* New York: Bantam Books.

Gravitz, H. L., and J. D. Bowden. 1985. *Recovery: A Guide for Adult Children of Alcoholics.* New York: Simon & Schuster, Inc.

Hetherington, E. M., M. Stanley-Hagan, and E. Anderson. 1989. "Marital transitions: A child's perspective." *American Psychologist.* 44, no. 2: 302-312.

Jewett, C. 1982. *Helping Children Cope with Separation and Loss.* Harvard, Mass: The Harvard Common Press.

Kalter, N. 1990. *Growing Up With Divorce.* New York: The Free Press.

Kubler-Ross, E. 1969. *On Death and Dying.* New York: Macmillan.

Kaufman, J., and E. Zigler. 1989. "The intergenerational transmission of child abuse." In *Child Maltreatment: Theory and Research on the Causes and Consequences of Child Abuse and Neglect,* ed. D. Cicchetti and V. Carlson, 129-50. New York: Cambridge University Press.

Lansky, V. 1989. *Divorce Book for Parents.* New York: New American Library.

Leite, E., and P. Espeland. 1987. *Different Like Me.* Minneapolis: Johnson Institute.

Lerner, H. 1985. *The Dance of Anger.* New York: Harper & Row.

McGinnis, E., and A.P. Goldstein. 1984. *Skill-Streaming the Elementary School Child.* Champaign, Ill.: Research Press Company.

Saunders, A., and B. Remsberg. 1984. *The Stress-Proof Child.* New York: Holt, Rinehart & Winston.

Schaefer, D. 1987. *Choices & Consequences.* Minneapolis: Johnson Institute.

Schmidt, T. 1993. *Anger Management and Violence Prevention: A Group Activities Manual for Middle and High School Students.* Minneapolis: Johnson Institute.

Schmidt, T., and T. Spencer. 1991. *Della the Dinosaur Talks About Violence and Anger Management (Grades K-6).* In the series *Building Trust, Making Friends: Four Group Activity Manuals for High-Risk Students.* Minneapolis: Johnson Institute.

_____. 1991. *Peter the Puppy Talks About Chemical Dependence in the Family (Grades K-6).* In the series *Building Trust, Making Friends: Four Group Activity Manuals for High-Risk Students.* Minneapolis: Johnson Institute.

_____. 1991. *Tanya Talks About Chemical Dependence in the Family (Grades 6-8).* In the series *Building Trust, Making Friends: Four Group Activity Manuals for High-Risk Students.* Minneapolis: Johnson Institute.

_____. 1991 *Thomas Barker Talks About Divorce and*

Separation (Grades K-6). In the series *Building Trust, Making Friends: Four Group Activity Manuals for High-Risk Students.* Minneapolis: Johnson Institute.

Wallerstein, J., and S. Blakeslee. 1989. *Second Chances: Men and Women and Children a Decade After Divorce.* New York: Ticknor and Fields.

Wallerstein, J., and J. Kelly. 1980. *Surviving the Breakup: How Children and Parents Cope with Divorce.* New York: Basic Books.

Wegscheider-Cruse, S. 1980. *Another Chance: Hope and Health for the Alcoholic Family.* Palo Alto, Calif.: Science and Behavior Books.

Weisinger, H. 1985. *Dr. Weisinger's Anger Work-Out Book.* Syracuse, N.Y.: Evaluation Research Associates, Inc.

Wolin, S., and S. Wolin. 1993. *The Resilient Self.* New York: Villard Books.

Resources for Help

JOHNSON INSTITUTE
7205 Ohms Lane
Minneapolis, MN 55439-2159
612-831-1630 or 800-231-5165

JOINT CUSTODY ASSOCIATION
10606 Wilkins Ave.
Los Angeles, CA 90024
310-475-5352

CHILDREN'S RIGHTS COUNCIL
220 I Street NE, Suite 230
Washington, D.C. 20002
202-547-NCCR

PARENTS SHARING CUSTODY
420 S. Beverly Drive, Suite 100
Beverly Hills, CA 90212-4410
310-286-9171

SINGLE PARENT RESOURCE CENTER
141 W. 28th St., Suite 302
New York, NY 10001
212-947-0221

STEPFAMILY ASSOCIATION OF AMERICA
215 Centennial Mall S., Suite 212
Lincoln, NE 68508
402-477-7837

STEPFAMILY FOUNDATION
333 West End Ave.
New York, NY 10023
212-877-3244

NATIONAL CENTER ON CHILD ABUSE AND NEGLECT
P.O. Box 1182
Washington, D.C. 20013-1182
202-205-8586

CLEARINGHOUSE ON CHILD ABUSE AND NEGLECT INFORMATION
P.O. Box 1182
Washington, D.C. 20013-1182
703-385-7565 or 800-394-3366

NATIONAL COUNCIL ON CHILD ABUSE AND FAMILY VIOLENCE
1155 Connecticut Ave., N.W., Suite 400
Washington, D.C. 20036
202-429-6695

CENTER FOR THE PREVENTION OF SEXUAL & DOMESTIC VIOLENCE
1914 N. 34th Street, Suite 105
Seattle, WA 98103
206-634-1903